Contents

Preface v

Part I: Orientation

Chapter 1:   What Is Spirituality and Why Is It
             Important? 3
Chapter 2:   The Social Destruction of Spirituality 21
Chapter 3:   Children's Spirituality –
             What We Know Already 40
Chapter 4:   A Geography of the Spirit 57

Part II: Investigation

Chapter 5:   How Do You Talk with Children
             about Spirituality? 79
Chapter 6:   Listening to Children Talking * 92
Chapter 7:   Identifying the Core of Children's
             Spirituality * 112

Part III: Reflection

Chapter 8: The Naturalness of Relational
            Consciousness 141
Chapter 9: Nurturing the Spirit of the Child 159

            Notes 176
            Bibliography 200
            Index 211

* These two chapters were written by Rebecca Nye.
  All the other chapters were written by David Hay.

Preface

Rather surprisingly, spiritual education has become newsworthy. One major reason for this is a growing public concern about the coherence of society as a whole, allied to an intuition that spirituality has importance in maintaining what Philip Selznick calls the 'moral commonwealth'. Unease about these matters was signalled in Britain at the beginning of 1996 by the setting up of a national conference on Spiritual and Moral Education by the Schools Curriculum and Assessment Authority (now the Qualifications and Curriculum Authority). Subsequently a national forum was appointed with a brief to create a practical educational response to the perceived crisis.

There are two major difficulties in understanding how best to develop spiritual education – lack of agreement on what spirituality is, and a shortage of detailed information about the spiritual life of children. When one considers the volume of research and theoretical reflection available on, for example, children's cognitive development, the lack of data is starkly obvious. In any other curriculum area such a deficiency would be considered unacceptable. The practical consequence of this impoverishment is that when teachers try to deal with spiritual education, they often feel they are talking into a vacuum.

The investigation reported in this book began as an attempt to clear away some of the uncertainty by finding out how ordinary children talk about their spirituality. Once we started the process of research it became apparent that spirituality is massively present in the lives of children. At the same time, however, it is hidden, because of a culturally constructed forgetfulness which allows us to ignore the obvious. If we are to take spirituality seriously we need to understand how it has come to be ignored and why it is sidelined in the educational system. These factors have governed the structure of the book.

In Part I: *Orientation*, I begin with a chapter explaining what I mean by spirituality, its complex relationship with religion, and its political importance. The second chapter is an attempt to set spiritual awareness, seen as a natural human predisposition, in the context of a cultural history which has had a severely destructive effect on its expression. I also return to its political importance, this time directly in relation to education. Chapter 3 then summarizes what little we already know about the way children's spirituality is expressed within this difficult social environment. Most researchers have assumed that spirituality will be made manifest in religious – usually Christian – language. In a secularized nation like Britain this means ignoring a large part of the spiritual lives of children. But then the problem arises of how to recognize this other, submerged part of spirituality. Chapter 4 identifies some ways of starting the process in an environment where traditional religious language is not always of much help.

Part II: *Investigation* is an account of the enquiry which grew out of the phase of orientation. Chapter 5 confronts the problem of researcher bias in a controversial area and explains the practical details of how we decided to go about the research. The field work and a major part of the data analysis were undertaken by my research assistant, Rebecca Nye. It therefore seemed appropriate to invite her to write Chapters 6 and 7, which present a vivid and subtly nuanced report of her findings. In Part III,

Reflection, I offer a theoretical meditation on the results. I suggest that they support a view of spiritual awareness as a natural human predisposition, often overlaid by cultural construction, but nevertheless a biological reality. I also identify the formidable difficulties facing an educational system which wishes to take spirituality seriously. The closing chapter makes four concrete proposals for an educational approach which may encourage children's spirituality and even permit it to flourish.

It is a pleasure to record my thanks to the three funding bodies which supported the work: the All Saints Trust, the Dulverton Trust and a third Trust which wishes to remain anonymous. Their generosity enabled me to employ Rebecca as my research assistant. I am profoundly grateful to her for her energy, the excellence of her work and the many rich insights she contributed to my understanding of children's spirituality. Towards the end of the project she was appointed to a post in the Divinity Faculty in the University of Cambridge and I was fortunate to be able to employ Kate Hunt as her successor. Between us, Kate and I brought the work to a conclusion and I am indebted to her for stepping into the gap.

Although the project was carried out at the University of Nottingham, it was given its initial impetus at a series of meetings of the Research Committee of the Religious Experience Research Centre at Westminster College, Oxford. My thanks are due to Michael Argyle, Nigel Bigger, Laurie Brown, Bernard Farr, Mike Jackson, Oliver Knowles, Carrie Mercier, Meg Maxwell and Gordon Wakefield for their support.

Guidance on setting up the project was given by my Nottingham colleague David Wood, and during the course of the work we were regularly advised by Margaret Donaldson in Edinburgh and Rosemary Peacocke in Oxford. Numerous other colleagues were generous with their time and support and I would particularly wish to record my thanks to Peter Davies, William K. Kay, Arthur Peacocke, Roger Poole, Roger Murphy and Michael Taylor for either offering advice or reading and criticizing draft chapters of the book. I owe a particular debt of gratitude to my friend Denis Rice for his detailed comments on all but two of the chapters of the book. Versions of some of the material have appeared previously in the *British Journal of Religious Education*, *The International Journal of Children's Spirituality*, *The International Journal of the Psychology of Religion*, *The Month*, *Religion*, *Research Papers in Education* and *The Tablet*.

Our greatest practical debt is, of course, to the children and staff in the primary schools in Nottinghamshire and Birmingham where the research was done. The kindness and consideration shown by all of them during numerous intrusions into busy school timetables merit our warmest thanks.

David Hay
Centre for the Study of Human Relations
University of Nottingham
July 1998

I

Orientation

1

What Is Spirituality and Why Is It Important?

> It is surely dangerous to invoke something whose meaning is no
> longer reasonably clear.
>
> MARGARET CHATERJEE[1]

Spirituality and religion

Few Westerners would have difficulty in guessing the subject
matter of a book entitled *The Spiritual Life*, written in France
and published in 1923 in Tournai, Paris, Rome and New York.
The identity of its author, the Very Reverend Adolphe
Tanquerey[2] confirms the expectation that it is about religion.
It is in fact a textbook of Christian theology, but theology of a
highly practical kind, applied to religious devotion and advance-
ment in the life of prayer. Tanquerey has a very clear, even
rigidly organized idea of his subject, and he begins by dividing it
into two parts. 'Ascetical Theology' is 'that part of spiritual doctrine whose proper object is both the theory and the practice of
Christian perfection, from its very beginnings up to the thresh-
old of infused contemplation.' 'Mystical Theology is ... the

theory and practice of the contemplative life, which begins with what is called the first night of the senses, described by St John of the Cross, and the prayer of quiet, described by St Theresa.'[3]

Tanquerey's equation of spirituality with Christianity is hardly surprising, given the history of Europe. But closer investigation shows that even amongst religiously committed Christians there are wide differences in people's notions of what is meant by the word. Tanquerey was writing as a Roman Catholic priest well before the days of modern Catholic attitudes to ecumenism, and he emphasizes his concern for the conversion of 'infidels and heretics'. Amongst such he no doubt included members of other Christian denominations who had a theological interpretation of spirituality at variance with his own. For example, I come from the north of Scotland, where traditional Calvinist culture holds to a notion of the action of divine Grace which implies a rather different understanding of spirituality from that found in Tanquerey.

Outside the world of professional theological dispute the word 'spiritual' has extremely vague connotations, although in recent years it has come to be widely used in the context of debates about the importance of spiritual education. That is why, although this book is about children, I need to begin by spending a considerable amount of time clearing the ground. It is necessary to be aware of the hidden agenda lying behind the various meanings – otherwise discussion is liable to get lost in a cloud of mutual incomprehension. There is also a need to bring the argument down to earth. Especially in scholarly works, spirituality tends to be approached in an abstract way, isolated from the concrete differences between ordinary people in their own social and historical setting.

In the course of the book I want to argue that children's spirituality is rooted in a universal human awareness; that it is 'really there' and not just a culturally constructed illusion. Although I believe I am right, I understand very well that people emerge from childhood into adult life having been educated formally or informally within all sorts of different cultures and subcultures.

The Spirit of the Child

In addition, each of us carries the baggage of a personal life history that is never exactly like anyone else's. These individual differences also affect the preconceptions which people have about spirituality and therefore the problem of setting limits to the term. In this first chapter I want to look more closely at meanings and also explain why I think spiritual education needs to lie at the heart of the school curriculum. In Chapter 2 I will reflect on the historical context within which today's children have to struggle to express their own spirituality.

Defining spirituality

Even amongst religious specialists we sometimes get wind of confusion over the definition of spirituality. The English educationalist Jack Priestley has a good story about this.[4] When the wording of the British 1944 Education Act was being debated, the then Archbishop of Canterbury, William Temple, was trying to create a draft text for the parts of the Bill concerned with religion. He wanted to find a form of words that would be found acceptable by the Members of the Houses of Parliament. Unfortunately, even the word 'religion' itself was rather troublesome. Partly this was because different kinds of Christians have different ideas about the nature of religion. It was also because he was well aware that quite a number of Members of Parliament had no time for religion at all. Temple's assistant, Canon Hall, hit on a solution:

> The churches were in such a state at the time [that] we thought if we used the word 'spiritual' they might agree to that because they didn't know what it was. They all had very clear ideas about what religion was and they all knew they didn't agree with anyone else's definition of it.

The meaning of the word 'spirituality' is probably even more obscure today than it was in 1944, but most people want to distinguish it from 'religion'. It is this contrast that makes 'spirituality' such a handy portmanteau word in political discussion. Even in the 1940s there were enough people with objections to the word 'religion' to make an archbishop think twice about using it in a text intended to receive general support in Parliament. By 1988, in a still more secularized Britain, the Education Reform Act successfully passed through Parliament with a reference to the necessity for spiritual education prominently highlighted on the opening page.

How did this happen? For some years I have used a 'brainstorming' exercise to help groups of students focus on how they understand the links between religion and spirituality. First they are asked to write on a large sheet of paper as many associations with the word 'religion' as they can think of in five minutes. They then repeat this procedure on another sheet of paper with the word 'spirituality'.

A few people see very little difference between religion and spirituality. Most make a clear distinction. Religion tends to be associated with what is publicly available, such as churches, mosques, Bibles, prayer books, religious officials, weddings and funerals. It also regularly includes uncomfortable associations with boredom, narrow-mindedness and being out of date, as well as more disconcerting links with fanaticism, bigotry, cruelty and persecution. It seems that in many people's minds religion is firmly caught up in the cold brutalities of history.

Spirituality is almost always seen as much warmer, associated with love, inspiration, wholeness, depth, mystery and personal devotions like prayer and meditation. This divergence is less than flattering to the religious institutions, but it is not just a critique made by outsiders. I know this to be so, because the same contrast has appeared when I have tried out the exercise with committed lay Christians and clergy. Sometimes, when working with groups of ordained priests, I have noticed one or two of them expressing a degree of anger with religion which would not have seemed out of place coming from a member of the British Secular Society.

At first these conflicting views disconcerted me. My own memories of the religion of my childhood in a remote part of Scotland are almost entirely benevolent.[5] I suppose I lived in a religious backwater, shielded from controversy. As I grew older and became aware of Christianity outside my immediate environment, it became clear that other people's experience could be very different, at times leading to a positive loathing of the religious institution. No one in touch with the mainstream of modern Western life can escape for long the negative attitudes and presuppositions about religion which are widespread in society.[6]

Yet anger is not the whole story. There is a final part to the brainstorming exercise which I described a moment ago. When the groups have completed the two sheets, I ask them to examine what they have written and to produce a representation of the relation which they see between spirituality and religion. In spite of their misgivings about religion, almost everybody wishes to emphasize that there is a real link. Often the groups will express their findings metaphorically, perhaps referring to spirituality as a journey and to religion as the mode of transport, or to spirituality as the fuel which enables the vehicle of religion to operate. One metaphor that turns up repeatedly is a drawing of a tree, with the roots labelled 'spirituality' and the leaves 'religion'. The roots transmit water to the leaves and support the tree as it grows larger. In turn the leaves manufacture food which nourishes the roots. Those who create this metaphor are always quick to point out that when this interchange falters the tree stops growing and is in serious danger of dying. It is as if most people, even those who have no time for the religious institution, see the need for some vehicle for spirituality. The spiritual life, they seem to be saying, has the opportunity to flourish when there is a degree of social agreement about its cultural expression. That in turn raises a question about the role of the school and the ways in which understanding about spirituality is transmitted to children, or even whether 'transmission' is the appropriate word.

Why is it that spirituality usually evades the criticisms levelled at religion? To make sense of this we need to turn to the range of uses of the word 'spirituality'. The thesaurus on my computer offers the following synonyms: 'devotion, holiness, piety, saintliness, sanctity'. These sound very like the kinds of connotation that the word would have had for Father

Tanquerey. They suggest a traditional idea of the practical means by which a person becomes 'spiritual'.

At one end of the scale, the dictionary definition is almost identical to that used by Tanquerey. It refers to human beings' awareness of their relationship with God and points towards the dramatic goal of mystical union with the Godhead. Of course, this definition is meaningless to an atheist and at least dubious to an agnostic. But the term 'spirit' is not necessarily without importance for an atheist; certainly not for the most influential of modern atheists, Karl Marx. He used it with great polemical intensity in his most famous attack on what he saw as the illusions of religion.

Religion, he wrote, is 'the sigh of the oppressed creature, the heart of a heartless world, *the spirit of a spiritless situation*'[7] (my italics). That is to say, in Marx's view, religion offers a painkiller or opiate – in fact, a false spirituality. Here 'spirit' carries connotations of what it means to be fully aware of our indissoluble membership of the human collective or, as Marx put it, to discover oneself as a 'species-being'.[8] Marx is implying that what the devoutly religious person experiences as intense desire for God is really a displaced expression of the human longing for a just and undivided community. So for some people terms like 'religion' and 'God' can actually get in the way of what they understand to be their spiritual life. In Chapters 2 and 3 I will explore more deeply how this view has come to seem plausible and how it affects the expression of spirituality in modern children.

Moving beyond such powerful differences of meaning, there is also a more innocuous use of the word 'spiritual', when we use it in relation to a person who demonstrates a refined aesthetic awareness of poetry, music or the other arts, or perhaps is sensitive to the needs of other people. This signification has the advantage that it gives the appearance of being politically and religiously harmless and is therefore widely acceptable in our secularized culture.

These very different senses of the word 'spiritual' mean that it can be used to conceal strong antagonisms about the validity and importance of religious belief, which is why it is useful in the drafting of parliamentary legislation. There is nevertheless an underlying degree of common ground, in spite of what appears to be a spurious linkage of meanings. The key point is that the three connotations – religious devotion; being fully aware of one's 'species-being'; being aesthetically or ethically aware – all refer to a heightening of awareness or attentiveness. Apparently widely disparate in meaning, they express a fundamental insight. Each of us has the potential to be much more deeply aware both of ourselves and of our intimate relationship with everything that is not ourselves.

This holistic notion of spirituality[9] is probably widely acceptable in a society whose de facto norms are highly secular, yet it leaves open a religious understanding of the word. From such a perspective, raised awareness itself constitutes spirituality, as indeed is taught in Buddhist *vipassana* meditation. But this understanding is not confined to Buddhism. It is implied in all forms of religious meditation, including Christian contemplative prayer where one places oneself as awarely as possible in the presence of God.

Alister Hardy on the biology of spirituality

I now want to consider the nature of this awareness or attentiveness a little more closely from the perspective of biology. From one modern viewpoint, spirituality is rooted in something as concrete as breathing or eating or seeing; that is to say, it is biologically natural to the species *Homo sapiens*. The first person to put this explicitly was the zoologist Alister Hardy.[10] In 1965, shortly after he retired from the Chair of Zoology at Oxford, Hardy was invited to deliver the Gifford Lectures at the University of Aberdeen. He chose to speak about the relationship between biology and religion. As a committed Darwinist he proposed the hypothesis that what he called 'religious experience' has evolved through the process of natural selection because it has survival value to the individual. An examination of his lectures shows that what he meant by religious experience is similar or identical to what I shall call 'spiritual awareness'.

Hardy's ambiguous use of language in an area where, as we have seen, most people are confused should not be allowed to conceal his fundamental assertion. What he is saying is that there is a form of awareness, different from and transcending everyday awareness, which is potentially present in all human beings and which has a positive function in enabling individuals to survive in their natural environment.

Hardy's hypothesis is revolutionary, because it shifts the ground on which scientific debates about religion and spirituality have tended to take place. Most of the currently prominent naturalistic hypotheses about religion are, at least in their ori-ginal intention, attempts to interpret Western monotheism reductively. They claim to explain how the error of religious belief came about. Thus I have already alluded to Marx's opinion that religion is an opiate which provides an illusory comfort to people who are oppressed and alienated in class society. Sigmund Freud suggested that religion is a neurosis,[11] whilst the French sociologist Émile Durkheim asserted that religious experience *is* the effervescence or excitement experienced at large religious gatherings.[12]

Hardy himself has been accused of reductionism – that is, of explaining away religion – but he had no such intention. As someone personally convinced of the reality of religious experience, he expressed his belief in the way most natural for a zoologist, by proposing the hypothesis that it is biologically based. From Hardy's perspective, the many religions of *Homo sapiens* are the richly varied cultural responses of human beings to their natural spiritual awareness.

Although he was the first to put it so explicitly, this is not a new idea. It is implicit in a whole series of thinkers belonging to the Renaissance and the Enlightenment, to some of whom I will refer in the next chapter. Amongst post-Renaissance writers on religion there is an intellectual link with Hardy's thought running back at least to the German Romantic theologian Friedrich Schleiermacher at the end of the eighteenth century. Schleiermacher tried to respond to the 'cultured despisers' of religion of his day by proposing a natural root for religious feeling. In suggesting that it is a 'feeling of absolute dependence' he seems to be implying that it is not simply an emotion, but something more like a perception.

Schleiermacher came from a Protestant pietist background which traditionally placed emphasis on religious experience, no doubt predisposing him to defend religion in this way. His cultural milieu was shared to a greater or lesser degree by most of the subsequent advocates of a view of spirituality which presupposes that it has a psychological or physiological basis. Prominent amongst them were the Harvard psychologist William James as well as German students of religion such as Rudolf Otto, Ernst Troeltsch and Joachim Wach.[13]

But there is a further and more radical shift resulting from Hardy's conjecture. If spirituality is biologically natural to all human beings, then it must be an expression of a bodily predisposition or process. Process can be associated with many different kinds of expression, so like any human universal, spirituality could be articulated in a multitude of languages, beliefs and religious or political doctrines. On Hardy's thesis, spirituality is not the exclusive property of any one religion, or for that matter of religion in general. Spiritual awareness could even be signified, and perhaps would be bound to be signified, in secular and even anti-religious language amongst those who for historical reasons are alienated from religious culture.

What Hardy added to the ideas of his forerunners was an evolutionary mechanism to explain the biological mode in which spiritual awareness emerged in the human species. In his lectures he drew upon data from Social Anthropology, Psychology, Animal Behaviour and, more controversially, from Psychical Research to support his contention that spiritual or religious experience contributes to the survival of the individual and has therefore evolved through the process of natural selection.

His quotations from the writings of early social anthropologists probably provide the most convincing circumstantial evidence. He included several references to Durkheim himself, believing that a close reading of his works demonstrated that he was less reductionist in his attitude to religious experience than is often assumed. Whether or not this was Durkheim's view, there is no doubt that he was convinced that religion gives a person strength, as demonstrated by the following quotations from *The Elementary Forms of the Religious Life*:

> The believer who has communicated with his god is not merely a man [sic] who sees new truths of which the unbeliever is ignorant; he is a man who is *stronger*. He feels within him more force, either to endure the trials of existence, or to conquer them. It is as though he were raised above the miseries of the world, because he is raised above his condition as a mere man ...[14] In fact, whoever has really practised a religion knows very well that it is the cult which gives rise to these impressions of joy, of interior peace, of serenity, of enthusiasm which are, for the believer, an experimental proof of his beliefs.[15]

In similar vein, the English anthropologist R. R. Marrett wrote:

> It is the common experience of man that he can draw on a power that makes for, and in its most typical form wills, righteousness, the sole condition being that a certain fear, a certain shyness and humility, accompany the effort so to do. That such a universal belief exists amongst all mankind, and that it is no less universally helpful in the highest degree, is the abiding impression left on my mind by the study of religion in its historico-scientific aspect.[16]

The language used by Marrett is striking. He suggests that people can 'draw on a power' and mentions the need for 'shyness and humility'. This is not the terminology of abstract belief; it is a reference to an awareness of some kind of directly discernible relationship. Hardy's lectures are an attempt to build an argument for the reality of such experience. It is important to add that although he often depends on professional opinions such as those of Durkheim and Marrett, he is also thinking autobiographically about his own spiritual experience in the light of his training as a zoologist.[17]

Religion and spirituality again

Even in secularized Britain, most people who have done the brainstorming exercise which I described earlier see a link between what it is to be spiritually aware, and religion. No doubt this is because for many hundreds of years the natural context for the expression of spiritual experience in Europe was through the terminology of Christianity. This alerts us to the fact that all of our human experience, without exception, is mediated to us and at least partially created by the social institutions of the culture to which we belong. But given the biological understanding of spirituality that I have been discussing, it ought to be possible to identify other means of expression, independent of formal religion, that are performing approximately the same task.

Whether the language is religious or secular, it is impossible even to begin to consider spirituality without the use of *some* symbolic medium. But that does not imply that what is referred to by the term 'spirituality' is merely an abstraction conjured up by language. This is disputed territory amongst theologians and one that I need to mention briefly because, once more, it concerns the relationship between religion and spirituality. The range of views has been outlined by the American theologian George Lindbeck,[18] according to whom there are three major theological theories of religion which currently find scholarly support.

❖ The first of these theories sees religions as having close affinities with traditional philosophy. It stresses the centrality of religious doctrine and its function in providing informative propositions or making truth claims about reality.
❖ The second major theory, corresponding approximately to the one with which Hardy had sympathy, focuses on what Lindbeck calls the 'experiential-expressive' dimension of religion. From this point of view, the different world religions are varied expressions of a common core experience. Indeed, it is their reference to this experience which identifies them as religions in the first place.

❖ According to the third view, which Lindbeck sees as particularly important, instead of deriving the external features of a religion from some prelinguistic core experience, experience itself is seen as growing out of the culture. To enter into religious experience involves becoming competent in the language of a given religion. Strictly speaking, it is necessary first of all to have a language, a means for expressing experience, in order to have that experience.

As I have said earlier, I do not dispute the primacy of language for giving expression to and opening up a person's imaginative response to their awareness, and hence, in a sense, for constructing experience. But to assign to it an exclusive explanatory role gives away too much to language, whilst quietly ignoring the biologically embodied nature of human beings.[19] We are not abstract language machines, free to create any kind of world we can imagine. We are living animals, adapted through the process of evolution to survive within the constraints of a real environment. Although the arguments of the supporters of this third theory[20] have probably gained rather than lost influence in recent years through the impact of postmodernism, there are sound reasons to insist on the contribution of biology to spirituality.

Firstly, much of the scholarly analysis of the contrasting accounts of experience in different cultures has been done by examining the language of historical texts (the Bible, the Qur'an, the Buddhist Sutras etc.). Religiously committed students of such texts interpret their meanings with the greatest of care because their function is to guard a long-standing orthodoxy. But our contemporary understanding of metaphor and the creation of meaning[21] leads us to understand that a very wide range of linguistic or symbolic expression and interpretation can appear in association with what appears to be a common experience. Consider, for example, the multitude of contradictory meanings associated with the preparation and eating of food in different cultures. Yet no one disputes that we need to eat food to stay alive. So it is at least conceivable that the things which different cultures have to say about spiritual awareness could at the logical level be utterly inconsistent with each other, though referring to the same human phenomenon.

Secondly, to suppose that religious or spiritual experience is, without remainder, the result of social construction is to place it in a realm of subjectivity very different from that which we deem appropriate for physical reality. But those reporting such experience, at least in Western culture, find that it does not easily fall into the category of subjective production or imaginings. In certain crucial respects it is much more like the perception of an objective reality.

Thirdly, we need not suppose that because different kinds of practices are used in the 'production' of (or, less reductively, 'opening the possibility of')[22] particular states of awareness, those states need necessarily be different from each other. It could be that a variety of methodologies will produce the same physiological state. There is evidence, for example, that experienced practitioners of Christian contemplative prayer and Zen meditation find that their experience is mutually recognizable.[23] This point will become important in Chapter 4 when I discuss the circumstances in which spiritual awareness is likely to be aroused in children.

What evidence is there of spiritual experience today?

These, of course, are continuing matters of controversy and debate. Alongside that, we also need to take note of the difficulty faced in testing a new and relatively unknown scientific hypothesis against the explanations of scholars like Marx, Freud and Durkheim, who have had a dominating influence in the formation of our contemporary culture. Their prestige pervades such a broad area of general understanding that a hypothesis which flatly contradicts their view is likely to be seen as upstart, perverse and without true authority.

Nevertheless, the fact that Hardy's view so clearly contradicts its major competitors makes it a good candidate for what the philosopher of science Karl Popper calls a 'daring conjecture'.[24] From Popper's perspective, the way that scientific knowledge grows is through the proposal of bold hypotheses which are open to refutation by scientific test. At the time of writing, Hardy's idea stands up well in comparison to these other more prominent reductionist conjectures: Marx's 'opium of the people' hypothesis; Freud's assumption that 'religious experience' is symptomatic of neurosis; and Durkheim's association of spiritual experience with social 'effervescence'.[25]

* Contrary to what could be predicted from Marx's postulate, at least in Britain, people who might be classed as 'oppressed' (the inner-city poor; the long-term unemployed) are less likely than others to speak of spirituality. In part this may be due to inarticulacy because of an underprivileged education, but it could also be seen as simply a further dimension of the psychological damage created by unjust social conditions.
* There is a statistically significant association between report of spiritual experience and good mental health and personal happiness.[26] This suggests that at the least we need to be wary of Freud's dismissal of religious experience (and hence perhaps spirituality in the sense in which we have been using the term) as symptomatic of neurosis.[27]
* Most people say that their spiritual awareness occurs typically when they are alone.[28] This sharply contradicts Durkheim's 'social effervescence' hypothesis, which suggests that religious experience 'is' the excitement experienced by people involved in large and enthusiastic religious gatherings.

In fact, spiritual experience is very widely reported in the adult population of Britain. Questions placed in a Gallup Omnibus Survey in Britain in 1986 revealed that about half those surveyed felt they had had such experience.[29] A series of in-depth studies on particular sub-populations in England,[30] where there was time to build up rapport and overcome the shyness of those being interviewed, suggests the probability that about two thirds of the population are aware of a spiritual dimension to their experience.

In broad terms then, Hardy's hypothesis has proved resilient under scientific testing. But a prudent caution is in order.

In coming to consider the ideas of the past masters against which Hardy's conjecture is pitted, we are always in danger of 'conceptual slippage'. Marx, Freud and Durkheim were writing about a poorly focused area of study that included both 'religion' and 'spirituality', often confused with each other. They were using the intellectual framework available to them in their time. It is not clear that they would be intolerant of spirituality in the wider sense to which I refer.[31] This is a complexity which it is important to acknowledge.

Why spirituality has political and social importance

These academic arguments have more than a theoretical importance. At the level of practical politics the most important single finding of my research over the past 20 years is the very strong connection there appears to be between spiritual awareness and ethical behaviour. Almost without exception, people link their spiritual or religious experience with a moral imperative. I have questioned literally hundreds of people about this matter. Typically they say that the initial effect of their experience is to make them look beyond themselves. They have an increased desire to care for those closest to them, to take issues of social justice more seriously and to be concerned about the total environment. Again and again people say things like 'I behave better; it touches the conscience.' One person said, 'I now have far more respect for my physical surroundings as well as fellow humans ... I don't think they were important to me before.'

Others associate their moment of spiritual insight with a radical shift in their life's purpose. A woman who gave up a job which was meaningless to her in order to look after delinquent children dated it from half an hour of sitting in the park on a sunny evening:

> quite suddenly I felt lifted beyond all the turmoil and the conflict. There was no visual image and I knew I was sitting on a seat in the park but I felt as if I was lifted above the world and looking down on it. The disillusion and cynicism were gone and I felt compassion suffusing my whole being...

Others find that once they have begun working in a caring role – for example, nursing the sick – their spiritual awareness becomes much deeper and confirms their choice of vocation.[32] American studies which parallel my own show similar effects: finding meaning in life, becoming concerned for a just society, losing racial prejudice, becoming less materialistic. In addition the statistics show that both in Britain and in America people in touch with their spirituality appear to be in a better state of mental health than those who are not.[33]

The philosopher Alfred North Whitehead once wrote:

> The misconception which has haunted philosophical literature throughout the centuries is the notion of independent existence. Every entity is only to be understood in terms of the way in which it is interwoven with the rest of the universe.

In the accounts of spiritual experience that I have investigated there seems to be a direct, almost perceptual recognition of that fact. The person discovers that the extreme individualism of modern Western society is an illusion. As a result the 'psychological distance' between oneself and the rest of reality disappears. With older people this is usually experienced as a realization that the love of God pervades everything and implies our stewardship of creation. Amongst younger people who are cut off or alienated from the religious institutions, it is increasingly expressed as a mystical insight that damage to any part of the fabric of reality is damage to oneself.

These findings give support to the traditional intuition that spirituality underpins ethical behaviour and encourages social cohesion. There is, however, a problem. Although spirituality is much more widespread than we once thought, it is also privatized. In a society in which the public face is one of alienation from spirituality, it is very often seen as an embarrassment, not to be talked about or even admitted to oneself. As a result the initial breadth of a person's insight often dwindles down and becomes constricted to little more than a source of private comfort in times of distress. Privatization dissipates the potential of spirituality to change society because it cannot feed easily into public understanding or political legislation. This is a major practical loss created by the decline of the religious institutions in the West. Even with all their potential for corruption or trivialization, they carry thousands of years of reflection on the moral and political implications of spiritual insight.

Somehow we need to learn how not to waste this stock of wisdom, whilst at the same time taking a broad view of the nature of spirituality, so as to incorporate its insights wherever they emerge. The distinction which I have continually drawn between religion and spirituality is an important one. In a public address given half a century ago, Lord Samuel expressed his alarm at the consequences of the disappearance of religion:

> All through the ages religion has been the principal source of the moral law and its mainstay, an incentive to noble minds, a guide to the peoples. The lives and teachings of the founders of Faiths, the prophets and sages, saints and martyrs, have bequeathed to mankind a precious heritage, exalted continually by poetry, music and all the arts. Imagine it gone: suppose the extreme case – the cathedrals deserted and fallen into ruin, like the mediaeval castles; the churches and synagogues, mosques and temples turned to other uses; their ministers dismissed, their zealous laity disbanded; suppose that heritage of centuries all dissipated and lost – how much the poorer would be the spirit of man.[34]

It is this perspective that is taken up by the Jesuit theologian Karl Rahner in one of his *Theological Investigations*, where he invites his readers to imagine a situation in which the kind of destruction imagined by Lord Samuel has taken place. More radically still, he suggests the possibility that there could come a time when even the memory of religion has gone and the word 'God' has disappeared from the dictionary:

> And even if this term were ever to be forgotten, even then in the decisive moments of our lives we should still be constantly encompassed by this nameless mystery of our existence ... even

supposing that those realities which we call religions ... were totally to disappear ... the transcendentality inherent in human life is such that [we] would still reach out towards that mystery which lies outside [our] control.[35]

This view of Rahner's points to the significance of distinguishing between spirituality and religion. He is expressing from his theological perspective much the same as Hardy says from a biological angle. The problem that remains, if Rahner's vision should ever come to pass, is how to reconstruct a culture so that it gives proper social and political expression to spiritual insight.

Conclusion

The findings I have been discussing in this chapter increase the plausibility of Hardy's hypothesis and also imply certain expectations about children's spirituality. If the suggestion is correct, one might suppose that in contemporary culture spirituality would be more prominent in childhood than in adult life. The process of induction into adult society may more often than not have the effect of closing it down. The pattern of modern Western assumptions has created an overlay which perhaps obscures, suppresses and in some cases represses the natural spirituality of the human species. It turns spirituality from something explicitly reflected upon, and therefore potent within political and social life, to something implicit and vague, disconnected from the mainstream of human activity. In the next chapter I shall address the reason for this state of affairs and the damage it does to children's spiritual education.

The Spirit of the Child

2

The Social Destruction of Spirituality

A contemptuous priesthood laughed at their simple devotion,
just as formerly in Italy the clergy, familiarised with the sanctuar-
ies, witnessed coldly and almost jestingly the fervour of pilgrims
come from afar.

ERNEST RÉNAN, VIE DE JESUS[1]

Once the human race has an experience which it has found to be
in part authentic, it does not let go.

OWEN CHADWICK[2]

The disillusionment of childhood spirituality

The adult world into which our children are inducted is more
often than not destructive to their spirituality. I am not thinking
simply of an inventory of the human woes that people wring
their hands about. I have in mind something that underlies this,
the process that goes on in the consciousness of children as they
assimilate popular culture. You will have seen it often enough.
Children emerge from infancy with a simplicity that is richly

open to experience, only to close off their awareness as they become street-wise. To be open is to be vulnerable. Its contrary is to 'know the score', to know how to look after yourself in a hostile environment.

Has this always been the destiny of innocence, the inevitable lot of naivety when it meets worldly sophistication? It is certainly not new. The human vulnerability of Jesus' disciples as portrayed in the New Testament is commented on by the French sceptic Ernest Rénan. In his *Life of Jesus*, he represents the group of rustic Galilean companions as having a childlike innocence, out of their depth, laughed at by the temple priesthood when they came south to enter the capital city. 'Jerusalem,' says Rénan, writing in 1863, 'was then what it is today, a city of pedantry, acrimony, disputes, hatreds and littlenesses of mind.' His vision of the members of the religious establishment was of a community of sophists who did know the score, experts in the most trivial matters of religious law. They were not naive, they were spiritually dead.

His biographer[3] notes that Rénan unwittingly included a large degree of autobiography in his writing, and there is obviously an element of projection in his *Life of Jesus*. As a boy, Rénan had himself been religiously devout and wished to become a priest. But like the Galileans, when he came south from his home in rural Brittany to enter the seminary in the metropolitan capital, he was shocked and bitterly disappointed. His teachers failed to provide him with the substance necessary to nurture the spirituality of his childhood. Where he had expected to find faith, he discovered dry intellectualism.

It seems perverse that in an attempt to save his spiritual life Rénan felt he had to distance himself from the institution that had mediated the expression of spirituality in much of Europe since the time of Constantine. But the nineteenth century is full of paradoxical stories like this. Rénan's sceptical predecessor, Auguste Comte (1798–1857), believed that human consciousness goes through three stages, each of which he had observed in his own life history. The religious faith of infancy, he said, is transcended firstly in youth by metaphysical speculation, then in maturity by scientific understanding.[4] Yet in his adult life, Comte's attempts to found a secular religion suggest that he continued to recognize the importance of his childhood spirituality. It could be contended that the secularism of Karl Marx (1818–83) was a necessary defence of the spiritual insight of his youth – that is, his belief in 'species-being'[5] – at a time in German history when the Church had deteriorated into little more than an arm of the secular power.

Something like Comte's experience is perhaps hinted at even in those Victorians who retained the religion of their early years. William Wordsworth (1770–1850), though a member of the Church of England all his life, regretted the fading of the spiritual awareness of childhood:

Heaven lies about us in our infancy!
Shades of the prison-house begin to close
    Upon the growing Boy,
But He beholds the light, and whence it flows,
    He sees it in his joy;
The Youth, who daily farther from the east
    Must travel, still is Nature's Priest,
    And by the vision splendid
    Is on his way attended;
At length the Man perceives it die away,
And fade into the light of common day.[6]

Behind these individual stories lies a set of complex issues rooted in the unfolding of European history. At least since the eighteenth century there has been a conflict between the demands of intellectual honesty on the one hand and the sustaining intuitions of the spirit on the other. It is therefore characteristic of modernity (and postmodernity) that total integrity in these matters leads honest seekers after truth into a state of uncertainty or discomfort.

There is an apocryphal tale that, many years after he abandoned Catholicism, Rénan was seen in a church in Rome kneeling at the altar rail, crying for his lost religion. Perhaps some cold and jesting priests witnessed the incident. Whether the story is true or not, it has contemporary currency because it illustrates the sense of equivocation that has surrounded the relationship between religion and spirituality in Western culture for much more than the hundred years since Rénan died.

How has this happened?

To try to understand what has happened, I need to consider the idea of 'secularization'. It is important to be careful in setting boundaries to the meaning of this word. Amongst sociologists of religion 'secularization' is a term used to describe the declining power and influence of religious institutions since the European Renaissance.[7] This includes the assumption that an increasing number of people will have lost belief in traditional religious doctrines. In a sense they have undergone a 'secularization of the mind'.[8]

In my usage of the term this does not necessarily have the added implication that spiritual awareness has been lost from the individual's consciousness. Survey research published in 1985 by Ann Morisy and myself suggests that probably a majority of our contemporaries are in a similar position to Rénan.[9] A rift seems to have grown up between their spiritual intuitions and the possibility of expressing them directly and simply through traditional religious doctrine and language.[10] In these circumstances secularization could sometimes imply the reverse of what it is commonly taken to mean. Like Rénan, people may choose to move away from a religious institution because they find it no longer sustains their spiritual roots. My work with Ann Morisy showed that many turn towards a secret or privatized belief which at least gives space to their spiritual experience.

There is a popular assumption that the loss of plausibility of the religious institution is the inexorable result of an increasing rationality in the way we conduct our affairs. Religion, so the argument goes, originally had a genuine social function. In the state of ignorance endured by our ancestors it served to reassure

The Spirit of the Child

and protect them emotionally from the terrors and brutalities of existence. But once people became aware of its irrational basis, religion ceased to serve this purpose and needed to be superseded. On this assumption, it follows that religion is at best a psychological defence mechanism, socially constructed out of the fears of ignorant people. Hence, like any other human creation, it can be deconstructed by the methods of an enlightened social historian.

Yet it is important to remember that reductionist explanations of religion are themselves socially constructed and in this respect have no privileged status. Secularism does not stand as an objective judge above the operations of history. It is equally as open as religion to the attentions of archaeologists of knowledge.[11] The very fact that secularism is primarily a European or Western phenomenon alerts us to the probability that this is so. Therefore it is equally as legitimate to ask what were the social factors that went into its construction as it is to enquire about the social construction of religion. This enquiry is important because it relates to the tearing apart of the bond between personal spirituality and traditional religion.

In the history of European attempts to understand religion, it is possible to pinpoint a sequence of stages in the emergence of an approach which looks at it from the disinterested perspective of an outsider. This line has been traced by Samuel Preus in his book *Explaining Religion*.[12] His intention is to defend 'methodological atheism',[13] and he gives a clear account of the social and political factors that went into the evolution of that stance. According to Preus, the political context which triggered off this process was the need to find a practical solution to the continent-wide chaos and slaughter caused by religious conflict following the Reformation. The first attempts were to retrieve a primeval purity of religion which was free of doctrinal dispute and was thus capable of leapfrogging over the squabbling errors of the time.

One such response in the seventeenth century was the 'deism' of Lord Herbert of Cherbury.[14] Herbert argued for a natural religion which could be agreed upon by all people, regardless of the historical differences between the faiths. He believed that everyone has certain innate ideas imprinted in their minds by God, including a knowledge that God exists and has a right to be worshipped, that virtue is the chief part of the worship of God, that crime is evil and we should repent of our sins, and that there will be rewards and punishments after death. He did not mean that an infant is born with these beliefs but that a normal person is bound to come to them as they reach a mature awareness.[15]

Whether Lord Herbert was implying some form of religious or spiritual awareness is not clear, but he had no wish to deny the possibility. He even said in his autobiography that the decision to publish his opinions was based on an insight following a prayer to God for a sign of approval:

> I had no sooner spoken these words, but a Loud though yet Gentle noise came from the Heavens (for it was like nothing on Earth) which did so comfort and cheer me, that I took my petition as granted, and that I had the Signe I demanded, whereupon also I resolved to print my Book ...[16]

Another of Preus' representative figures is Giambattista Vico.[17] Vico's main work *The New Science*, which was published in the first part of the eighteenth century, was intended to be religiously orthodox and was dedicated to the Pope. Nevertheless, Vico sounds very like Herbert when he identifies certain human institutions that he believes are universally found, including religion, marriage and the burial of the dead. He differs in that he insists on the need for a socio-historical account of the creation of those institutions. He also adds that the religions have a secular function, since they are necessary for the maintenance of civilization. Preus comments:

> What is really revolutionary about Vico ... is the tendency of his system to explain providence *away* without remainder, except as a category of meaning. There is, however, one final 'remnant', one element of providence in Vico's scheme for which he does not

explicitly offer any naturalistic explanation – the idea that there is an innate sense of divinity. This ... is the most durable remnant of traditional theology not only in Vico but in the study of religion until today and demands close attention.[18]

In Preus' opinion the Scottish Enlightenment philosopher David Hume disposed of this last theological remnant, most clearly in *The Natural History of Religion*, published in 1757.[19] Innateness implies universality and Hume tries to demonstrate, within the limits of his eighteenth-century knowledge, that whilst religion is very widespread it has never been so universal as to admit of no exceptions. He adds that there is no uniformity in the ideas which have derived from religious belief. In this way the supposed 'sentiment of religion' differs from a genuine instinct or impression of nature. Examples of these ideas might be 'self-love', 'resentment of injuries' and 'the passion between the sexes'. These really *are* universal, says Hume, and rather contentiously claims that they transcend culture because (he believes) they are expressed through the same ideas everywhere. Preus' view is that Hume was pivotal in providing for the first time a thoroughgoing naturalistic explanation of religion. Hume finally offered a genuine alternative to theology by objectifying religion as a problem to be solved. Thus the primary task of the student of religion at last became what it is today, that of explaining a natural (and almost universal) human error.

At the end of his book Preus makes an appeal to the representatives of theology to cooperate in the investigation of religion as a natural phenomenon instead of

staking out its own privileged universe of discourse and, so far, failing to show how that universe intersects with the one constituted by the rough consensus of the academy at large. The issue is not whether 'transcendence' refers to something extramentally real, but whether the study of religion wishes to enter as a full partner in the study of culture.[20]

There is here an assumption that Preus' version of academic consensus is correct and should be submitted to gracefully. It is to just such a submissive giving over of the tasks of theology, in this case to natural science, that the historian Michael Buckley ascribes the rise of European atheism at the beginning of the seventeenth century.[21] Buckley detects a critical shift in the way theologians thought about religion following the Reformation. Instead of reflecting directly on their spiritual experience as the major source of their convictions, they began to call upon the methods of natural philosophy (physics) to defend their belief in God. They felt that the reasonableness of religious belief could best be demonstrated by pointing to design in nature. Exemplars of this shift in strategy are the Jesuit Leonard Lessius at the University of Louvain and the Franciscan Marin Mersenne in Paris, both of whom were writing at the beginning of the seventeenth century.

Philosophy had been employed as the handmaid of theology before, most famously in St Thomas Aquinas' proofs for the existence of God. But Aquinas created his proofs within an already existing context of faith. In other words they had purposes other than that of producing religious conviction.[22] By the time Lessius and Mersenne were writing, they felt they needed to combat what they saw as the errors of atheism, feared to be growing as a product of the uncertainties created by the Reformation.[23] Presumably one of the reasons why atheists were atheists was because they felt their spiritual life gave them no grounds for belief in God. Therefore it must have seemed to apologists for religion that if unbelievers were to be convinced it would have to be as the result of arguments drawn from the appearance of physical reality. Avoiding an appeal to kinds of spiritual experience which atheists claimed did not exist, they turned instead to the natural world, over the existence of which there was no dispute.

Buckley does not say so, but one might hazard a guess that there was another, political, motive for not putting too much weight on spiritual experience. This was alarm at the political chaos created by the untutored, often somewhat crazy fideism of the Radical Reformers who emerged from a ruptured Christendom. Amongst educated people in seventeenth-century England it generated a distaste for most kinds of religious subjectivity, labelled as 'Enthusiasm'.[24] John Locke repudiated these manifestations in his *Essay Concerning Human Understanding* published in 1690, where he stated that 'Enthusiasm' was a fallacious ground of assent to a proposition because 'it takes away both reason and revelation and substitutes ... the ungrounded fancies of a man's own brain ...' Enthusiasts are those who 'cannot be mistaken in what they feel ... they are sure because they are sure, and their persuasions are right, only because they are strong in them.'[25] Similarly, Isaac Newton, though deeply and rather eccentrically religious himself, felt a revulsion at the outpourings of 'all enthusiasts, ranters, men who spoke with tongues'.[26]

In this political context, says Buckley, the most convincing 'warrant for the personal god was the impersonal world: the strongest evidence for the personal god was the design within nature.'[27] Accordingly, the task of the defence of religion was given over in particular to the natural philosophers, a responsibility willingly accepted by both Isaac Newton and René Descartes. It seemed that as the result of a loss of morale, numerous mainstream theologians no longer believed they had the means to establish their own cognitive claims. But this giving up of spiritual experience in the defence of religion eventually generated the destruction it was meant to avoid:

> For if religion itself has no inherent ground upon which to base its assertion, it is only a question of time until its inner emptiness emerges as positive denial ... Eventually the self denial of religion becomes the more radical but consistent denial that is atheism. If religion has no intrinsic justification, it cannot be justified from the outside. The very forces mustered against atheism will dialectically generate it, just as the northern tribes enlisted to defend Rome and its empire eventually occupied the city and swept the empire away.[28]

Buckley concludes that this tactical error of the theologians in the seventeenth century is a major root of modern atheism.

There are other, later roots. By the nineteenth century the secularization of the European mind had taken on a many-faceted form. Owen Chadwick, in his 1973–4 Gifford Lectures at Edinburgh University,[29] explored this complexity. Secularism is not one thing. Like the many different cultural manifestations of religion, secularism must be understood as a social construction with a variety of origins. The important questions are 'What changes in economic or social order lay under the willingness of a society to jettison notions which hitherto were conceived as necessary to its very existence?'[30]

Among the phenomena discussed by Chadwick as possible influences on the process during the nineteenth century are:

- The rise of religious toleration, which led eventually to the toleration of secular and atheist ideas.
- The influence of the Marxist interpretation of religion as a phenomenon generated by the oppressions of class society.
- The practical experience of the working class that the religious institution was used by the Establishment as an instrument of social control.
- The rise of anti-clericalism following the publication of the Syllabus of Errors appended to the Encyclical *Quanta Cura* of Pope Pius IX.[31]
- The perception of a conflict between science and religion.

In the midst of this complex tissue of secularizing influences, the defence of religious belief offered by the Established Church continued stubbornly to be what it was before, primarily by an appeal to the very approach which Buckley criticizes – the argument from design. It was in this form, for example, that Charles Darwin studied Christian apologetics when he was a Theology undergraduate at Cambridge. The standard text was William Paley's *Natural Theology*.[32] Paley expounds his case by an invitation to reflect upon the extraordinary adaptations of animals and plants to their environment as evidence for the

The Spirit of the Child

intervention of a creator. Paley had many contemporary critics, but his argument is commonly perceived to have been finally discredited when Darwin published *The Origin of Species* in 1859.[33] Darwin's proposal that evolution operated through the natural selection of random variations removed the necessity for direct intervention by a creator. The cumulative strength of this attack led at length to a decay of Darwin's own Christian beliefs, though apparently he did not embrace outright atheism.[34]

The survival of the spirit

Michael Buckley's central theme is the peculiarity of defending religion by an appeal to the appearances of nature rather than a direct reference to personal and communal spiritual awareness. He has no wish to dismiss the role of science but wants to place it more appropriately than did the apologists for religion in the seventeenth century – that is to say, in the context of a reflection on the experience of transcendence:

> A doctrine of god can arise within such an inquiry when the namelessly transcendent is approached as its asymptotic horizon, or as the never-comprehended 'lure of transcendence' or as that which essentially is, giving context and intelligibility to every-thing else encountered and understood but remaining endlessly other. God has emerged again and again in the history of wisdom as the direction towards which wonder progresses ... There is a depth at which human beings confront the great issues of life that lies far beneath the formal separation of the sciences and of the sciences from the humanities. Indeed the various disciplines emerge from this experience.[35]

Like Karl Rahner, Buckley is speaking of the ordinary human experience of wonder which, when it is profound enough, shifts imperceptibly into spiritual or religious awareness. The history which he describes led to such awareness becoming increasingly split off from philosophical or scientific speculation, indeed being dismissed from serious consideration.[36]

There were, however, a number of countercurrents, suggesting that at least some people were unhappy that human realities were being denied or ignored. This is illustrated in the life of Blaise Pascal. Though he was himself a significant contributor to the rise of physics during the seventeenth century, he did not subscribe to its use in the defence of religion. In his maturity Pascal had a striking conversion experience which gave him an unshakable conviction of the validity of his religious faith. A modern Marxist writer offers a reductionist account of the origin of Pascal's *Memorial*, the piece of parchment on which was recorded his conversion:

> The impetus came from a dramatic incident which took place in Neuilly at the beginning of November 1654, when he slipped under the hooves of a shying horse and very nearly lost his life. In the full flush of the emotional turmoil this caused he wrote down a few sentences on a scrap of parchment, highly agitated sentences in which the crisis of the last few months came to a head; it is now directed to loving Jesus Christ.[37]

There is some uncertainty as to whether this incident actually took place,[38] but there is no doubt that Pascal went through a 'second conversion'. His own interpretation, found after his death on the piece of parchment which was sewn into his clothing, opens with the lines:

> The year of grace, 1654.
> Monday, 23rd. November, Feast of S. Clement,
> Pope and Martyr,
> and of others in the Martyrology
> Vigil of S. Chrysogonus, Martyr, and others,
> From about half-past ten in the evening until about
> half past twelve
> FIRE
> God of Abraham, God of Isaac, God of Jacob,
> not of the philosophers and savants
> Certitude. Certitude. Feeling. Joy. Peace.[39]

Though Pascal was a natural philosopher, it was not a remembrance of God as the end point of a philosophical argument that he chose to wear about his person for the rest of his life. He insists that his encounter was with the God of Abraham, Isaac and Jacob, and *not* the God of the philosophers. He is therefore speaking concretely and personally, from within an historical culture. As he says in the *Pensées*, he believed that a purely speculative knowledge of God was worse than no knowledge at all; it was positively harmful.

Pascal was not alone in his opinion. Following the Reformation, the idea that spiritual experience is the true ground for religious belief was clung on to with particular insistence by the Puritan and Pietist traditions within Christianity. There are historical reasons for this which are connected with the theology of John Calvin.[40] Calvin taught that from all eternity people have been predestined by God for heaven (the 'elect') or hell (the 'reprobate') in the next life. It is understandable that for people committed to Calvin's doctrine, uncertainty about which side of the divide lay their eternal soul generated a pastoral need for some way of reducing the anxiety induced.

One response was to work and pray for the psychological experience of religious conversion as evidence of being saved. Thus in English Puritanism of the seventeenth century a new emphasis on feeling as a testimony to election appeared.[41] A characteristic figure was William Perkins, who laid emphasis on the need for the experience of conversion:

> None can be a lively member of Christ till his conscience condemn him, and make him quite out of heart in respect of himself ... Herein stands the power and pith of true religion, when a man by observation and experience in himself, knows the love of God in Christ towards him.[42]

Conversion had achieved the position of a central rite of passage into adult society in the eighteenth-century New England of Jonathan Edwards.[43] Edwards, Calvinist preacher and one of the founding fathers of the psychology of religion, puts the motivation clearly in the introduction to his most famous book, *The Religious Affections*:

> There is no question whatsoever that is of greater importance to mankind, and that it more concerns every individual person to be well resolved in, than this: *What are the distinguishing qualifications of those that are in favour with God, and entitled to His eternal rewards?*[44]

Edwards, as a student of John Locke, represents a stance that still wished to prevent a tearing apart of religion understood as the fruit of spiritual experience, and Enlightenment philosophy. It was a strategy that was to become more and more submerged by the secularizing forces of the Enlightenment itself. By this time the life of the spirit was beginning to find another sanctuary that was relatively independent of orthodox religion. R. D. Stock[45] charts a survival route through literature and the arts, especially with the rise of the Romantic movement at the end of the eighteenth century. This helped to ensure that spirituality was never truly submerged by rationalism.

To British ears, the expression of romantic feeling is clearest in the poetry of Wordsworth. His most famous lines on the subject, composed a few miles above Tintern Abbey, include the following:

> *I have felt*
> *A presence that disturbs me with the joy*
> *Of elevated thoughts; a sense sublime*
> *Of something far more deeply interfused,*
> *Whose dwelling is the light of setting suns,*
> *And the round ocean, and the living air,*
> *And the blue sky, and in the mind of man,*
> *A motion and a spirit, that impels*
> *All thinking things, all objects of all thought,*
> *And rolls through all things. Therefore am I still*
> *A lover of the meadows and the woods,*
> *And mountains; and of all that we behold*

From this green earth; of all the mighty world
Of eye and ear ...[46]

Wordsworth's biographer Stephen Gill notes that '"therefore" is the pivotal word in this declaration.'[47] People were worried about Wordsworth's philosophical consistency; they even felt he did not grasp its arguments properly. But as in the case of Pascal, his defence of the realm of the spirit is not through philosophical abstraction but by direct appeal to experience.

The most obvious difference between Pascal and Wordsworth is that whilst Pascal speaks from within a Judaeo-Christian context, Wordsworth completely avoids all such reference. This detachment between orthodox religious language and spirituality on the part of a practising member of the Church of England is something that we have already seen more radically expressed in Rénan's complete break with the religious institution.

The politics of spiritual education

I have offered some illustrations of the tangled history of the relationship between spirituality and religion. The confusion persists to this day, and it has created a cultural crisis. Though spirituality continues to express itself strongly, if obliquely,[48] in the realm of the arts, the message is easily missed. The arts are reduced to being a commodity providing diversion or entertainment, and their spiritual power is diluted or lost. But as I said in the previous chapter, spirituality has a vital social and political function, and when it no longer finds an overarching means of cultural expression, social coherence is threatened.

Fears about social disintegration are perennial in human history. No doubt they are a permanent source of neurosis in any human group that is too large for face-to-face communication between all its members. But as Samuel Preus remarked, such worries began to emerge with particular force in Europe following the overt loss of religious community at the time of the Reformation. Already in the early seventeenth century John Donne's anxiety is evident in his observation, 'Tis all in pieces, all cohærence gone.'[49] Three hundred years later, in a still more fragmented environment, W. B. Yeats expresses the same thought in terms of spiritual deafness:

Turning and turning in the widening gyre
The falcon cannot hear the falconer;
Things fall apart; the centre cannot hold;
Mere anarchy is loosed upon the world,
The blood dimmed tide is loosed, and everywhere
The ceremony of innocence is drowned;
The best lack all conviction, while the worst
Are full of passionate intensity.[50]

By the beginning of the 1990s in many parts of the Western world apprehensiveness had reached a point where responsible commentators were voicing fears about the large-scale break-down of the moral community. Writing about the United States in 1993, Philip Selznick talks of a deterioration in the subtle and intimate complexity of human relations.[51] Mass society, he says, is able to survive and even flourish when density of population is accompanied by what he calls a 'density of social texture and relatedness', as was the case in traditional China or India. But in modern mass society we feel ourselves to be little more than mobile, interchangeable units, only loosely bound together. The fabric of relationships becomes very thin, and as a result there are fewer and fewer constraints on the excesses of individualism. People lose intimate connection both to other people and to what he calls 'sustaining ideas', meaning the religious and philosophical resources of traditional cultures.

One outcome of these attenuations is the the rise of meaninglessness and consequently the weakening of moral consensus, with its accompaniment of social dislocation and crime. In the preface to the 1995 British edition of *The Spirit of Community* the American sociologist Amitai Etzioni[52] suggests that these matters should be of some concern to the citizens of the United Kingdom:

True, the United Kingdom has not yet reached the levels of moral anarchy and the crumbling of social institutions that we witness in the United States, but the trends point West-ward. Increases in rates of violent crime, illegitimacy, drug abuse, children who kill and show no remorse and, yes, political corruption, are all indications. It matters little if these portents are old or new, or that other societies are more decayed; it only matters that by any measure the readings of social ill health are far too high for a civic society. The best time to reinforce the moral and social foundations of institutions is not after they have collapsed but when they are cracking. Does anyone truly believe that they have not yet cracked in the United Kingdom?[53]

There are indeed similar fears in Britain. At the beginning of 1996 a large Symposium was convened in London by the School Curriculum and Assessment Authority (SCAA – now part of the Qualifications and Curriculum Authority), the statutory body charged with responsibility for advising the British gov-ernment on all curricular matters. The theme of the meeting was 'Education for Adult Life with particular reference to the spiritual and moral dimensions of education'. The 300 or so delegates were drawn from all sectors of the community: government, parents, employers, academics, trade unionists, the police and representatives of the different faith communities.

In his welcoming speech to the delegates Sir Ron Dearing,[54] the Chairman of SCAA, expressed his acute misgivings at the decay of social coherence in Britain. He echoed the fears mentioned by Etzioni, at least partly triggered by concurrent news of a spate of well-publicized incidents of random violence. There are differing opinions about crime levels in Britain. A current report shows that annual rates of crime have begun to drop, perhaps because of a fall in unemployment. The fact remains, as was pointed out in one of the recent publications of the British ESRC, that on average over several years now, the annual *increase* in reported crime is greater than the annual *total* of reported crime during the 1950s.

Nicholas Tate, the Chief Executive of SCAA, identified the cause of the problem as the growth of moral relativism: 'If ever a dragon needed slaying, it is the dragon of relativism.' According to Tate, one of its major sources is the decline of religious faith:

> Although many can accept that truth in moral matters can be independent of God, the loss of the religious basis for morality has weakened its credibility. As the Archbishop of Canterbury has recently said, people ever since the Enlightment 'have been living off the legacy of a deep, residual belief in God. But as people move further away from that, they find it more and more difficult to give a substantial basis for why they should be good'. This is one reason why religious education must continue to be a vital part of every child's curriculum ... It is also a reason why children's spiritual development is so important, as the origin of the will to do what is right.

This is a familiar point of view and one with which I sympathize, but the situation is unfortunately not as straightforward as Tate suggests. Ten years after the trauma of the Second World War, when the steep decline in the power of institutional religion was clear to everyone, the psychologist Margaret Knight gained notoriety as the first person to create a truly national debate in Britain on the relationship between morals and religion.[55] The trigger for her celebrity was two short talks which she gave on BBC radio in 1955, suggesting that moral behaviour does not require a basis in religious belief. In one newspaper she was headlined in two-inch capitals as 'The Unholy Mrs Knight'.[56] The article went on to complain that the BBC had 'allowed a fanatic to rampage along the air lanes, beating up Christianity with a razor and bicycle chain'. The over-the-top outrage in the media betrayed the depth of public anxiety about the sources of morality.

Seen from a vantage point nearly half a century later, what was concerning both Margaret Knight and her religiously committed opponents was the need for a plausible basis for social coherence. In spite of her views, in most people's minds then and now, morality is still associated with religion. There is good reason for this. The literature of religion is full of references to the importance of love of one's neighbour, justice, honesty, care for the poor. The religious institutions carry within them many hundreds of years of reflection on the nature of the human spirit, how it becomes corrupt, how it is revived and sustained, and how it relates to political reality. These reflections are illustrations of the 'sustaining ideas' to which Selznick refers.

But I have been arguing that morality has its source at a deeper level than specific religious adherence, since it arises in the first place out of spiritual insight. My guess is that at some level Margaret Knight was aware of this, though as a secular humanist she would no doubt be unhappy to use my rhetoric. The problem is that no obvious alternative to religion has emerged with sufficient power to act as a vehicle for the nurture of spiritual awareness. It is because of this that spiritual education has become such a salient issue in the school curriculum.

How are we to ensure that our children grow up to be morally responsible members of the community? If spiritual awareness is a necessary basis for moral behaviour, then for many years the educational system has been disastrously neglectful of its responsibilities. Of all the curricular areas highlighted in the opening paragraphs of the 1988 British Education Reform Act, Spiritual Education is given the least overt attention and the least resources.[57] The danger is that the loss of religious coherence is only the surface appearance of a more profound loss or suppression of spirituality which begins in childhood. In the next chapter I want to review the research evidence which we already have about the spirituality of children.

3

Children's Spirituality – What We Know Already

> For myself, I would sooner know what contrition feels like, than how to define it.
>
> THOMAS À KEMPIS[1]

I spent the last two chapters explaining the context in which the spirituality of today's children has to survive and, if possible, flourish. I now want to turn my attention to what we already know from research on children's spirituality. Immediately we run into snags, the most important of which is the shortage of competent research.

In the English-speaking world towards the end of the nineteenth century a small but important school of psychologists of religious experience emerged in the north-east United States, led by William James and G. Stanley Hall, the first president of Clark University. The motivation behind this development seems to have been, at least partly, concern for the validity of the Puritan conversion experience, which was still an important rite of passage in New England at that time. Given space, the empirical study of children's spirituality should have flourished, especially as several members of the group were interested in religious education. But the school was soon to suffer eclipse because of the increasingly powerful critique of religion which I discussed in the previous chapter. Under the hostile influence of early psychoanalysis and behaviourist psychology, serious study of religious experience had more or less died out by 1930.[2]

A second difficulty is the intellectual bias of much of the modern psychology of education. During the 1960s one of the most influential students of religious education in the English-speaking world was the psychologist Ronald Goldman. He launched an important debate about the way in which the mental development of children relates to their ability to grasp the meaning of religious narrative, particularly the text of the Bible. Goldman was a follower of the cognitive psychologist Jean Piaget, and his personal assumptions led him to ignore the possibility that spirituality might feature in the lives of children.

In the second chapter of his most important book, *Religious Thinking from Childhood to Adolescence*[3] Goldman took the view that 'the mystics, who claim to have direct sensations of the divine, are exceptions, but as they are extremely rare cases, rarer in adolescence and practically unknown in childhood,'[4] he would ignore them. The mistake he made was to assume that spiritual awareness is always something extraordinary, equated with mystical ecstasy, instead of holding open the possibility that it might be a very ordinary aspect of young children's everyday experience. For anyone who thought Goldman was right, it followed that their research efforts should be directed away from spirituality to subjects that are of more immediate educational significance.

Goldman's opinions continue to have influence, despite sustained critiques of his position by a number of scholars.[5] In more recent times the leading figures in developmental theory as it affects children's religion have been the American James Fowler[6] and the Swiss Fritz Oser.[7] Their work is sophisticated and it would be much too dismissive to say that they do not take account of spirituality. Nevertheless, I believe their stress on the development of intellectual and moral *reasoning* in children means that they downplay the spiritual dimension.

There is a third difficulty. This is to do with the words people use to communicate and, to a degree, construct their experience. As I have emphasized, reality is always and inevitably interpreted in terms of a particular cultural medium. Consequently, Western researchers who have looked at spirituality have almost always focused on the language of Christianity as the criterion for identifying their subject. If Alister Hardy is right and spiritual awareness is universally found in human beings, this kind of limitation is in danger of distorting the accuracy of the findings very seriously. In a multi-faith and highly secularized nation such as Britain, the spirituality of most people is liable to be overlooked.

What do we know of the spirituality of childhood?

Following the collapse of the New England School, one of the first signs of a revival of psychological interest in spirituality came not from America but from Sweden. In 1959 the child psychologist Gote Klingberg published a study of what she identified as the religious experience of 630 Swedish children aged 9 to 13.[8] She had asked them to write compositions completing the statement, 'Once when I thought about God ...' When she read their essays she found she could classify the situations into four types. In order of frequency, they were (a) situations of distress; (b) experiences in nature; (c) moral experiences; (d) formal worship experiences. Of course, thinking about God is not the same thing as awareness of God. Nevertheless, Klingberg felt that the tone of the essays suggested an immediately felt spiritual dimension to the descriptions provided by the children. This was most likely to be the case with prayer experiences, which seemed to involve the deepest emotional reactions.

In 1962 the Elkinds, a husband-and-wife team, published an account of a piece of psychological research copied from Klingberg's study.[9] Their subjects were American teenagers and thus older than the group with which I am mainly concerned. But the research is interesting because of the way the Elkinds altered Klingberg's question to make it key in more directly to experience. The 144 ninth-grade students were asked by their English teacher to write a paragraph directly and personally in answer to each of two questions: (a) When do you feel closest to God? (b) Have you ever had a particular experience when you felt especially close to God?

The students responded to the request willingly and in a variety of ways. Some of the situations written about were 'recurrent' – that is, the writer claimed they happened often. In order of frequency the contexts in which they often felt close to God were described as: church, solitude, anxiety, fear, worry, prayer, moral action. Other kinds of situations were what the Elkinds called 'acute' – that is to say, memorably intense and unusual occasions. In order of frequency of report these related to: thanking God, meditation, initiation, grief, revelation.

One curious difference between the Swedish and American findings is that the position of the church as a setting for spiritual experience is reversed, being bottom of the list in Sweden and top in the United States. Is this because of the fact that Sweden is much more secularized than the United States, or could it be a reflection of changing attitudes to formal religion on entering adolescence? The former interpretation seems more likely, and it reminds us yet again of the influence of cultural context on the way spirituality is expressed. At any rate, these relatively modest pieces of research by Klingberg and the Elkinds suggested that spiritual awareness was perhaps not as absent from childhood and youth as Goldman was about to claim in a few years' time.

In 1967 David Elkind, along with two other American psychologists, Long and Spilka,[10] published some research that complicated the picture. They were looking at differences between children and adolescents in the nature of their religious understanding and experience, particularly in relation to prayer. They found that before the ages of 10 to 12, prayer tended to follow a mechanical formula and consisted mainly in making requests to God. In teenagers prayer was more likely to be understood as a private conversation with God, sharing intimacies and confidences, whilst petitionary requests were of only secondary importance.

The findings imply that as children move into puberty there is a growth in religious or spiritual awareness. This, incidentally, agrees with the results of investigations reported at the beginning of the twentieth century by G. Stanley Hall and some of his colleagues in the New England School with regard to the typical age of religious conversion. Conversion tends to coincide with the age of sexual maturation.[11] This may indeed be the normal pattern of development for children growing up within a community where religious assumptions are not strongly questioned. It is not what usually happens in other, more secularized circumstances, as I have hinted in previous chapters and as we shall see more clearly later in this book.

During the 1970s and 1980s, evidence of the reality of spiritual awareness in early childhood began to flow from the work of Edward Robinson, the successor of Alister Hardy as director of the Religious Experience Research Unit in Oxford. Robinson noticed that a sizable proportion of the 5,000 or so accounts of religious experience which had been sent in to the Unit were reminiscences of events occuring in childhood, sometimes in very early years. As a result of pondering on these stories, he published an account of them in his book *The Original Vision*.[12] This was a pioneering attempt to question the educational validity of the Piagetian model as applied by Goldman to the area of religious understanding.

What first impressed Robinson was the way that these childhood experiences had remained vivid in the memories of his correspondents for the whole of their lives. People repeatedly spoke of them as having the greatest personal significance when they were contemplating their personal identity and the meaning of their lives. No doubt there had been a considerable development in the interpretation and perhaps embellishment of these experiences as the individuals thought about them over the years. Yet Robinson found it hard to ignore the power of the initial impact of the event which had generated this wealth of reflection. Could it be that Goldman and his followers were giving a great deal of attention to the language and thought forms of religion, whilst ignoring the direct awareness out of which it grows? Robinson began to suspect, as had Wordsworth before him, that the vision of childhood could perhaps be locked out of awareness as we enter the secularized world of adult life. The Orkney poet Edwin Muir, from whom Robinson drew the title of his book, also believed that the original vision of childhood was usually forgotten:

> a child has also a picture of human existence peculiar to himself, which he probably never remembers after he has lost it: the original vision of the world. I think of this picture or vision as that of a state in which the earth, the houses on the earth, and the life of every human being are related to the sky overarching them; as if the sky fitted the earth and the earth the sky.[13]

Robinson's research movingly demonstrated that in spite of the pressure to neglect it, the vision is not always forgotten. But perhaps in the social circumstances of our time the dominant beliefs are such that they very often do not permit the development of a mature understanding of the original vision. Could spirituality become suppressed or even repressed out of consciousness?

Edward Robinson depended for his data on reminiscences of childhood by adults, some of whom were very elderly. There is no way to assess the reliability of such long-term memories, or to check up on the elaboration that must inevitably have gone on with repeated reflection upon the story over many years. In the second half of the 1980s, two brief American investigations began to tackle this problem. In *The Children's God* David Heller[14] describes his exploration of children's ways of understanding and communicating with God. His relationships with the children seem to have been fairly short. He had only one meeting with each of them and based his conversation on a previously prepared interview schedule. His personal perspective was overtly religious, but he was careful to ask the children to use their own terms and to relate them to other issues of personal significance.

Jo-Anne Taylor's study *Innocent Wisdom*[15] is still briefer, but in many ways it is just as impressive. It contains a set of very sensitive individual interviews and analytic comments with a small sample of children from a range of faiths, aged 4 to 12. Her interpretations are placed in the context of Christian religious literature, but this is done creatively, exploring the children's use of metaphor and also the way that their drawings amplify their verbal expression.

Robert Coles' book *The Spiritual Life of Children* was published in 1992. This is an ambitious account of an important large-scale study which does not suffer from the limitation of Robinson's work.[16] Over many years Coles, based in Harvard University, had had numerous conversations with children from many different countries and cultural backgrounds. Like Robinson, he sees it as a mistake to give priority to intellectual operations in our attempts to understand children's spirituality. In his dialogues he insisted on listening actively to the descriptions of the children's experience and, as far as possible, refusing to lay his own interpretations on them. He showed that when you listen directly to what children have to say instead of setting them Piagetian tests, you hear a different kind of story, one concerned with living personal experience.

As a result of talking with children of many faiths and none, Coles found himself thinking inevitably of spiritual awareness as a universal human attribute. In his attempts to understand in naturalistic terms what the children mean when they talk of their experience of God, he begins from a psychodynamic perspective, following quite closely the ideas of the American psychoanalyst Ana-Maria Rizzuto.[17] What Rizzuto has in mind is the concept of 'transitional space', a term invented by the English psychoanalyst Donald Winnicott.[18] It is intended to describe the all-important realm *between* illusion and reality, in which many of the most significant human experiences, such as creative and religious impulses, appear to find expression both in childhood and adulthood. As such, the notion of the transitional space offers an important potential source of spirituality which takes respectful account of both inner and outer worlds, reducing spiritual experience to neither.[19] In the end though, Coles is rather uncomfortable with Rizzuto's continued use of the word 'illusion' to refer to spiritual experience, since even if 'illusion' and 'reality' are not contradictory, as she asserts, they are not identical.

I do not wish to dismiss the psychoanalytic contribution to our understanding of children's spirituality, particularly its account of the role of projection in creating children's images of God. The work of many researchers shows that their images of God contain a strongly projective component, usually drawn from the parents. But the Finnish psychologist Kalevi Tamminen has recently reminded us of the ambiguity of this evidence.[20] If Freud is correct that God is a projected parent figure and if children normally prefer the opposite sex parent, it follows that boys should be more concerned with a motherly deity, girls with a fatherly God. According to some researchers[21] the father figure is more dominant in girls' idea of God, but others[22] find that the dominant figure is either the mother or, alternatively, the parent who is closer to the child. Clearly, the situation is more complex than a simplistic interpretation of Freudian theory would lead us to suppose. It could be that the apparent significance of one or other parent figure depends on the contribution which that person makes to the child's experience of personal relationships, of self-knowledge and of being known. Each of these are recurrent themes in the progression towards spiritual enlightenment in most faiths.

Two German approaches
At approximately the same time as some of the earlier pieces of research to which I have referred, rather different methods were being used by two German-speaking researchers. Their approaches are philosophically subtle and more interpretive in style, and they allow the possibility of exploration in depth. By the same token, they are also more open to question on methodological grounds. Theophil Thun's study of groups of Catholic and Protestant children in the first four grades of school was published at almost the same time as Klingberg's

Swedish work.[23] Thun's research procedure owes a good deal to Karl Girgensohn, the major figure in the Dorpat (Tartu in modern Estonia) school of religious psychology. During the early years of the twentieth century, Girgensohn devised a systematic method for experimental introspection into religious experience, which Thun has partly borrowed.

He offered the children a series of what were, within the Christian cultural context, existential questions to reflect upon: What was Jesus like? What is the nature of prayer? How did they experience meeting death? Instead of being asked to reply immediately to Thun's questions, the children were invited to sit quietly with their eyes closed whilst they contemplated the theme presented. After this request to get in touch with a dimension of knowing which is perhaps deeper than that provided by an immediate reflex response, they discussed their replies to the questions. Thun noted that from the second grade onwards the children demonstrated the capacity for wonder, or an awareness of the *mysterium tremendum* and the *mysterium fascinans* (these are terms which were used by the German philosopher and theologian Rudolf Otto to explain the meaning of the word 'numinous', which he coined to refer to the experience of the overwhelming presence of God).[24] At the same time it also became clear to Thun that in the third grade the first hints of religious scepticism were creeping in, as evidenced by occasional critical comments made by the children. In a later study of adolescents published in 1963, Thun showed how religious awareness had become absolutely foreign for the majority of those he questioned.[25]

In 1965 Maria Bindl, whose thinking was also influenced by the work of Rudolf Otto, produced a study of over 8,000 drawings on religious themes by Roman Catholic school pupils aged from 3 to 18 years.[26] Otto had emphasized the centrality of a nonrational element in religious experience which goes beyond words. Bindl felt that examining children's drawings might help her to reach further into those depths. With young children, drawing also has advantages over speech as a means of expression, because of the limitations in the children's verbal and

The Spirit of the Child

conceptual ability. To interpret the drawings Bindl adapted a method devised by Ludwig Klages for analysing handwriting.[27]

She felt she was able to detect four developmental phases. The first extended till about the age of seven, and was labelled by her as 'naive relatedness to the Wholly Other'. At this stage God is experienced very simply, in an I-Thou relationship. In her second stage, 'decline in spontaneous experience of the numinous', which may appear as early as the age of six, the powerful experience of the wholly other begins to fade as reason displaces fantasy. At puberty the third phase, 'narcissistic reversion toward one's own self' takes over. Self-preoccupation closes off awareness of the 'Wholly Other'. Bindl did, however, note that in some cases in the later teenage years there was a return to a 'consciously striven for relation to transcendence'. Her findings are interesting, not least because they suggest that in the appropriate environment late adolescence can be a time when there is an attempt to recover what had been lost in childhood. Unfortunately her use of Klages' graphological method of assessing the children's drawings has been severely criticized as invalid.[28] Nevertheless, Bindl's interpretations need not necessarily be ruled out entirely. There is, for example, evidence that the interpretation of drawings has been used successfully in the diagnosis of severe physical illness and psychological problems in children by Susan Bach and her colleagues.[29]

Some doubts about developmental theory

The research I have been discussing is in accord with the findings of a more recent large scale study of religious development in childhood and adolescence published in 1991. Kalevi Tamminen noted very high levels of report of religious or spiritual experience in children up to the age of about 12 or 13 years, followed by a steep decline.[30] These data are in accord with those of the British researcher Leslie Francis, who has charted the collapse of religious interest in British children from the ages of 8 to 15.[31]

In Chapter 2 I suggested that the process of secularization is a social construction peculiar to Europe and rooted in the history of that continent. The findings I have discussed are in harmony with that interpretation. It is around the age of 12 that children in Europe typically have their first serious induction into the scientific tradition of the Enlightenment, with its associated religious scepticism. That children are now often receiving scientific instruction from a much younger age may have the effect of inhibiting early spirituality at an even more sensitive, vulnerable stage. Tamminen's identification of declining reports of spiritual experience with age can therefore be assimilated to a hypothesis that the 'blotting out' of spirituality is a socially constructed phenomenon. This hypothesis directly contradicts a sceptical opinion which might argue that spirituality itself is socially constructed and therefore only gradually in evidence as children are artificially inducted into this otherwise 'unnatural' sensibility. In my opinion the research evidence reviewed here does not support the sceptical view.

The notion of the development of religious understanding in children has surely always been of concern to devout parents and teachers. Recently, F. Schweitzer has shown that formal ideas about religious development were already present in the writings of the sixteenth-century Reformers,[32] and he traces a train of thought emerging steadily in Luther, Comenius and Francke. But he goes on to suggest that in the seventeenth century the philosophers Rousseau and Locke had transmuted this concern into a conscious and highly rationalistic interest in the theory of knowledge. Schweitzer notes that amongst religious writers it led to a paradoxical avoidance of the spiritual dimension of human experience, a theme which echoes my remarks in the previous chapter.

No one can sensibly dispute the importance of intellectual understanding in relation to any aspect of reality, whether it be spiritual experience or the data of the physical sciences. Cognitive theories of religious development offer such understanding and are important as far as they go. Even so, the cumulative feeling I am left with after reviewing what we know about childhood spirituality is an uneasiness about the adequacy of developmental theory to give an account of it.

The continuing legacy of avoidance of spirituality shows itself in the power of mainstream psychology to set the bounds for acceptable research. The plausibility of cognitive psychology as a means of gaining self-understanding has meant that developmental theories of religion have tended to follow rather tamely in its wake.[33] I do not deny that stage theories have their uses. The major problem is their narrowness, coming near to dissolving religion into reason and therefore childhood spirituality into nothing more than a form of immaturity or inadequacy. If cognitive development is central, it also puts out of court the work of Henri Bissonnier,[34] who writes about the profound spiritual awareness he has observed in people who are mentally retarded. Similarly, it rules out Jean-Marie Jaspard's discussion of the comprehension of religious rituals among male and female mentally handicapped adults.[35]

Intellectualist theories of religion need to be complemented by a similarly strong interest in the nature of spiritual awareness. For example, Jaspard hypothesizes that amongst mentally handicapped people, ritual is the major way in which spiritual awareness of God is mediated. I believe his hypothesis can be extended. When we examine the total phenomenon of religion directly, rather than theorize about its cognitive aspects, we find that central to its *praxis* is the use of rituals or exercises which in many cases have developed over thousands of years and are highly sophisticated. They can be seen as designed to enhance awareness through meditative or contemplative techniques. Such awareness appears to be an extremely subtle and delicate phenomenon, but one which I have been claiming is rooted in our biological make-up.[36] The fact that the expressive dimension of religion is marked by a particularly rich emphasis on ritual, as well as symbolism and metaphor, seems to be related to this holistic awareness.

In its preoccupation with the profoundest questions of existence, religion is the most extreme form of the human desire to know. Though in its arguments it may use linear logic, it cannot be confined by logic and needs to turn to other modes of expression. As I mentioned earlier, Donald Winnicott argued that these aspects of human behaviour occupy the 'transitional space' between fantasy and reality. Hence, though they may have their roots in the physical world, their articulation necessarily borrows qualities from the creative imagination.

In recent years there has been a number of attempts by researchers in the field of religion to reinstate the validity of ritual and symbol as dimensions of thinking. Hans-Günther Heimbrock,[37] for example, asks whether, in religion, symbolic thinking is truly inferior to linear logic. Elsewhere[38] he questions the apparent belittling or ignoring of ritual, especially by his Swiss colleague Fritz Oser. Oser appears to accept the view that ritual is primitive, a stage which we grow out of, yet it is central to the mediation of spiritual experience in many religious groups, not least in Oser's own Roman Catholic faith. By insisting on intellectualization as the most valid criterion for assessing religious understanding we are perhaps assimilating assumptions of developmental psychology which may not correspond to human reality.

Modern students of religious development are tempted to fall into a well-known error, alluded to clearly in a perceptive article by Lorelei Farmer.[39] Discussing the results of a small study of adult reminiscences of childhood spiritual experience,[40] Farmer points out that no amount of refinement and blending of the cognitive theories of Piaget, Kohlberg or Erikson will bring us closer to understanding religious knowledge. The mistake is one of false philosophical categorization. Spiritual or religious *knowing* is very different from knowledge of factual information, or speculation about religion. It is much more like a direct sensory awareness.

The distinction between 'direct knowledge' and 'knowledge about' a subject is a familiar one. Farmer notes that our care in separating these two kinds of knowledge (religious knowing and knowledge about religion) suggests that we must also allow the possibility that direct knowing may be independent of the growth of intellectual abilities and emotional capacities. What we *can* do, she says, is consider the functioning of the intellectual and emotional processes which we bring to bear on the contents of religious awareness. That means much more than being able to give a logically correct explanation of a passage from scripture, or solve a moral conundrum.

All of the adults Farmer talked with spoke of a process of slowly coming to understand (in some kind of quasi-rational way) through being faithful to the truths they perceived (in some other way) in their early transcendent experiences. She suggests that an important area for research must be to investigate the form in which such experience is held by children at the time, before it becomes the subject of a lifetime's reflection. How, if at all, do children articulate or at least store such memories which are later recalled as spiritually significant? And how much more experience is forgotten in the absence of any context which allows its expression?

A new direction for spirituality research?

What is implied in the criticisms made by Farmer is the necessity to turn to a more holistic model of human spirituality, which sees it as something larger than any individual religion. So far I have insisted on taking religious (and particularly Christian) interpretations of reality seriously. It has involved me in hopping rather uncomfortably between the terms 'religion' and 'spirituality' because of their close historical linkage. I now want to go on to say that the bond between spirituality and the Christian religion is itself a constriction of meaning which has had serious practical consequences in the school curriculum. The rapid de-Christianization of British society has created a legacy that makes for considerable difficulties in implementing the requirements of the 1988 Education Reform Act in regard to spiritual education.

Most of the pieces of research I have discussed have either an overt or a hidden assumption that spirituality, if it is to express itself, must do so via the language and concepts of Christianity. The implication of taking Hardy's view seriously for an understanding of children's spirituality is very different. He implies that there is in every child a spiritual potentiality, no matter what the child's cultural context may be. Of course, it is certain that the specific context will play a central role in shaping, nurturing or stunting this innate potentiality, just as the specific language environment serves to shape the linguisitic expressions made possible by our human capacity for language – the innate potential that Noam Chomsky[41] refers to as our 'language acquisition device'.

Social institutions like language offer both possibilities and constraints. Karl Rahner in discussing what, from his Christian perspective, is the experience of God today, speaks of religions as 'conceptual reflections on, and social institutionalizations of our experience of God'.[42] He adds that conceptual reflections always fail to capture the experience, *just as it is possible to talk about God without being spiritual* (my italics). The difficulty with almost all research on children's spirituality up to the very recent past is that it focuses on God-talk, or in Goldman and his descendants' case, the Piagetian development of God-talk. Given that the religious contexts surrounding children today are typically much less explicit than in the past or even absent, in order to uncover the innate spiritual potential children may possess, research needs to take a different direction. Researchers need to focus on the perceptions, awareness and response of children to those ordinary activities which can act as what Peter Berger calls 'signals of transcendence'.[43]

I have complained of the lack of a research tradition that has looked at children's spirituality from this broader perspective. But recently there are signs of a move in this direction. Elaine McCreery in her work on 'talking to children about things spiritual'[44] is enquiring about the spiritual notions of children as young as four or five. She reminds us that the people who gave accounts of their childhood experience to Edward Robinson[45] were unable to articulate it at the time that it happened. They did not have the language available and it is only in adult life that they were able to retrieve it as a spiritual experience.

McCreery's straightforward definition of spirituality is 'An awareness that there is something Other, something greater than the course of everyday events.' She has tried to identify events in the home (birth, death, love, trust, joy, sadness, special occasions, religion), at school (nature studies, stories, danger, failure, reward, companionship, success; also activities such as painting, drawing, sorting, matching, play, story, singing) and on television (cultural difference, violence, death, social taboos, nobility, despicable behaviour, suffering, charity) which might relate to her definition.

It is notable that in her conversations with children, she is keen to give no verbal cues which might trigger off standard religious phraseology – that is, theoretical talk *about* spiritual experience rather than direct reference to personal spirituality. Thus she considers that the question 'What do you think happens when we die?' is too leading. McCreery feels it is better to tell a story involving the death of an animal, perhaps a pet, and invite the children to give their reflections on it – for example, by asking them how they would console the owner.

In their work on children's spirituality, Clive and Jane Erricker stress the problem of identifying an immutable spirituality in a social context where normal spiritual or religious language is either absent, suppressed or repressed because of problems of plausibility in modern, scientific culture.[46] The Errickers and their colleagues ask, 'How can we converse in an informed way about such notions as spiritual and moral, unless we have an understanding of the views, attitudes and concerns of children nurtured in a plurality of social, religious and educational environments?'[47] They give an account of talking to two ten year old boys (one a Muslim, the other a Sikh) about their interest in *bhangra* dancing and how it acts as a metaphorical expression of the individuality and spiritual self of the boys.

The task of the Errickers' research is to reach towards the understanding of reality and the metaphorical frameworks of the children with an 'open ear', ready to catch the elusive dimension of spiritual awareness. One of their descriptions is of work with Stage-2 children in an inner-city comprehensive school in Southampton. In their conversations they focus on existential themes such as loss and conflict and how children attempt to resolve these issues with the personal narratives available to them. From the perspective of the Errickers, there is a need to deconstruct the children's storytelling in the process of bringing their own spirituality to their awareness. The Errickers believe they have identified a set of 'genres' – that is, ideas and attitudes constituting an identifiable package – that children tend to take up, and presumably within which their spirituality must find expression. Children can switch genres and it is interesting that the research team have not at the time of writing identified a genre purely based on religious tradition (though surely this would be the case at least with some Muslim children). Four genres that are fairly clear are:

- ❖ 'My little pony' – a Disneyesque approach concentrating on the welfare of animals.
- ❖ 'All-American kid' – theme parks, McDonalds and consumerism.
- ❖ Family-centred.
- ❖ The hard man.

The pieces of research I have discussed are examples of a very small area of work which is still at an early stage. No firm conclusions can yet be drawn from the data. It is notable, however, that the assumptions held by the researchers and the validity of their findings appear to depend much more on a notion of in-built spiritual awareness than on any of the contemporary variants of developmental theory.

In my view research of this kind does not, as some critics claim, attenuate or damage religious understanding. On the contrary, by drawing attention to a realm of human awareness commonly avoided in school, even in the RE classroom, it may help children to appreciate the experiential perspective of the religious believer. Religious understanding can grow out of a recognition by individuals of the existence of such spiritual experience within themselves. In the next chapter I will go on to discuss the theoretical framework that underlies the work of the Children's Spirituality Project at the University of Nottingham.

4

A Geography of the Spirit

It is possible to talk about God without being spiritual.

KARL RAHNER SJ[1]

The epigraph to this chapter can be supplemented with the remark that it is also possible to be spiritual without talking about God. I have been at pains to emphasize that knowledge *about* religion and the ability to use religious language is not the whole story when we are thinking about spirituality. It is important not to get caught into the assumption that spirituality can only be recognized by the use of a specialized religious language. I have spoken about the difficulty with almost all research on children's spiritual life, up to the very recent past, in that it has been focused on God-talk rather than spirituality. I have also presented a notion of spirituality as something biologically built into the human species, an holistic awareness of reality which is potentially to be found in every human being. Although historically it has very close links with religion, it is logically prior to religion, at least when religion is conceived of as a set of beliefs, doctrines and practices held by a particular human community.

But if people don't use traditional religious language to talk about their spiritual life, how can we recognize it? Now that teachers are being asked to give proper attention to the spiritual dimension of the curriculum, it is a basic requirement for an intelligent approach to this field to discover in which areas of language and behaviour we need to be alert if we are to find evidence of spiritual awareness.

You will gather from what I have said previously that in principle there is no area of human experience which is not potentially open to spiritual awareness. But the history of any human society means that its assumptions and expectations about reality will close off spiritual awareness in some areas of life, whilst leaving others intact. This is so even for the religious believer. Christians who have been brought up traditionally will almost certainly have been taught that God is everywhere. Yet the habit of regular churchgoing in a devout family, perhaps along with an emphasis on the importance of silence in religious life, may mean that someone from that background feels closest to God in the quiet of an empty church. At the other end of the scale, it is at least feasible that someone who is well aware that they have a spiritual life may have had a life history that leads to an angry distaste for formal religion. Many years ago a clergyman's son told me, 'One thing I detest more than anything is to go into a church. Man is in charge.' His spiritual life, if it was to emerge, would have to do so in some context other than an empty church.

The tangled and contradictory history of religion in the West means that the task before us is to map the geography of a novel spiritual terrain. The landscape is likely to be vaguely and tantalizingly familiar because many of its features have been identified and named long ago in the language of traditional Christianity. The task is also confusing because in post-Christian society we have very little idea of the ways that children deal with their experience in this area. How do they speak about it? What 'spiritual dialects' do they use? How do these languages relate, if at all, to religious language? We need to learn to become at home in this landscape and used to the vocabulary and practices of the children in their own exploration if we are to help them to protect their spirituality.

In the end, the only way an accurate map can be drawn is to listen to what children have to say and, from what we hear, to create an empirical account of the contexts of childhood spirituality. By trial and error we will be able to identify the omissions, assumptions and mistakes which we have made and, eventually, to create a coherent scientific picture.[2] Once teachers are equipped with this information, the curriculum can be sensitively built around the realities of the children's experience.

But to begin with, we are in the unenviable position of having to start without a starting point. Where shall we begin to look and listen? I want to suggest as a provisional beginning a set of three interrelated themes or categories of spiritual sensitivity or awareness which Rebecca Nye and I have worked out. Because there simply is no unambiguous starting point, these categories will provide an initial 'something to look for'.

We believe they must play a part in anyone's spiritual life. They are hinted at in the converging evidence of other writers on spirituality and on child psychology, as well as in our own reflections on what children said during the pilot stage of the research which will be described in later chapters. As will become clear, by inviting children to talk about these ordinary areas of human experience, we were indeed able to uncover a rich landscape.

Categories of spiritual sensitivity

Awareness-sensing	Here-and-now
	Tuning
	Flow
	Focusing
Mystery-sensing	Wonder and awe
	Imagination
Value-sensing	Delight and despair
	Ultimate goodness
	Meaning

(After Nye and Hay, 1996.)

Awareness-sensing

The word that kept recurring when we were discussing the practicalities of spirituality was 'awareness'. In modern English usage it has an ambiguous meaning. My dictionary defines it as 'a dim form of consciousness' – in other words, not full consciousness. This is almost the opposite of what I mean. The word comes from the Old English root *wær*, 'to be wary or cautious', suggesting a state of high alertness. Although we can become alert involuntarily, as when we are startled or find ourselves suddenly in danger, we can also choose to be aware by 'paying attention' to what is happening.

Psychologists use the term 'attention' in this way, and quite often they are thinking of the awareness we have when we are attending carefully to a practical task that we are performing. The awareness to which I am referring can include this, but it also refers to a more reflexive process – being attentive towards one's attention or 'being aware of one's awareness'. This kind of awareness is of great importance in spiritual practice. I have chosen four examples of contemporary interest in heightened awareness to illustrate the pervasiveness of this phenomenon and to show how it relates to an understanding of childhood spirituality.

Here-and-now   Much of the time our thoughts are spent considering abstractions that have no physical existence in our current life. We muse upon pleasurable or painful things that happened to us in the past, or wonder and plan about the future. But quite apart from these ponderings which take up a great deal of our waking life, there is also the experience of being in the *here-and-now*. The Edinburgh developmental psychologist Margaret Donaldson notes that babies under eight months or so appear to have no memory of an extended past stretching out behind them. Nor, apart from the briefest anticipations, do they appear to have any conception of the future. Donaldson talks about this 'here-and-now' awareness as the 'point mode'.[3] She identifies it as the most basic mode of the mind's operation, and as such it continues to have prominence in children even when they have acheived the 'line mode' – that is, the ability to focus on the 'there and then' of the past and future.

Here-and-now experience is characteristically vivid. One morning when he was very young our son Simon called excitedly for me to run to the window. When I hurried over he pointed triumphantly out of the window and ecstatically cried out 'Grass!' One only has to think of how frequently small children are transfixed by the moment in this way to realize how natural and universal the point mode is to childhood.

There appears to be an overlap between Donaldson's 'point mode' and what the Soviet psychologist Lev Vygotsky has to say about the nature of the consciousness that emerges at the point in childhood just before there is a synthesis of language and thought.[4] Vygotsky suggested that this core of our consciousness is characterized by the absence of 'marked' time (past and future), and the content is highly symbolic – the language of 'pure' meaning. This level is normally inaccessible since, as we reconstruct it into the language of the culture to which we belong, time is 'marked' and the intense quality of the original meaning is diluted.

This intensity and immediacy of awareness referred to by Vygotsky and Donaldson is celebrated and taken to very high levels of sophistication in the practical life of great religious cultures, both Eastern and Western. In Theravada Buddhism, for example, the principal religious practice is *vipassana* or awareness meditation, in which the novice learns to maintain a highly disciplined attention to the here-and-now, by observing as carefully as possible either the act of breathing or the body's movements in walking. 'Single-pointed' awareness is of central importance throughout Buddhist culture and not only in the Theravadin tradition. The intensity of awareness of mind which is required of the true adept is illustrated in the following well-known story taken from a Buddhist Sutra:

A man travelling across a field encountered a tiger. He fled, the tiger after him. Coming to a precipice, he caught hold of the root of a wild vine and swung himself down over the edge. The tiger sniffed at him from above. Trembling, the man looked down to where, far below, another tiger was waiting to eat him. Only the vine sustained him.

Two mice, one white and one black, little by little started to gnaw away the vine. The man saw a luscious strawberry near him. Grasping the vine with one hand, he plucked the strawberry with the other. How sweet it tasted.[5]

Religious interest in the here-and-now of human experience also appears in certain traditions of contemplative prayer in Christianity. This is most obviously seen in those approaches which stress awareness of the presence of God in all things. The eighteenth-century French Jesuit, Jean Pierre de Caussade, speaks directly of the 'sacrament of the present moment':

We are well instructed only by the words God speaks to us personally. It is not by reading or historical study that we become wise in the science of God: such methods alone produce but a vain, confused and self-inflating science. What instructs us is what happens from moment to moment ...[6]

To summarize, at the same time as the 'point mode' is the object of widespread and sophisticated religious interest, it is also universally available in childhood, and we need to be alert to it when we talk to children. Traditional pedagogy concentrates on feats of memory such as learning tables, formulae, historical dates and the like. But Donaldson draws attention to the fact that even 'good' education, where children are encouraged to develop extended thinking skills, very often ignores this mode. Important as thinking skills are, they can lead to a forgetfulness of what is experienced immediately – the vividness of the here-and-now.

Tuning   Another contemporary metaphor for the experience of raised awareness is that of *tuning*. This term has been used in particular by the sociologist Alfred Schutz.[7] He understands tuning as the kind of awareness which arises in heightened aesthetic experience – for example, when listening to music. When we listen attentively to a piece of music, says Schutz, we are involved in a different activity from listening to someone talking to us. Speech requires a humanly constructed language, or what Schutz calls a 'scheme of expression' used by the speaker and a 'scheme of interpretation' used by the hearer. But hearing musical sound involves a direct, shared inner time, or *durée*. So, when a pianist plays a piece of music and someone else hears it, both pianist and hearer are participating in an immediate simultaneous stream of consciousness. Indeed, Schutz believes there is a sense in which this stream of consciousness is also shared with the composer of the music.

It has been pointed out by two American sociologists, Mary Jo Neitz and James Spickard, that 'tuning in' to the immediacy of musical experience has much in common with the way people often describe their religious or spiritual experience.[8] By extension, instances where awareness manifests itself as profound empathy or sensitivity to the ebb and flow of experience could also be termed tuning.

Feeling 'at one' with nature is a commonly reported context for adult recollection of childhood spiritual experience and seems to be an illustration of this type of awareness.[9] Research by Edward Robinson and Michael Jackson on a large sample of British and Irish teenagers suggests that around four fifths of them recognize this kind of experience in themselves.[10] Apparently more ordinary events in a child's life could promote a similar sense of unity – for example, through an intense sense of belonging experienced at a family celebration. In contrast, experiences of alienation such as those precipitated through bullying, may be found to prompt spiritual crises.

Flow   A special type of awareness which can be identified as poten-tially spiritual is what the social psychologist Mihaly Csikszentmihalyi calls *flow*.[11] An idea of what he means can be gained by reading some of the questions which he and his colleagues have used to identify flow:[12]

❖ Do you ever do something where your concentration is so intense, your attention so undivided and wrapped up in what you are doing that you sometimes become unaware of things you normally notice (for instance, other people talking, loud noises, the passage of time, being hungry or tired, having an appointment, having some physical discomfort)?

❖ Do you ever do something where your skills have become so 'second nature' that sometimes everything seems to come to you 'naturally' or 'effortlessly', and where you feel confident that you will be ready to meet any new challenges?

❖ Do you ever do something where you feel that the activity is worth doing in itself? In other words, even if there were no other benefits associated with it (for instance, financial reward, improved skills, recognition from others, and so on), you would still do it?

❖ Do you ever do something that has provided some unique and very memorable moments – for which you feel extremely lucky and grateful – that has changed your perspective on life (or yourself) in some way?

Flow, says Csikszentmihalyi, is what we sometimes feel when, for example, we read a good book or play a good game of squash or get lost in a fascinating conversation. There is an experience of concentrated attention giving way to a liberating feeling of the activity managing itself, or being managed by some outside influence, so that an activity that previously demanded an effort-filled attentiveness transforms into a single flow. Action and awareness become merged. Csikszentmihalyi gives other examples of the subjective reports of skiers, actors, rock-climbers, musicians and chess players. The factors essential to flow seem to be firstly, the preceding challenging nature of the activity contrasted with the release of the flow, and secondly that this is experienced as something transcending the self and valued for that quality.

The flow quality of consciousness can have a more long-lasting spiritual significance. One of the contexts which Csikszentmihalyi suggests is that of religious ritual. It has also been proposed by Isabella Csikszentmihalyi that the Jesuit Rule and the Spiritual Exercises created by St Ignatius Loyola constituted a formal attempt to generate the experience of flow. They 'provided an optimal set of conditions by which young men could live the entirety of their lives as a single flow experience'.[13]

When we consider the life of a young child, filled almost daily with the mastery of new skills – crawling, standing, walking, speaking, learning to read and write, riding a bicycle, learning arithmetic – it is obvious that this kind of awareness is potentially very familiar. Not all moments of flow contribute to a conscious spirituality, but some may, and nearly any activity might be experienced by the child as special in this way.

Focusing A fourth sub-category is *focusing* on what the American philosopher and psychotherapist Eugene Gendlin[14] calls the 'felt sense'. When he began practising as a psychotherapist, Gendlin noticed a difficulty in working with some of his clients, especially those who – like university academics and other members of the professions – had been highly trained in one of the intellectual disciplines. Quite often they had a problem in getting in touch with their bodily feelings, sometimes claiming not to have any. They preferred to get into an academic debate with Gendlin about their problems, and in such cases he found it was not possible to help them. In response, he devised a methodology which he called 'focusing' as a means of teaching people how to get in touch with the 'felt sense' of their situation. Once they were able to do that, they were better able to tackle their personal predicaments.

Gendlin's view is that our cultural history leads us into the temptation to ignore our bodies as sources of knowledge. We have a tendency to restrict knowing to the manipulations of the intellect. But in fact we encounter and act upon the world with the whole of our bodies; our awareness includes bodily awareness. If we have learned to ignore or suppress this awareness in favour of cool intellectual detachment, we may find we are unable to attend to the wisdom of the body in helping ourselves to cope with our personal difficulties and to be sensitively aware in our relationships.

Getting in touch with the felt sense of the reality which each of us inhabits is very like, and perhaps identical to, opening up our holistic awareness. It is therefore no surprise that focusing has been developed as a spiritual discipline within the Christian tradition.[15] It implies a recovery of respect for the body as a source of spiritual knowledge. The important point in the present context is that from Gendlin's perspective, all of us are quite naturally and simply holistically aware in early childhood. Focusing on the felt sense is the natural knowing of young children before they become inducted into the intellectualism that is our inheritance from classical Greek philosophy, but more particularly in the seventeenth century from René Descartes.[16] It is therefore an area of experience that children of primary age are much more easily in touch with than adults. This may partly help to explain the evidence from Tamminen[17] and others which I discussed in the previous chapter, that spiritual experience is commoner among children than older people.

Mystery-sensing

The notion of transcendence is closely associated with ideas of spirituality, but it is not always easy to see how to talk in a practical way about this with children. Mystery offers a way into this difficult area. Mystery involves the awareness I have already discussed, but in this case awareness of aspects of our life experience that are in *principle* incomprehensible. To take the simplest and most profound mystery of all, why is there something rather than nothing? A key feature of human intelligence is our desire to find pattern and order in our experience of the world, and we spend much of our time, especially during school years, learning to categorize and classify complex information into manageable chunks. To encounter the mystery of existence in the midst of all this rational activity can be a jolt to the system. At the same time that we bring into view the vast mystery of our existence, we also learn about ourselves as limited.[18] I offer two examples of areas of life where our encounter with such mystery is very clear.

Wonder and awe   Rudolf Otto[19] identifies two sides of our experience of the mystery of the sacred: fascination or *wonder*, and fear or *awe*. These feelings are familiar enough in the life of most adults from time to time, and perhaps particularly so in people who for professional reasons have reflected deeply on the larger questions of our existence. In the conclusion to his *Critique of Practical Reason* the philosopher Immanuel Kant gives one of the classic accounts of such feelings:

> Two things fill the mind with ever new and increasing admiration and awe, the oftener and the more steadily they are reflected on: the starry heavens above me and the moral law within me.[20]

A consideration of the vastness of the universe strikes awe in us. Similar feelings may arise for the devout believer in relation to religious ritual – for example, at the moment of the consecration of the elements in the Catholic Mass, or for the Muslim, hearing the divine thought incarnated in the words of the Qur'an being read aloud in Arabic. These are profound moments and, in inviting us to consider the 'holy', Rudolf Otto is meditating upon the ultimate mystery.

For young children the distinction between the commonplace and the profound may not yet have any meaning. Their sense of mystery can be awakened by much more down-to-earth and familiar phenomena – simple events such as a flame appearing when a match is struck, or a light being switched on, or water coming out of a tap. I myself remember my feeling of utter amazement and awe when it was demonstrated to me in the classroom that air has weight; before that time I had somehow got the idea that air was simply 'nothing'.[21]

Rebecca Nye points out that in the past the rising and setting of the sun was considered appropriate adult material for the consideration of 'ultimate mystery'. She suggests that adult interpretations of what will count as adequate material for proper 'theological' reflection on mystery may illegitimately exclude the perspective of the child. Could it be the case that children's perceptions of mystery in situations where, from an adult perspective, there is a simple explanation, arise from as profound an experience as those of the contemplative philosopher or the theologian?

Here an important discrimination needs to be made. Young children initially sense that much of life is incomprehensible and therefore mysterious. For the older child, the explanations provided by education may imply that there are answers to everything, and displace or even repress the true mysteriousness of existence. Frequently science is identified as the bogeyman here. If it is badly taught it may indeed offer a restricted picture of the world, cut off from the larger context of our holistic experience as human beings. But if it is well taught, with an awareness of the philosophical basis of the scientific method, this need not happen. This could mean, for example, considering how scientific explanations might be presented in terms of further questions or causes for wonder. It could also mean seeing the scientific hypothesis through the eyes of Karl Popper, as a conjecture which may at any time be refuted, rather than a thesis to be proved.[22] In this way the child's perception of mystery develops into a mature insight into the human condition, rather than being dismissed as infantile thinking.

Imagination   Another way in which everyday experience is transcended is through *imagination*. To investigate mystery requires the imagination to conceive what is beyond the known and what is 'obvious'. The use of the imagination is thus important in scientific creativity, as is beautifully illustrated in *The Double Helix*, James Watson's lively account of the human side of the process of discovering the structure of DNA.[23] Such creativity is closely allied to what is often called our fantasy life, an area first explored fully in this century by the analytical psychologist C. G. Jung. Like several other people whom I have mentioned, Jung was critical of the highly cognitive, rationalized lifestyle of many people in the Western world. He believed that it was likely to split them off from a large part of their awareness of reality.

In response he developed the technique of 'active imagination' for working with his patients. This involved them imaginatively recovering dreams and fantasies that they had experienced in the past and exploring what personal meanings they might be conveying. It is important to note that Jung saw getting in touch with the symbolic meanings conveyed in fantasy as a means of dealing with emotional disturbance. That is to say, it is the avoidance of our fantasy life, rather than attention to it, which tends to create psychological difficulties.

Imagination is central to religious activity through the metaphors, symbols, stories and liturgies which respond to the otherwise unrepresentable experience of the sacred.[24] In Christianity, this is particularly obvious in the method of prayer developed by St Ignatius Loyola in his *Spiritual Exercises*.[25] People undertaking the exercises are encouraged to enter imaginatively into scenes from the Bible. They are advised to notice what is happening to them, using all the senses, and to explore their feelings in relation to the characters in the story as it unfolds freely. Those who have experienced the exercises typically say that their insight into the meaning of scripture has been greatly deepened because of the opportunity to use the whole of the imagination in their meditation, rather than simply the intellect. Parallel use of the imagination occurs in many other religions, for example in Shingon Buddhism[26] and also perhaps in the spirit journeys which feature in many of the Shamanistic religions.[27]

The free use of imagination is very evident in children's play, where an old cardboard box can become a car, a house, a spaceship, or practically anything else. Studies of children's ability to enter into fantasy in classroom exercises show they have a powerful capacity for (and enjoyment of) letting go of material reality. Indeed, their natural ability to become absorbed in a guided imaginative exercise is so evident that teachers are urged to use such methods with care and only after appropriate training.[28] Nevertheless, when used sensitively, work with the imagination provides a powerful way to discover meanings and values in response to children's experience, especially experience for which their language is inadequate. In children's imagination, seen in their play, stories, art work and perhaps also their fears and hopes, we may at times be encountering a window on this aspect of their spirituality. The mystery-sensing created in imaginative acts is perhaps as much or even more significant than children's responses to what 'adult' religion has defined as sacred.

Value-sensing

The term 'value-sensing' was coined by Margaret Donaldson.[29] As an eminent cognitive psychologist and student of Piaget, she nevertheless found herself critical of the heavy emphasis given to cognitive skills by modern psychology, whilst tending to ignore feeling or 'affect'. The undervaluing of feeling in our culture, often dismissed as 'mere' emotion, is something that had previously been commented on critically by another Edinburgh scholar, the philosopher John Macmurray.[30] He pointed out that the supposed objectivity of scientists is in fact driven by feeling. If it were not, they would never embark on their research in the first place. Feeling is a measure of what we value.

Donaldson has shown that as we mature there is a progression leading from self-centred emotion to an experience of value which transcends personal concerns, and is perhaps implied in the ecstatic experience of the great religious contemplatives. Clearly, the conscience or moral sense of children is related to this idea, perhaps in a way that is prior to and more profound than Kohlberg's cognitive approach.[31] I give as examples three dimensions of value-sensing.

Delight and despair   Value-sensing is experienced as emotion. Hence those things that matter to us most are associated with feeling at its most profound. For this reason I want to focus particularly on the experience of *delight* and *despair*. These feelings have an obvious association with religion because of the frequency with which they are mentioned in manuals of religious practice. Within Christianity they are sometimes referred to by the technical terms 'consolation' and 'desolation'. For the devout person the experience of consolation is associated with

The Spirit of the Child

an awareness of the presence of God. Desolation, on the contrary, occurs when the devotee feels abandoned by God. The extremity of these feelings has been described by people who have 'been there' as ranging from ecstasy to what St John of the Cross called the dark nights of the senses and of the soul.[32]

Margaret Donaldson suggests that spiritual enlightenment is an advanced outcome of the education of value-sensing and that this has a link with the religious meaning of worship, as pertaining to worth. Children readily express their ideas of worth or value in the intensity of their everyday experience of delight or despair. The latter is particularly interesting. Children's (hopefully) modest experiences of personal despair contain the potential for the development of greater general sensitivity, which in turn may form a significant step on the path of spiritual enlightenment. In our pilot studies, a common indicator of wider despair was children's great interest in environmental concerns. These are often associated with the child's personal experience of being taken for granted or used, supporting the notion of a linked progression between personal concerns and values and more general and potentially ultimate concerns.

It also seems possible that the particular attention given by children to environmental issues may in part derive from an animistic tendency to attribute or project their own emotions and thought on to animals and things, as noted by Piaget.[33] This so-called childish phenomenon may in fact be a tool in advancing a shift from seeing things primarily from the perspective of personal gain and worth, to appreciating a wider, holistic perspective.

Ultimate goodness   The sense of *ultimate goodness* may seem beyond the experience of young children. On the contrary, the American sociologist Peter Berger suggests that such a sense is transmitted to children from the earliest age. In his book *A Rumour of Angels*[34] he imagines a scene familiar in every family:

A child wakes up in the night, perhaps from a bad dream, and finds himself surrounded by darkness, alone, beset by nameless threats. At such a moment the contours of trusted reality are blurred or invisible, and in the terror of incipient chaos the child cries out for his mother. It is hardly an exaggeration to say that, at this moment, the mother is being invoked as a high priestess of protective order. It is she (and in many cases, she alone) who has the power to banish the chaos and to restore the benign shape of the world. And, of course, any good mother will do just that. She will take the child and cradle him in the timeless gesture of the Magna Mater who became the Madonna. She will turn on a lamp, perhaps, which will encircle the scene with a warm glow of reassuring light. She will speak or sing to the child, and the content of this communication will invariably be the same – 'Don't be afraid – everything is in order, everything is all right.'[35]

Berger goes on from the ordinary experience of the child being comforted by its mother to raise a more profound question, 'Is the mother lying to the child?' He suggests that 'the answer, in the most profound sense, can be "no", only if there is some truth in the religious [I would say "spiritual"] interpretation of human existence.' 'The reassurance, transcending the immediately present two individuals and their situation, implies a statement about reality as such.' 'The formula can, without in any way violating it, be translated into a statement of cosmic scope – "Have trust in being."'[36] This, it seems to me, is an expression of holistic spirituality, which is thus easily available in any normal family during early childhood.

Psychoanalysts have pointed out that this experience of order may be interpreted by the child to relate to the omnipotency of the parent, at least in the younger years.[37] So we should not be surprised to find practical evidence of the apparently sentimental claim that, with what Winnicott calls 'good enough' parenting, young children's lives are characterized by much more pure delight than those of more mature years. Delight is in a sense closer at hand, mediated by the parents (and especially the mother) seen as the source of all-powerful goodness.

Meaning   Finally I come to *meaning*, and the endless curiosity and meaning-making of children. A number of students of religion, with predominantly cognitive interests, have taken this as their guiding category, including James Fowler[38] on faith as a meaningful personal framework, and Daniel Batson[39] on the spiritual quest as a search for ultimate meaning. I certainly endorse the centrality of 'meaning' amongst the collection of features we have identified as pertinent to the study of children's spirituality. At the same time I criticize the proponents of a purely cognitive approach for their tendency to ignore what appears to be the experiential basis for the creation of religious meaning. There is also a deeper 'sensed' meaning which is characteristic of spiritual or religious experience, as in the following example which is drawn from the archive of experience gathered in Oxford by Alister Hardy:

> One day years ago I went for a walk in the fields with my dog. My mind suddenly started thinking about the beauty around me, and I considered the marvellous order and timing of the growth of each flower, herb and the abundance of all the visible growth going on around. I remember thinking 'Here is mind'. Then we had to get over a stile and suddenly I was confronted with a bramble bush which was absolutely laden with black glistening fruit. And the impact of that, linked with my former reasoning, gave me a great feeling of ecstasy. For a few moments I really did feel at one with the Universe or the Creative Power we recognize. I know it was a feeling of oneness with something outside myself, and also within. I must have been confronted with the source of all being, whatever one should call it. I have often told my friends about it, though it seems too sacred to talk about. The experience has never been forgotten. It was quite electric and quite unsought.

There is much more in this quotation than the logical deductions of William Paley's natural theology which I discussed critically in Chapter 2. It is an expression of spirituality in which the person, perhaps consciously, uses some of the language of natural theology to refer to direct intuitive knowing, but does not wish to relate it to conventional religion.

To summarize, the search for and discovery of meaning may directly form an aspect of developing spirituality. In childhood in particular as a sense of identity is sought for, established and deepened, questions are raised which are essentially spiritual: Who am I? Where do I belong? What is my purpose? To whom or what am I connected or responsible?

These apparently cognitive signs of spiritual activity are in many cases the secondary products of spiritual stirrings found in awareness-sensing, mystery-sensing and value-sensing. A task for spiritual education may be to help children to investigate their identity, and to delight in other forms of meaning-making and meaning-sensing. But it will be important to understand the foundational experiences suggested by the categories outlined here, through which issues of meaning may become salient to the child.

Conclusion

We have now completed our brief tour of a landscape that turns out to be much more familiar in contemporary experience than might at first be expected. Again and again the theme of 'raised awareness' has emerged, even in the unlikely territory of 'meaning'. Here are those realms of human experience to which Karl Rahner refers as 'the transcendentality inherent in human life'. An artificial constriction of ordinary human awareness, created by a culture that has got out of touch with large areas of life's experience leads us to avoid, ignore, even be bored by this transcendentality. In exploring these regions, what we have uncovered is a communal nervousness and lack of trust in our general awareness as a source of reliable knowledge. It is here that spirituality faces its stiffest test of plausibility.

In the face of these anxieties we may wonder how well children are able to express their spiritual experience, and the languages they use to articulate it. Our exploration of the geography of spirituality allows us to be optimistic in the hope of discovering that children do still 'reach out towards that mystery which lies outside our control'. This is a question to which we will now turn in the next three chapters.

II

Investigation

5

How Do You Talk with Children about Spirituality?

Knowledge in the human sciences always has something of self-knowledge about it. Nowhere is deception so easy and so near as in self-knowledge, but nowhere does it also mean as much, where it succeeds, for human existence [Sein]. Thus it is legitimate in the human sciences that we are confronted not only with ourselves – as we are already known to ourselves – but with something else as well: it is legitimate that we experience a provocation [Anstoss] from them that leads us beyond ourselves.

HANS-GEORG GADAMER[1]

The myth of objectivity
During the three years when we were researching children's spirituality, Rebecca Nye and I were not neutral observers located at some Archimedean point outside the universe, detached from all personal concern with spiritual or religious issues. At the weekends Rebecca was running the children's Sunday School in St Philip's Cathedral in Birmingham. During the same period I had become attracted to the *Spiritual Exercises*

of St Ignatius Loyola and spent just over a year undertaking the exercises in daily life (sometimes called the 'Nineteenth Annotation').[2]

According to some people, these interests must mean that we were entirely unfitted to make an academic study of spirituality because we were unlikely to be able to retain a detached attitude towards the object of our research. The question of detachment is problematic in all forms of social research.[3] It has proven to be particularly controversial in the study of religion because of the strength of feeling which surrounds the subject. Rebecca, with an academic background in psychology, once commented to me appositely, 'Who cares about the personality of personality theorists?' Yet we almost always find ourselves suspicious or curious about the religious beliefs of people who study religion or a closely allied subject like spirituality.

Freud famously offered the opinion that 'where questions of religion are concerned people are guilty of every possible kind of insincerity and intellectual misdemeanour.'[4] There is no doubt that he had religious believers in mind, not atheists. From the perspective of our critics, the fact that we were studying children's spirituality rather than their religion makes little difference. The link between the two is historically so strong that it could be assumed that our evangelical urge must outweigh any claim to balanced objectivity.

But what would the situation be if the research were to be undertaken by people whose personal stance was one of atheism or even agnosticism? The fact that atheists are often seen as suitably objective in matters of religion tells us much about the *de facto* stance of contemporary popular culture. Atheists too have their biases and expectations about the nature of reality.

The two commonest standpoints with regard to research on people's beliefs are the 'myth of the outsider' and the 'myth of the insider'.[5] According to the first myth, outsiders to a belief system are the only ones who can be objective about the phenomena they encounter. Because they are outsiders they are less likely to lapse into interpretations which are value laden with the beliefs of the group being studied. On the other hand,

The Spirit of the Child

supporters of the 'insider' perspective suggest that only an insider has the sensitivity to understand truly the structure of the beliefs and motivations of the believer. Ernest Rénan, whom we have met in an earlier chapter, offered a third alternative. He thought that the best kind of investigator of religion was someone who had formerly been religiously committed but then abandoned their beliefs. Such a person would, so to speak, straddle the two worlds. But, as was pointed out by Wilhelm Schmidt,[6] this appearance of neutrality conceals an emphatic decision about the falsity of religion.

Crossing cultural boundaries is an everyday event not confined to differences in matters of religion. One of the benefits of the postmodern movement, which in some of its dimensions has encouraged a destructive relativism,[7] is the clarity it gives to our understanding that there is no such thing as an objectively situated neutrality in human affairs (perhaps we *should* be interested in the personality of personality theorists). Everyone, without exception, is situated within a context of beliefs and values which both blinds and enlightens them to aspects of reality.

It is very easy to underestimate how difficult it is to enter into an understanding of someone else's culture or beliefs. Yet it is a process we are having to undertake more and more frequently in an environment where migration and the instantaneous communication of TV and the Internet has highlighted the multicultural nature of the human population.[8] The sheer range of difference, often with its entailment of bloodstained tribal hostility, may make us forget or minimize the misunderstandings that can exist, even within a single community. Rapid cultural shifts may mean that there is a significant gulf between different generations in the same small-scale human environment. It may be the case that adults who attempt to comprehend the spirituality of children within their own society may require some of the same skills as those employed by ethnographers investigating a culture remote from their own.

But there are other difficulties raised by the inevitability of bias. Two extreme possibilities immediately spring to mind.

Sometimes social researchers may find themselves, or may even choose to be, advocates on behalf of the people who are the subject of their research. This might be the case, for example, where they are trying to understand what has happened to abused children or people who have been the targets of racial prejudice. At the opposite extreme, ethnographers who adopt a postmodern stance in attempting to deconstruct the texts presented to them by a religious or political agency, may in effect be attacking the credibility of the views of the people being studied. Choosing to do research on what children have to say about their spirituality means that one is quite unequivocally entering this value-laden world. In turn this implies that what we are doing takes on a political dimension, since our findings could potentially affect what goes on in the field of education. We therefore have to accept responsibility for the political and social implications of our interpretations of the research material.

To summarize, every act of research involves a choice of some kind. One's personal stance means that certain aspects of the subject under investigation will be highlighted and other aspects will be neglected. The pretence that one is being completely open can lead to a denial or a blindness to the fact that one is inevitably looking at one's theme from a particular perspective. Even openness itself can be seen as a type of commitment. On one occasion when Rebecca was talking about our work to a religious group she was identified as having a bias on the grounds that the openness of our approach was in fact implicitly 'atheist'.

It is clear that it is no good any researcher in the social sciences claiming to embrace a superficially neutral, open position, especially in a field like that of spirituality. The most important preliminary statement one needs to make is about integrity; the necessity to affirm a belief that the primary goal of research is knowledge, even though the findings may ultimately have educational and political implications. Honest acceptance of this requirement means that there is a reduction in the likelihood of our personal bias distorting the data to fit preconceptions about how the world ought to be. If we are to behave ethically in the role of researchers we need to record the other person's point of view as accurately as possible. This implies an acknowledgement that we may be surprised or disconcerted by what is discovered; that we are likely to have to change our minds.

Instead of denying one's perspective, one needs to use it constructively. Here I am depending on the insight of the German philosopher Hans-Georg Gadamer, who insists not merely that every human being is inevitably prejudiced, but that 'prejudice' is necessary for effective understanding.[9] If we were hypothetically to suspend our prejudice (an impossibility, since what Gadamer calls our 'horizon of effective understanding' is not one that we consciously acquire), it is not clear how we could move to a freely chosen neutral point from which to begin. We need a horizon in order to 'place ourselves within a situation'.

Gadamer talks about a 'forestructure' of understanding that the individual brings to a situation, a prejudice which permits the researcher to have a topic of conversation in the first place. Another way of looking at this is to see one's perspective as supplying potentially 'sensitizing concepts'[10] which may alert one to aspects of reality which would otherwise be missed or ignored. Of course, the dialogue that goes on in a research conversation may produce information that contradicts the assumptions of the researcher, showing up their limitations and the necessity to change one's understanding. On the other hand, the introduction of the forestructure or sensitizing concept may also move understanding forward by shedding new light on what the informant has to say.

The aims and practical approach of the research

In this and the preceding chapters I have tried to make clear what my own 'forestructures' are, with their accompanying sensitizing concepts as well as their potential for blindness. Given these strengths and limitations, the overall intention of the investigation was to develop a theoretical perspective – an interpretation – of children's spirituality, based on reflections on what they have to say in conversation with a field worker, in this case Rebecca Nye.[11]

The initial pilot work was done in a Church of England primary school in a commuter village near Nottingham. In large part this was due to the fact that we were known in the school, and also to my (correct) assumption that the subject of our research would be welcomed because the school has a religious foundation. But the ultimate aim was to be able to speak to groups of children that would be reasonably representative of the range of religious and secular perspectives likely to be found in state schools in Britain.

To whom should we speak? Ideally it would have been appropriate to have conversations with children of all school ages below the secondary stage and belonging to all major cultural groups. In practice, time and money put a strict limit on this possibility, so we decided that the conversations would be with children who were coming up to Key Stages One and Two in the primary school – that is to say, aged 6 to 7 and 10 to 11 years of age. There was a pragmatic reason for this choice. My intention was that the findings would be helpful to teachers and inspectors when they have to face up to the controversial task of making a judgement about the quality of spiritual education in a school at those Key Stages.

The children with whom we wished to talk were selected at random (apart from a proviso to include equal numbers of girls and boys) from classes in a state primary school in each of two large industrial cities in the English Midlands (Nottingham and Birmingham). The schools were chosen on the basis that they were typically urban, not associated with any religious group, and known to be accessible from previous research contacts. The catchment areas served were predominantly lower middle class. We took care to gain the approval of the headteachers and to discuss the content of the research programme with them. This included an explanation of the fact that the topic was somewhat undefined and that the research was intended to clarify our understanding. We sent letters to the parents of all the children with whom we wished to talk, asking for their permission. The letters did not, however, mention the word 'spirituality'. The reason for this was the feeling that it would be liable to misinterpretation in the ways I have discussed in Chapter 1, particularly in the assumption that the research was limited to a concern with institutional religion.

Altogether 38 children had conversations with Rebecca – 18 aged 6 to 7 and 20 aged 10 to 11. Of the 38 children, 28 were classified by us as having no religious affiliation – that is, approximately three quarters of the total. Judging very crudely from the ethnic origins of this group (one child was of Afro-Caribbean origin, and all the rest were Caucasian), it could be surmised that they represented secular or 'lapsed' Christians. Or, to put this more accurately, since the children had not necessarily taken up a personal position on religious matters, they probably came from lapsed or secular families. Of the quarter of the group which did belong to religiously practising families, four children were affiliated to the Church of England, four were Muslim and two were Roman Catholic (see the table below).

Table 1: Religious affiliations of the research sample

	6–7 year olds	10–11 year olds
Church of England	1 male 1 female	2 female
Muslim	1 female	2 male 1 female
Roman Catholic	1 male	1 male*
No affiliation	7 male 7 female	7 male 7 female
TOTAL	18	20

* The family of this boy was not practising, but he had attended church regularly with a neighbour until recently.

Rebecca spent a preliminary half day as a helper in each of the classes from which the children were drawn, in order to ensure that she was not encountered as a total stranger. In addition, she attended school assemblies on most of the days when she was involved in conversations with the children. She had up to three meetings with each of the children, and each tape-recorded conversation lasted about half an hour. Usually she spoke with four children during the course of one day's visit and collected each child from their classroom and took them back afterwards. This allowed some time for a brief friendly chat before and after the research conversation, which was always held in a quiet place where talk could not be overheard.

The question of putting the children at their ease was also an issue when considering whether to talk with them in groups or alone. In a recent piece of research which has some similarities to ours, Clive Erricker and his colleagues[12] chose to speak with children in small groups rather than individually, when asking them about their world-views. The rationale was that it was less intimidating for the children to be with friends than to be alone with an adult researcher.

In our programme we decided to have the discussions on a one-to-one basis. Our reasoning was grounded on my previous research on the spiritual experience of adults. This had shown that people are often extremely shy of talking about spirituality in public for fear that they will be thought stupid, or even mentally disturbed.[13] I have discussed the historical reasons for this in an earlier chapter. On balance, in view of Rebecca's ability to enter into a friendly and trusting relationship with the children, it seemed important to offer the privacy necessary to talk about matters which they might feel reticent to share with other children.

Having gained permission to speak with the children, the next problem was to decide what we wanted to talk about with them. Most other researchers to whom I have made reference in earlier chapters used explicitly religious, usually Christian, language in their investigations of spirituality. We were not happy about restricting our study in this way. But it did seem possible that religious vocabulary could be useful in directing children to our area of interest, simply because it is the traditional vehicle for exploring the spiritual dimension of life. This was probably a correct assumption, since we found in practice that many of the children, even those who were highly secularized, resorted to religious language without prompting when they were referring to spiritual matters.

On the other hand, the disadvantage of encouraging children to talk in religious terms was that it tended to trigger off impersonal 'learned' responses rather than reference to the child's personal experience. This often meant that the conversation moved away from the personal spirituality of the child towards conventionalized 'God-talk'. A paradoxical result was the sense we had at times of the spirituality of children from conventionally believing backgrounds being circumscribed and limited by standardized religious language. The spontaneous and religiously unconventional language of children from more secularized environments could sometimes come across as more impressive and genuine.

To try to accommodate these dilemmas, the solution we chose was to split the conversation with the children into three parts. The first section was a very loosely structured, light chat about the child's interests and life story. Especially with the younger children, this was often facilitated by inviting them to do a drawing of some aspect of their world that was important to them. The act of conversing whilst the drawing was proceeding in itself tended to put the children at their ease. If all went well, this led to the development of a friendly atmosphere which enabled the conversation to move on to phase two, concerned with spirituality, and eventually to a third phase concerned with the child's own experience.

The practical method of shifting the discussion from general issues towards spirituality was guided by the 'sensitizing concepts' which I discussed in Chapter 4. The themes of *awareness-sensing*, *mystery-sensing* and *value-sensing* were approached most typically (but not always) by inviting the children to talk about one of a set of photographs. The pictures were chosen because they had the potential to generate reflective conversation on one or more of these themes.

One picture was of a girl gazing into a fire, and another of a boy looking out of his bedroom window at the stars. A third picture was of a girl looking tearfully at her dead pet gerbil in its cage. Another picture was of a boy standing by himself in a playground, ignored and perhaps unhappy. Another was of a boy standing on a wet pavement, having dropped some food on the ground, looking upwards with his hands spread out, perhaps saying, 'Why me?' We also used some photographs of the beauties of nature – for example, scenes of waves whipped up in stormy weather.

In each case the pictures were used in a non-directive way to encourage the children to speak personally about their own thoughts and experiences. Thus, with the first two pictures, Rebecca might wonder aloud what the girl was thinking about as she stared into the fire, or what was going through the mind of the boy as he gazed at the stars. In the case of the girl looking at her pet gerbil, the question raised might involve wondering what to say to help her to cope with her loss. At least in part, the kinds of thoughts the children shared with Rebecca could include reference to their own ponderings in such circumstances. In other words, they were quite likely to give a projective response which could then lead on naturally into further reflective conversation on the spiritual aspects of the child's experience.

During the major part of the discussion there was no overt mention of religion or religious experience unless the subject was brought up spontaneously by the child. But towards the end of the sequence of meetings, if religion had not emerged as a topic it was introduced, usually by asking about school assembly. It was also here that any references to specific instances of religious or spiritual awareness were gently explored. The theme might be led into by discussing one of the photographs for example, the one of the boy looking upwards, which could potentially be interpreted as illustrating a spontaneous prayer of frustration. Finally, if it seemed appropriate, direct reference to religious or spiritual awareness might be mentioned and the child might be asked whether they found such a thing recognizable or resembling anything in their own experience.

This aspect of the conversation was probably the most difficult one to handle. Partly this was because of the taboo I have already mentioned. But it is also problematical because of the unspecifiability of 'spiritual experience'. In my judgement there is at the very least an extremely permeable boundary lying between the kinds of vivid spontaneous spiritual experience which people tend to remember for the rest of their lives, and the low key spiritual awareness someone aspires to as a permanent personal life stance. Having undertaken research in this field for more than 20 years, I have come to believe that these are parts of a continuum rather than distinct kinds of human experience. The feature which varies along the continuum is one of intensity of awareness. Since one of my guesses about contemporary culture is its tendency to close down spiritual awareness, it was both interesting and important to listen particularly carefully to what the children had to say about this.

There was one final explicit reference to religion. The children were asked about their religious background so that we had some evidence about the cultural context from which they were speaking (see Table 1 on p. 85). This is because formal adherence to a religiously believing community is bound to make an important difference to the children's consciousness. In most state schools, children from religiously practising backgrounds will usually find themselves in a minority, and this was the case with our research sample. Being aware of their position may have contradictory effects on the way they will express their spirituality, according to whether their perception of their status tends to make them adhere more strongly or break away from their faith community.[14]

The spiritual dimension of qualitative research
There is no practical or ethically acceptable way to regulate most of the variables when you are investigating the opinions and experiences of a group of children. In this respect it is no

different from any other qualitative study of the personal life of human beings. Whilst the headteachers and staff in the schools we visited were extremely helpful and accommodating, the realities of life along with the professional priorities of the staff meant that many factors were outside our control. These included such matters as the general mood and social dynamics of the school, the detailed make-up of the specific classes selected for investigation, the personality and influence of the teachers of the classes selected, the time of day when the children were seen, and the decor of the room available for private conversations. In addition there could be no control over the weather, or the mood of the children at the time they were invited to have a conversation, or their personal judgements about the personality and motives of the researcher, or the stories they would tell their classmates when they returned from the research conversation.

These are only some of the variables that immediately come to mind. Furthermore, standardizing the content of the conversation so that it was duplicated in each case would have been totally inappropriate. The sheer complexity of human life means that qualitative research depends as much on the rationality of feeling[15] as quantitative research depends on the rigorous control of variables. Rebecca's task was to be accepting, facilitating a relaxed conversation and giving the children as much opportunity as possible to talk in their own terms. Flexibility of approach was a central necessity if we were to be able to make an intelligent attempt to understand their perspective.

In such a situation the researcher is not a neutral sounding board. A more appropriate analogy might be to consider the 'total awareness' of the researcher as if it were an instrument engaged in understanding and interpreting the information that emerges as a result of the bond created with the child. This means noting how the relationship affects one's feelings of comfort, insecurity, anxiety, confusion, excitement or any other emotion, and the bearing that these experiences have on understanding the data. It is a matter of holistic awareness. Indeed there is a sense in which the skills needed to conduct the research have close affinities with what I have been describing as spiritual awareness. In the next two chapters Rebecca will give an account of what emerged from her conversations.[16]

6

Listening to Children Talking

By Rebecca Nye

Cor ad cor loquitur.

J. H. NEWMAN[1]

Introduction

My role as a comparative stranger, visiting two primary schools, was to encourage children to share their feelings and thoughts with me. Their willingness and enthusiasm to talk with an adult whom they hardly knew was in itself a demonstration of a generosity of spirit. But in almost every case something more was present. Throughout the process of data collection I had the repeated 'sense' that a child's unique spirituality was being expressed in how and what they spoke about. With a little practice, encouraging children to talk in ways that activated what I perceived to be their spirituality became relatively easy.

What is more difficult is to articulate those features of our conversations that produced this sense in me. Once transcribed, the research interviews comprised over 1,000 typed pages which I read and re-read, annotated and compared in a variety of ways.

This daunting mass of data required considerable organization and interpretation (as well as condensing) in order that my firm sense that it contained evidence of children's spirituality might be communicated to others.

By way of introduction, it will be helpful to note that this chapter has some special characteristics. It is an account of the procedures I adopted to shed light on the character of children's spirituality. If one is to get under the surface of the challenging topic we chose to investigate, it is important to attend to these procedures. Merely turning to a 'results section' will not provide enough of a genuine feel for the central ideas arising from the study. The chapter outlines the analytical and reflective processes arising from my inevitably personal sense of spirituality. As such, the approaches to discernment described here may provide useful guidelines to those wishing to explore spirituality with other children, whether or not they accept the interpretative framework of results that I will be proposing in the next chapter.

The role of the researcher's subjectivity in this kind of research has been discussed in the previous chapter. Here it is sufficient to note that the application of my personal qualities as a 'human instrument'[2] in the analysis phase of the research was specially influenced by my recollection of the direct experience of meeting each child and my opportunity to engage with some intimate aspects of their lives. My stance also reflects my background in child psychology, influencing the kind of questions I ask and the developmental psychological approach to evidence through which I seek to describe children's behaviour.

The chapter has an intentional emphasis on the presentation of children's voices. This is essential if I am to convey in a convincing way how spirituality was manifested in the talk of ordinary school children. These voices are heard in two brief sketches of individual children presented in the first main section below, where the broad character of children's spirituality (as a personal signature rather than a reflection of type or group) is discussed. Examples of how the children talked are also in evidence in the second main section of the chapter, where I describe the 'compare-and-contrast' discernment process of analysis which I applied to different kinds of conversation that arose during the research.

The individuality of children's spirituality

I had spoken to each child individually and in private, so the initial phase of analysis lent itself well to a case-study approach. This proved to be an illuminating way of appreciating the layers of significance that each set of conversations presented. Focusing on separate individuals helped to sensitize me to the phenomenon being studied. On the other hand, with a view to saying something about children's spirituality in general, the particularity of case studies might constitute a handicap. A different kind of approach might be necessary: examining children's spirituality through a cross-section of the data. One obvious way of doing that might be to look at classifications of different types of children and their spirituality.

Thus, in the process of trying to represent what was spiritual in these conversations with children, I identified a basic question. To what extent was it legitimate to forgo an individually informed account of each child in favour of an account of group features? In the process of determining an answer to the question I identified a fundamental characteristic of children's spirituality. Even in these rather constrained research conditions, the expression of spirituality had a markedly individual character that seemed to reflect the unique disposition of each child. In fact, the primary influences on a child's spirituality appeared to flow from his or her personality. One could identify a kind of personal 'signature' for each of the children that pertained to their spirituality as well as the more general features of their conversation and interests. Influences that might be ascribed to group or type effects, such as age or gender, seemed to be of secondary use in the search for a way to conceptualize spirituality amongst these children.

Although a cross-sectional examination of the data is required, this basic feature of individuality demands special attention. The presentation of 38 case studies would be hopelessly unwieldy, so I

The Spirit of the Child

have decided to present two illustrative sketches of the material gathered through conversations with one of the younger girls, Ruth, and an older boy, Tim. They illustrate this 'signature' phenomenon of children's spirituality and the individuality of its expression.

Ruth[3]   Ruth appeared to be a quietly happy, articulate six-year-old from a stable home. She attended a Church of England Sunday school, but she did not recall this weekly activity spontaneously when asked about her weekend routine. Her comments about her experience of church indicated that it was not a source of spiritual inspiration for her: 'Somehow I never want to go, because it is so boring.'

However, she had a pronounced sense of wonder and delight, and an active religious imagination – elements within the categories described in Chapter 4. Her individual way of expressing this was primarily in terms of a multi-sensory, aesthetic and nature-inspired framework. For example, this was how she imagined heaven:

A mist of perfume, with gold walls, and a rainbow stretched over God's throne ... but a transparent mist, like a ... I can't explain it. Like a smell. A real cloud of smell, a lovely smell ... like the smell that you get when you wake up on a dull winter morning, and then when you go to sleep, and you wake up, the birds are chirping, and the last drops of snow are melting away, and the tree-tops, shimmering in the breeze, and it's a spring morning ... [Then she added:] I suppose it's not a season at all, not really, because [it's] just a day in delight, every day.

Ruth's imaginative response, drawing on nature, her senses and an appreciation of the mysterious transformations that occur in life, pervaded many of her comments in other 'non-religious' contexts. This could be traced to the opening remarks in her first interview. When offered the choice to draw 'anything at all' while we chatted, she replied: 'I like nature ... [Why?] ... just because I like it. I don't know. And it's so beautiful to be in the world.'

This demonstrates how Ruth's own individual signature – an aesthetic appreciation of the natural world – directed the form of her spiritual response which, in her case, was expressed often in explicitly religious contexts, such as an image of heaven, or receiving a blessing. Furthermore, she seemed to some extent to be conscious of this patterning of individual disposition and spiritual response. For example, when considering the kinds of moments in her life which might lead her to think about God, she suggested: 'When I see um ... the trees burst into life. In spring I like that. But when I see the lambs in Wales, oh ... it makes me ... oh ... leap and jump too!'

The intensity of her responses suggested to her that she might have what she termed 'different senses' that allowed her to be attuned to such things – that spiritual perception was a precious gift. In fact her whole attitude seemed to be one of gratefulness for nature, for beauty and for her abilities to appreciate these things. Certainly, the sensory connections which she mentioned making, including 'hearing the sun', did suggest a kind of synaesthetic capacity, or at least a capacity to make meaningful connections very readily from this framework. In contrast, in her everyday experience, other people sometimes seemed oblivious to this: 'It's so nice, the world, the environment, but people destroy the beauty of it ... like once my mummy told me that she'd seen someone just dump some rubbish on the road.'

It is important to note that in other respects Ruth resembled many of her peers in terms of struggling with ideas about death and afterlife, and her tendency to construe a sense of mystery by drawing on Disneyesque types of fantasy. She also exhibited some selective reliance on authoritative world-view conceptions (e.g. see her reference to 'mummy' in the quote above). Such shared features were overshadowed, however, by her individual efforts to express her sense of the spiritual according to her own disposition.

Tim   Tim was 10 years old and rejected any religious affiliation, in line with his family, of whom only his grandmother was perceived by him to be a Christian. Even this was thought to be simply because she was old and it was her 'last chance' to get to heaven. In such a case (and in contrast to Ruth above) it was therefore less appropriate to probe Tim's conception of traditionally 'religious' spiritual notions such as heaven, blessings and experiences of the presence of God. Despite this, much of Tim's conversation did touch on themes broadly connected to religious matters – such as animal reincarnation, polytheism, afterlife, morality and free will.

The distinctive characteristic that coloured Tim's discussions was a sense of inner struggle. In stark contrast to Ruth's framework, his allusions to the spiritual were framed as conflicting hypotheses representing a special kind of mental work. As with many of the other children, this individual 'signature' was present in some of his earliest responses concerning quite ordinary contexts. For example, when Tim looked at the first of our pictures (a young girl sitting pensively by the fire) he assumed she was lonely and worried, possibly thinking about her parent's divorce, struggling to make sense of some kind of problem which could not be talked about with others. This framework of discomfort and struggle also characterized Tim's senses of wonder, awe, meaningfulness and mystery.

The following excerpt illustrates two of his spiritual dilemmas, 'Is there a single true God?' and 'How can we cope with the mystery of infinity?':

> I sometimes think about if there is one God and there is ... everybody, well ... most people believe in one God and um ... there's um ... different people believe in different gods. Which God's real? Um ... I just can't figure that out. And I sometimes think about after the universe, what's ... uh ... what's the universe um .... going on for ever. I just don't know. [What does that feel like?] Well, when I'm thinking about the universe, that gets me quite annoyed sometimes because I can never think about um ... get the right answer or get even near it and um ... then, well ... things ... you just wonder.

His frustrated and struggling, rather than joyous, inspiration was clear here. At another point he described having had an answer to prayer about which he felt equally undecided and frustrated. He weighed up the options of it being a real answer or a coincidence, concluding: '[It] gets annoying trying to think about it ... just 'cause you can't find the answer and you think your brains is gonna get all scrambled, like.'

There were other situations that gave him cause to wrestle mentally with the spiritual. For example, he wondered whether religious behaviour was a genuine response or mere 'habit' (as prompted by the picture of the boy in need seeming to address the sky – or was it, perhaps, God?). He attempted to define 'spiritual' as a feeling of being emotionally moved, and recalled that he might have had 'a lot' of experiences when younger of something like God's guiding, an influence 'shaping your life'. He quite readily described unusual experiences and feelings which he had had when visiting churches and sacred sites, and when thinking his thoughts alone at night. However, these feelings were predominately negative, and he used words such as 'spooky', 'shiver' and 'cold' in a manner consistent with his overall framework and disposition. Each time these special moments were balanced by a sense of struggle as to the underlying validity and meaning contained in such mysterious and thought-provoking experiences. He suggested that quite probably they were due to his 'eyes playing tricks' on him or were 'an illusion of the mind', 'coincidence' or 'chance'.

He described his perception of life's qualities in terms of a feeling ('I just love that feeling') that humans have broken free from a bondage that would otherwise have trapped them in an endless routine of mere living. Here also there was a strong sense of difficult mental work being involved. This view seemed to me to be particularly insightful, so I gently asked how he had come by it. He explained, 'Just ... um ... [by] thinking about it. Kept on thinking and found it.' This reiterates the primacy of mental effort in his approach to this and other areas.

Finally, he indirectly commented on the contrast between his 'thinking and struggling' spirituality and that of others, which is more direct and emotional, but potentially short-lived. I had asked him to consider whether children of his age could have religious experiences such as a sense of the presence of God or something like that, and he replied: 'I think they just look at it and think *Wow!* and uh ... forget about it, really ... Or just um ... think about it, but don't think how they were made.' In other words, such children would not, in his view, pursue their thinking far enough for it to qualify as spiritually meaningful, according to his individual framework of inner struggle and facing up to the problematic questions.

The 'signature' phenomenon   These two children presented quite different kinds of spirituality, yet the spirituality of each was active in its own way. From this alone the need for a multi-dimensional characterization of spirituality seems warranted: neatly simplistic accounts that might force individual differences into grouped patterns are in danger of misrepresenting it.

Others have alluded to the role played by an individual's psychological make-up[4] in their spirituality, but here I suggest it is given a central position. The practical implication is that one needs to enquire carefully about and attend to each child's personal style if one is to 'hear' their spirituality at all. At a theoretical level this implies that we cannot neatly distinguish the spiritual aspects from the psychological features of a child's life. Indeed, it seems plausible to suppose that this dependency of spirituality on the individual contours of personal psychology may be especially pronounced amongst children. After all, children are less aware than adults of the religious tracks along which spirituality has traditionally been routed. They depend far more on their own resources (and resourcefulness).

In the context of the whole research sample, neither Ruth nor Tim were exceptional cases. Other children were equally forthcoming and thoughtful on some occasions, reticent or flippant at other times. Although the summaries I have offered represent different genders and age groups, their personal 'signatures' could not be explained simply in these terms, nor by any other discernible classification such as membership of a religious institution or family structure.

However, it would be foolish to suggest that age or other categorizations have no role to play in helping to understand the expression of children's spirituality. In drawing conclusions about children's spirituality, it seems important to avoid misreading as features of spirituality itself differences which are primarily reflections of age or cognitive development (or gender, or class, or religion). To do so may be at the expense of uncovering more fundamental core features of such spirituality. One difference suggested by the contrasting examples of Ruth and Tim is the ability of the older child to reflect more intentionally on experiences, thoughts and feelings. In Tim's case, this reflective process was a key to his spirituality, which was dominated by mental struggle. On the other hand, the absence of this ability from Ruth's repertoire does not impede the intensity of her spirituality. Where Tim capitalizes on his reflective awareness about matters spiritual, she capitalizes on a direct awareness of spiritual significance.

Discerning spirituality through different kinds of data

The categories identified in Chapter 4 as a guide to the research conversations were each well represented by examples in the children's talk. Nonetheless, it began to be clear that a different kind of 'superordinate' core category was needed to provide an interpretative key. Whilst it was clear that each child had a very individual spiritual approach, there was equally something uniform about the resounding 'sense' of children's spirituality which I had during the conversations, and again when reading and re-reading the transcripts.[5] A core category gradually emerged as I reflected on the analytical and interpretative processes I had applied to reading and selecting different kinds of passages from the original mass of data. The following section describes some of the reflective processes prompted by various kinds of conversation.

A basic question I found necessary to ask myself was about the particular aspects of the conversation in which children's spirituality seemed to be most clearly expressed. A considerable amount of these conversations could be classified as 'casual chatter', in which everyday exchanges took place, such as comments about the lunch menu or the rules of a playground game. This kind of chatter had served an important role during the data collection itself, relaxing the children and dissipating the impression that a formal interview with set questions and answers was taking place. It also served as a kind of 'control' material as I came to analyse what could be said about children's spirituality. Chatter gave a rough measure of each child's oral abilities against which to compare any instances of spiritual talk.

In addition to this, the 'bread and butter' of the research conversations, it was clear that there were certain passages that seemed especially significant; passages that activated my sense that here was something indicative of children's spirituality. Such passages were drawn from two different kinds of conversation: (1) dialogue that employed religious ideas and language; and (2) non-religious dialogue that implicitly conveyed that the child was engaged in something more than the casual or mundane. It was helpful to reflect further on what was going on in these different kinds of contribution.

'Religious' dialogue   It is, of course, entirely possible to speak about religious matters in ways that are not indicative of spirituality, something that was evident in much of the children's religious talk. Therefore, this kind of conversation called for distinguishing between passages which were merely made up of religious information and those that seemed more personally grounded. Accounts of children's own religious experiences, religious sentiments and personal constructions of faith were natural candidates for the latter category, and constituted the clearest evidence of explicit spirituality at least as it is conventionally recognized in adults. Here are two examples illustrating this kind of material, from a younger boy and an older girl.

John (aged 6) had been explaining his religious beliefs to me. These were clearly Christian and supported by his family, though neither they nor John attended church more than twice a year, at Christmas and Easter. I asked how he came to hold his beliefs. In his response he described a religious experience:

> I worked about it and I received ... one day ... I was with my mum and I begged her ... um ... for me to go to um ... some church. And we did it and ... I prayed ... and after that praying ... I knew that good was on my side. And I heard him in my mind say this: 'I am with you. Every step you go. The Lord is with you. May sins be forgiven.'

And later on he described his encounter with the Holy Spirit:

> Well once I went um ... in the night and I saw this bishopy kind of alien. I said, 'Who are you?' And he said, 'I am the Holy Spirit.' I did think he was the Holy Spirit.

When, in his shock, he called out to his mum and explained what had just happened, John was told that the Holy Spirit looks like a ball of fire, and his version of events was rejected.[6] He seemed to accept his mother's authority concerning this sighting, though he added, 'But I often felt the Holy Spirit in me.'

Maggie (aged 10) mentioned moments of both intense doubt and belief in God. Belief was bolstered by explicitly religious experiences of God in special moments she could recall.

> [What are those moments like?]
> Weird, because I think like he's talking to me. But I never know whether it's him or whether it's just what I want him to say, and that's my conscience. I never know.
> [What sort of times does that happen?]
> When I'm upset or worried about something ... it feels all comfortable and tingling ... I don't know ... it just ... I can't describe it ... it's just weird ... it's nice.
> [Does it last very long?]
> Well, I normally feel it like at night, I mean when I'm on my own and near the end of the day when I'm tired, so next day it's all gone...

[And do some things that you see remind you of it?]

No, but churches remind me, and I feel all that when I go to the church ... same feeling.

Conversation employing explicitly religious language was likely to be pivotal in the analysis, as a touchstone for indentifying children's spirituality which expressed itself in other ways. However, recollections of dramatic religious experiences were not common in the sample. More often children couched their responses in terms of a recognition that experiences such as these could happen or had happened to them, but their memory was vague. They were also often able to project themselves imaginatively into what such an experience would be like, making use of religious language to express this sense of the spiritual. For example, they could imagine their feelings (e.g. 'warm kindness', 'amazed and trembling') on encountering God or an angel in ways that echoed the feelings reported by adults who actually recollect such experiences.

Earlier chapters have described how it was an intention of this research to attempt a study of children's spirituality that went considerably further than the accounts of children's religion that others have provided. Here spirituality was approached as a natural phenomenon that is not wholly dependent on religious teaching and understanding. However, special attention to how children used religious reference in conversation was illuminating in our study's attempt to identify the multi-dimensional characteristics of children's spirituality. This attention resulted in a number of interesting observations reflecting some general features of the children's spirituality.

First, it was noticeable how readily this largely secularized sample of children introduced religious terms in the course of our conversations. Their readiness to use religious language was all the more intriguing given the considerable gaps in the children's knowledge and understanding. For example, Katie (aged 6), told me she had recently become the owner of a Bible but said she had never been inside a church. I asked what she thought about God, and she replied: 'I don't know yet, because

I haven't read it very long. [Did you know about God before you got your Bible?] No, not at all.' This established that she had little coherent understanding of formal religion. However, earlier on, when discussing a picture of a starry sky, she had commented that 'You [i.e. Rebecca] couldn't even reach that high ... no one can, except God.' And at another point, when discussing whether some aspects of a person might be entirely personal and private, Katie was asked, 'What sorts of things could somebody know about themselves that nobody else knew?' and she replied, 'God knows everything.' In yet another moment, reflecting on how we know things, she suggested that her moral knowledge of when she's being good or bad was God-given. Additionally, she decided that other kinds of knowledge are beyond human understanding, but may be a special kind of knowledge available to God, such as the mystery of 'Like ... how um ... we get alive.'

This readiness to draw on religious conceptions in the task of meaning-making, despite a background of lack of knowledge of formal religion, was especially noteworthy. It seemed to reflect a need for a language to articulate a domain of which most children had at least some degree of perception (about which more is said below).

In tandem with this note about readiness, it was also possible to observe children's reluctance to stay with religious dialogue for very long. Even amongst children such as six-year-old John (mentioned above), who relished expressing his theological ideas, there came a point when using traditional religious discourse became overwhelming, and the subject was changed either by request or simply by default. In the following excerpt John suddenly changed the subject when he was in full flow describing how he 'saw' God:

With my mind and with my eyes. Sometimes I feel that ... um ... I am in um ... a place with God in heaven and I'm talking to him ... And um ... there's room for us all in God. He ... God's ... well, he is ... in all of us ... He's everything that's around us. He's that microphone ... He's that book. He's even ... He's sticks ... He's paint ... He's everything ... Around us ... Inside our heart ... Heaven. By the way, have you seen *Indiana Jones and the Temple of Doom*? [a film that had been on television the previous night].

Can an awareness of this reluctance to pursue religious conversation help us to understand children's struggles to express spirituality? For some, resisting religious language may have been due to a crisis of confidence in using terms and concepts which they could not fully understand, let alone articulate. Several of the older children were able to express their difficulties with this kind of language. For example, Jenny (aged 10) commented on a hymn which she found meaningful, but when asked to explain this she said, 'You think it's quite easy [when singing it], but when you try to explain it ... you don't know which words to use.'

For others it was apparent that embarrassment was at the root of their reluctance. They were cautious of straying for too long beyond the acceptable confines of secular discourse.[7] Some children admitted that they were afraid of being laughed at or thought stupid or even mad, not only by their peer group but also within their families (including 'religious' families), if they talked about their personal sense of the religious in their lives. Thus, even in the privacy of the research conversations, being seen to talk at length about religious matters was to be avoided.

In a few cases this ambivalent response – a readiness to choose, then abandon, religious language – may have been a facet of their spiritual awareness itself. The dual potential of spiritual experience to attract or to disturb is a core feature in Rudolf Otto's account.[8] It seems that an encounter with the spiritual may prompt desire and love, or fear and flight from the perceived stimulus. For some children a wish to disengage from a conversation that triggered such memories may have indicated something of their insight into their personal spiritual pasts.

It is too easily forgotten that spiritual experiences are not inevitably 'cosy'. Therefore it is probably important to leave open any final interpretation of children's tendency to 'shut down' whilst talking in this way. There is a need to respect children's reticence (perhaps evident in a disinclination to engage consciously in spiritually expressive discourse at all) as potentially spiritually informed, rather than as indicative of an absence of spiritual awareness.

In spite of these obstacles, leading to a wariness of religious language, many children's readiness to use it suggests their perception of its symbolic function. It seemed to be a necessity in expressing something distinctive about their own experience. For example, Jenny expressed how her recourse to religious language happened for her in the ordinary context of thinking about who she is and why she is here. She referred back to a conversation we had had about her memory of sitting in a tree reflecting on the nature of self-knowledge. It was prompted by her own thought on seeing a ladybird and wondering if it knew where it was in time and space: 'Well, there was the time I told you that I stop and think, "How did I get here and that?" Well, that's when I switch on to God. That's when I start thinking about him.' Thus, for her the area where the personal meets the existential is one which calls on a special language – religious language.

Implicitly spiritual discourse: associative and isolated types Reflecting on those conversations in which there was an overt use of religious language was helpful when it came to recognizing the contours of a children's spirituality expressed without the use of religious language. It is to these accounts that I now turn.

My comments on the symbolic function of religious language need to be qualified. It was clear that for a substantial number of children, religious reference had lost its potency. Some children had a suspicion that religious explanations were 'just too easy', and thus failed to capture the inherent complexity and mystery for which they sought an expression. Several children who apparently rejected religious dialogue as a means of expressing their spirituality called upon other languages to fit an analogous purpose. For example, one six-year-old boy's sense of ultimate mystery was stirred more by the incomprehensibility of human nature than by any questions about God that occurred to him. Another, older, boy found religious language untenable, but repeatedly located his comments about ultimate meaning in messages he had had in dreams, the symbolic language of the unconscious.[9]

At the beginning of this chapter I referred to the 'sense' I often had of a spiritual reference in children's talk. This was frequently prompted by passages that lacked any clearly expressed traditional religious or metaphysical terminology, and it was these passages that required the most intuitive treatment. I already had the 'working map' categories as guides to how implicit forms of spirituality might plausibly be manifest amongst children. However, just as with religious talk, it was clear that spirituality was not necessarily being tapped just because the conversation touched upon, for example, mystery or values. Furthermore, there were plenty of instances that seemed to fall outside the working-map categories, but which nevertheless seemed (intuitively) significant to the child's spiritual make-up. I distinguished two forms which this kind of conversation took: *associative* and *isolated*.

In a number of cases the process of identifying these implicitly spiritual instances was helped by converging patterns in the data. This was the situation when a child's discussion of what seemed to be an implicitly spiritual theme echoed or foreshadowed a more explicit articulation. It was the association with more explicit or traditional religious langauge and ideas that provided a key to its identification as 'spiritual'.

For example, Freddie (aged 6) repeatedly discussed friendship and reconciliation in his own life and in his fantasies. He did this in a way that suggested these themes represented something that was of both personal and universal concern in his view – themes fundamental to his world-view and, by extension, to his 'spirituality'. This could be confirmed in a conventional sense in his case. On one occasion his implicitly spiritual discussion of friendships and mutual respect seemed to have been prompted by thoughts about his view of creation and God's role in that. In another passage he followed up a discussion about the value of friends, good relationships and his difficulty in maintaining these, that seemed implicitly spiritual in his case, with the comment, 'God's the kindest person I know, I think ... because he never shouts or tells you off, because he never even speaks to you apart from perhaps when you're dead.'

In both instances, associated evidence suggested that his discussion of aspects of his personal and social world was spiritually significant for him, since they were linked in his own mind with his personal faith. Material was judged to be implicitly spiritual when such associations could be discerned. Identifying these associations often added depth to the different passages of a child's interview, bringing the religious dialogue to life through these personal modulations, and vice versa. This process produced a kind of subtext to include in the overall accumulating body of evidence of what children's spirituality is like and how it might be 'heard'.

This sort of confirmation was not always available. Yet many passages, isolated from any association with traditional religious language, seemed to carry an implicit spirituality, characterized by emotional sensitivity or philosophical reflection. Whilst it was moving and impressive to encounter the quality of such material in children so young, there was no obvious rationale for labelling it as 'spirituality' *per se*. The intuition that these passages were representative of children's spirituality had to be justified in another way. This was through a process of searching for a common thread underlying such passages that was also shared by explicitly religious dialogue or by the 'implicit associative' passages which I mentioned above. Finding this common thread was decisive in identifying a core category, to be described in the next chapter, by which the general realm of children's spirituality might be recognized.

Examples of this isolated form of spirituality are illustrated in Jackie's (aged 6) and Harriet's (aged 10) interviews. Jackie expressed an insightful emotional sensitivity to her experience. This was evident in her sense of values, for example. Unlike some six-year-olds, who were unable to suggest anything that was special to them or others, except perhaps such things as sweets, Jackie replied, 'It's hard to choose because I've got so many things that are special.' She went on to list a precious china house she cherished, certain people, and her pet dog. In a similar vein, whilst she professed conscious indifference to formal religion encountered at school, she admitted to a vaguely 'nice feeling' during assembly prayers, though she didn't participate in them. She tried to explain this as 'It seems like ... um ... no unkindness', and proceeded to describe how she had become aware of her own unkindness to a friend and had been prompted to put a stop to it.

Harriet, a very matter-of-fact 10-year-old, had said very little of interest in her first two interviews. I had been unable to spark off a conversation with her that tapped enthusiasm or emotion in other areas, and she was clearly unimpressed with religion in so far as she had heard about it in school. In her final interview, however, Harriet suddenly came alive with philosophical questions, though not of a traditionally spiritual kind. Her flow of questions covered the nature of thought as never ending, leading her to wonder about the relationship between mind and brain. This was immediately followed by queries about the nature of language and how things came to have their names. In turn, this flood of unanswerable questioning (largely uninterrupted by me) led her to wonder about the origin of the universe and of human beings (stopping to mention her rejection of the biblical explanation along the way). Finally she suggested that, faced with such mystery yet yearning for meaning, 'Perhaps we've got to, like, ask the clouds. The clouds have been there millions and millions of years.' This perhaps echoes Native American forms of spirituality. I then asked if she felt there was some organizing principle behind it all, and she replied, again drawing on images from nature:

> Well, there must be somewhere, somehow – or else, how would it keep reproducing? Like it [?] made a flower, a dandelion. Where did the wind come from to blow all the petals off to make them fall on the floor to make more? ... (*in a whisper*) It's puzzling.

The reflections of these two girls illustrate how children some-times express profound, personal, sensitive and, as in this last example, searching philosophical reflections concerning their existence. Yet they hold back from anything one might confi-dently identify as traditionally spiritual. It seems important for such kinds of deep pondering to find a place in an account of children's spirituality.

The experience of interviewing many different children sug-gested that there is a continuum. At one end are those who per-ceive spiritual matters in terms of questions or principles. Then there are those who go on to make unconscious or conscious associations with the traditional spiritual language of religion in their attempt to articulate these questions and find meaningful ways of answering them. Finally, at the other end of the continu-um are those who have experienced their spirituality directly and personally in the form of religious insights. The kinds of com-ments made by a child like Harriet do not lie outside the field of spirituality, merely because they did not lead, as in other chil-dren, to the construction of traditionally religious answers or meanings. In other words, to accommodate these various points on the continuum, children's spirituality required a description that could handle both explicitly 'spiritual experience' and the implicitly spiritual passages described in this section.

Conclusion

Seeking ways to identify, condense and make sense of the spir-ituality which the children had shared with me was an extremely challenging task. This process began with attention to each child's conversation as a case study in its own right. Reflecting on the insights gained from this approach, it became clear that children's spirituality could not be divorced from their individuality. Attending to the personal style and idiosyncratic preoccupations of each child often revealed a 'signature' or key that unlocked the layers of meaning otherwise hidden from the naive listener.

As I attempted to move beyond these individual cases, it became necessary to make comparisons between children. One direction which my reflections took was to consider the contribution made by different kinds of conversation. This analysis demonstrated that the traditional spiritual language provided by religion still plays a surprisingly prominent role in contemporary children's spiritual expression. However, it was also clear in thinking about these passages that more sensitive criteria were needed to distinguish those occasions when religious talk was spiritual from those when it was not. Such criteria needed to accommodate a broader range of significant material, particularly that which seemed 'implicitly spiritual', sometimes through association with religious material, but on other occasions in apparent isolation from this.

The important consequence of these thoughts was that I became aware of a converging property in all the passages where I had experienced an initial intuitive sense of children's spirituality. I began to perceive what it was that ran through each of the diverse examples; the essence by which children's spirituality might be known. This property became the 'core category' of the theoretical framework proposed in the next chapter.

7

Identifying the Core of Children's Spirituality

By Rebecca Nye

And calling to him a child, he put him in the midst of them and said, 'Truly, I say to you, unless you turn and become like children, you will never enter the kingdom of heaven.'

MATTHEW 18:2–3

All knowing is consciousness of knowing.

JEAN-PAUL SARTRE[1]

Introduction

Hearing the children's voices in the last chapter may have conveyed some sense of the richness of their conversation. Despite snags like the limitations of language, relative lack of experience and social taboos, it seems that children can provide their own evidence of what their spirituality is like. Many passages are so alive that additional commentary is rather pale in comparison. The impressive wealth and individuality of spiritual expression which we had uncovered made it important to find a way to talk about this systematically. Would it be possible to build up a general picture that could help us and others to 'get a handle' on what children's spirituality was like?

To analyse the conversations I followed a 'grounded theory' approach.[2] The data and the results of our attempts to analyse it – theoretical memos about different themes, line-by-line analyses of texts, computer searches for particular words and patterns – were repeatedly scrutinized. We wanted to see if it was possible to expose a core category that would 'tell the story' of the phenomenon being studied. Following this extensive search,[3] the category which drew together all the different kinds of seemingly relevant data was a compound property which I called *relational consciousness*. This reflected two patterns, indicated in key passages of data similar to those serving as illustrations in the previous chapter:

- ❖ An unusual level of *consciousness* or perceptiveness, relative to other passages of conversation spoken by that child.
- ❖ Conversation expressed in a context of how the child *related* to things, other people, him/herself, and God.

The kind of consciousness identified in every case was qualified by reference to a specific 'relationship'. In brief, children's spirituality was recognized by a distinctive property of mental activity,[4] profound and intricate enough to be termed 'consciousness', and remarkable for its confinement to a broadly relational, inter- and intra-personal domain.

It must be emphasized that superficial readings of the terms 'consciousness' or 'relationship' do not apply here. 'Consciousness' refers here to something more than being alert and mentally attentive. It also implies more than what was described by the category of 'awareness' in our guideline categories (see Chapter 4), which focused on discrete moments of unusual awareness. Very often the quality described here suggested a distinctively reflective consciousness or, as it is termed in developmental psychology, 'meta-cognition'. This entailed some degree of awareness on the part of the child of the remarkable nature of his or her own mental activity in certain contexts. It was often this apparently objective insight into their subjective response which fostered a new dimension of understanding, meaning and experience (of meta-consciousness) in itself. The sense of being objectively aware of themselves as 'subject' seemed particularly important in encouraging the children's ability to perceive their world in relational terms.

'Relational' was not applied in a narrow sense either. Its reference was not limited to family, friends or foes. In a broad section of the data the dual patterning included not only 'I-Others' but also 'I-Self', 'I-World' and 'I-God'. In each case the child's awareness of being in relationship with something or someone was demonstrated by what they said and, crucially, this was a special sense that added value to their ordinary or everyday perspective. Sometimes this was explicitly expressed as having a distinctive form of awareness. In this 'relational consciousness' seems to lie the rudimentary core of children's spirituality, out of which can arise meaningful aesthetic experience, religious experience, personal and traditional responses to mystery and being, and mystical and moral insight.

Illustrating relational consciousness at a general level

I now want to illustrate in a general way the dual patterns that comprise the core category by returning to some of the examples of data already presented in Chapter 6, beginning with the children described in the two brief sketches.

Six-year-old Ruth's conversation (p. 95) included a sensual description of heaven. She referred to the key elements in her spiritual response as 'waking up' and 'noticing', both of which suggest that a different quality of consciousness was crucial to her experience. The relational component in this was a strong feeling of connection to the natural world as something which was full of gifts for her and deserved her respect and love in return. This sense of intimacy also had reverberations in her relationship with herself, as seen in her self-conscious perception of a symmetry between her own joy and the joyful leaping of the lambs.

In the other brief sketch (p. 97) many of 10-year-old Tim's comments were about the different kind of consciousness the spiritual domain seemed to engender in him, for instance the uncomfortable awareness of his brains feeling 'scrambled'. The relational component in his case was represented mainly in terms of struggling to achieve a comfortable relationship within himself. Many of the themes he pondered, such as the eternity and creation of the universe or the existence of a single true God, were directed back to questions about and feelings of his own sense of identity. The central relational issue that appeared to colour his rather anxious, struggling expression of spirituality was that of trust. Were the feelings and insights associated with these products of his own consciousness 'trustworthy partners', so to speak, with whom constructive relationships might be made, or were they merely 'tricks of the mind'?

Maggie, Tim's 10-year-old classmate (p. 102), also struggled over the nature of trust in her relationship with insights and feelings. Were they merely the machinations of conscience, one form of consciousness, or something more divinely inspired? In her attempt to isolate features that might distinguish the more mundane consciousness from the other, she notes the 'comfort-ing' quality of what might be her spiritual experiences. Such a property is a natural one exchanged between friends, thus sug-gesting her sense of a special defining relational quality to these forms of consciousness.

John, aged six (p. 102), was the precociously religious child who had described 'hearing God in my mind' when praying in church and seeing the Holy Spirit in bed one night. In explain-ing his experiences he favoured images of conscious activity: God was 'in my mind', 'with my mind', 'felt in me'. One good reason for this might have been his recognition that others could not so easily tamper with his experiences as they did in the case of his Holy Spirit vision. He insisted that he had nevertheless 'felt the Holy Spirit in me', redefining the kind of consciousness this experience had prompted. In each of John's descriptions of 'religiously' spiritual experience, a close personal presence was suggested. Thus in his case 'relational consciousness' was manifested as a sense of relationship with God.

Bob, aged 10, was memorable for his repeated references to dreams in his conversations. Where other children had located the spiritual in special activities (often relational) of their conscious minds, Bob suggested that a more radically different kind of consciousness represented his experience of spiritual matters. Contemplating his sense of ultimate mystery and meaning, he described the feeling as: 'Pictures going through my head, like dreams or something ... they all seem to fit together like a big puzzle ... like one dream in all, like telling me things.' Once again, this different sense of consciousness is credited with relational qualities, as a means of communication within and between himself and life's mystery. Referring to dreams, as Bob did here, was a way many children (more than one third) used to express the unusual nature of their consciousness of the spiritual.

As has been stated above and illustrated amongst the examples here, defining the consciousness associated with spirituality as 'relational' is not limited to talk about relationships *per se*, although in the following examples this was the case.

For Jackie, aged six (p. 109), heaven conjured up the relational concept of 'no unkindness', and prompted self-conscious recognition of her own shortcomings with friends. Andrew, also aged six, shared his vivid images of heaven and hell, represented in his mind by a circle and a square respectively. The derivations of his innovative metaphors were given in terms of God's unending love for us (like the unending property of circles) and the devil's inferior, finite 'love'. This encapsulated not only his perception of the nature of God's relationship with us, but also led him to reflect on the potentially sacred nature of relationships between people: 'God made us and God gave us love, so we can love each other.'

The power of this relational property as central to Andrew's spirituality was especially remarkable because earlier on he had stated, and given his justifications, for being an atheist. Yet at the closing stage of his final interview, having found himself expressing his ideas about unending circles and love, he qualified his previous statement by saying: 'I believe in God's love.'

At the very end of the interview he was asked to imagine that he might have three wishes and to choose what these could be. All of these displayed a clear relational ethic: 'Nasty people would be good people'; 'Rich people [would] give some money to the poor people'; and whilst the final wish would be 'Something for myself', he concluded that he would 'share it with someone else'. It is suggested, therefore, that simply by identifying and examining his personally meaningful images, his special sense of the value of relationship was brought into consciousness and gave us access to his spiritual code.

Finally, six-year-old Freddie (p. 107) epitomized how talk about relationships captures spiritual consciousness. Having slipped into religious language as a way of conveying his sense of the physical world's existence (i.e. God had made the world, except for those parts his dad had built), Freddie then effortlessly moved into a discussion about his own difficulty in relating to others in a positive way (he had a habit of attacking other children), as if religious discourse and relational insights were totally equivalent in his mind. This conversation included his recent insight into himself in relation to others by means of an interpretative identification with Grumpy's transformation of self in the film version of *Snow White and the Seven Dwarfs*:

> The earth's so good [that God made], but sometimes somebody feels really sad, and like on *Snow White*, you know, Grumpy like, he feels very sad and grumpful ... but when he gets into know[ing] about life, he thinks more better about it, about Snow White and things like that, because Snow White being in trouble by the Evil Queen, then he cares and when she dies, then he really cares, and when she comes back alive again, he cares even more. So I think Grumpy and Snow White learned about how clever and good life can be. At the start he doesn't know nothing about life, so he don't like life and the planet of God and really later on he finds out all about it ... Sometimes I get really grumpy at school and then I thought about how life could be and how happy I could be if I started to try and not to be grumpy no more.

It appears that when Freddie considered his religious views about creation, his personal conception of spiritual values was triggered. Through this story-ing about relationships we glimpse both his emerging and transformative self-consciousness, as well as some hints of his 'God-consciousness' suggested in his comment about Grumpy's realization that he is a citizen of the 'planet of God'.[5]

From core category to a framework of its dimensions
Through a number of examples of different children's talk, I have tried to show that 'relational consciousness' is a common thread tying together the spirituality of these ordinary school-children. This way of referring to what seemed to be the concentrated essence of the various kinds of spiritual discourse paid further dividends. It gave a central reference point around which the very many themes might be organized and further described. Subsidiary questions could now be asked about the different kinds of context in which this aspect of children's lives seemed present. Likewise, it became possible to ask about any special patterns that conditioned its expression – for example, the opportunities which religious language seemed to afford. Another set of questions examined the ways in which relational consciousness was governed over time – the strategies and processes which kept it going or curbed its course. Lastly, the types of consequence that followed on from encounters of this core category were examined. In this way a framework arising from this empirical study of children's spirituality was built up comprising contexts, conditions, strategies, processes and consequences, all describing the pivotal features of the area of relational consciousness.

There is great diversity underlying the uniform presentation of children's spirituality as 'relational consciousness'. Each of the dimensions in the framework was represented by many different kinds of that element, as illustrated in Figure 1 (p. 120). It is unlikely that light will be shed on the spirituality of a child by considering any of these dimensions in isolation. Insight more often lies in their distinctive and unique combination. One type

The Spirit of the Child

of context – for example, 'child-God consciousness' – might be given a distinctive character by quite different conditions, such as a language of religious faith or a game. It could be yet further altered by different strategies of, for example, imagining or reasoning. It is little wonder that so many different consequences were also represented in this data.

Nevertheless, the lists of different features that characterize each dimension are informative. They help to specify the rangeof sources which children can draw upon to express their individual spirituality. In turn, this helps us to identify the different functions and roles played by the various manifestations of the spiritual in children's experience. It is also significant that many, if not all, of the attributes within these lists are normal processes forming the conventional content of child psychology (e.g. playing, imagining, games, stories, autobiography). This firmly locates children's spirituality within the reach of the ordinary child.

Illustrating the dimensions of the core category

Contexts This dimension reflects the broad forms or contexts in which our core category of children's spirituality (relational consciousness) appeared. These can be divided into four different types: child-God consciousness, child-people consciousness, child-world consciousness, and child-self consciousness.

Child-God consciousness. In this type of context the material was framed in terms of the child's sense of relationship to God. This was naturally the closest to traditionally conceived notions of spirituality and could describe the explicitly religious experiences that a few of the children reported. Many more children were able to imagine what it would be like to have such an experience.[6] In a looser way, this type related to cases where the child simply talked about their concept of God, and the meaning and emotion it prompted, since this was also a criterion for

Figure 1: The dimensions of relational consciousness: a framework for children's spirituality
Relational consciousness

Contexts
child-God consciousness
child-people consciousness
child-world consciousness
child-self consciousness

Conditions
religious language
language of beliefs, incl. beliefs
    about death
autobiographical language
language of fiction
language of play and games
language about time and place
language about values and
morals
language of science and
technology
language of the natural world

Processes
avoidance
sidetracking
'third-personizing'
sliding between contexts
forcing a conclusion
magnification
self-identification
interiorizing
forgetting
changefulness

Strategies
Explicit:
mental/physical withdrawal
focusing, concentration
seeking relation or dialogue
seeking/exploiting aesthetic/
    sensory stimulation
'philosophizing'

Implicit:
meandering questions, puzzling
imagining
reasoning
searching for meaning
moralizing
staying with a mood
dreaming
playing, escaping reality
concrete/abstract combining

Consequences
calmness and peacefulness
holiness
goodness
oneness
impressed
wonder
quest for understanding
new clarity
sense of worth
thankfulness
strangeness
perplexed and frustrated
inner conflict
embarrassed
ridiculed
undermined
search for supportive comparison

NB: This is a comprehensive list based on the entire body of research data. It is not possible to discuss every one of these manifestations in the text of this chapter, but they are included here for reference.

recognizing that the excerpt belonged to this context. Beth's (aged 10) account of her prayer experiences following a period of religious doubt is an example:

> So I just half believed in God and half didn't, and then I had to pray extra hard to get his love back because I had been really mean to him. I had not prayed to him for ages, and so I was really mean to him, so I had to give him extra love, and I felt really good after that, but when I wasn't praying I felt really, really bad.

She went on to elaborate on the emotions she associated with the context of a relationship with God. Though these included a pleasant sense of peacefulness, she also said:

> Sometimes I feel very lonely when I am alone with God because I can't see God and I can't hear God. I just think about God. I feel really lonely, so I like being with people sometimes.

This context is the most straightforward and least novel of the ones we have identified: children's spirituality as reflected in their feelings and thoughts about their relationship with God. But the data suggest that provision for such reflection need not be confined to children committed to religious faith and therefore able to speak from a standpoint of being 'in' a relationship with God. Spirituality may be explored in the ponderings of atheists and agnostics as they consider how their views shape their denial of, or uncertainty about, the possibility of relating in this way.

Child-people consciousness. Discussion about the child's sense of relationship to others often formed a bridge to and from the child-God context. I noted this in Andrew's case, which was described earlier. Conversation about his image of heaven and God's love became a reflection on his wish for interpersonal relations.

Some comments made by Natasha (aged six) also illustrate how this context frames relational consciousness. Her very first comment in the interview had been in response to the general question about what struck her as really special. For her, 'people' headed this list. God came further down and was mentioned only after discussion of a number of other things. At a later point she was invited to think of a time when she had felt God's special nature in some way. In conversations with other children this was usually seen as a prompt to chat about the child's sense of relationship to God, but Natasha replied with an autobiographical anecdote about making a new friend with whom she shared her sweets, sandwiches and playtimes. Another way of describing this could be the spirituality of fellowship. A Christian analogy to her example might be the shared bread of Communion that expresses this (amongst other things) for adults.

This type of context seemed especially 'available' to children; much of their interest is naturally focused on their social world. Its capacity to provide a vehicle for spirituality suggests that particular note might be taken of how children construe interpersonal relations as a means of glimpsing something of their spiritual life.

Child-world consciousness. Examples of this type indicated that spirituality was experienced through the child's sense of relationship to the natural world. Ruth (aged six; p. 95) illustrated this context to some extent in her profound responses to the sensual beauty in nature. In her case this was often more in the context of a sense of relationship to God, with characteristics of the natural world providing a secondary contextual effect.

However, for Louise (aged 10) relating to the natural world was the primary context of her spiritual consciousness. Her main source of amazement was the birth-and-growth process which she had witnessed in small animals. She expressed profound wonder in contemplating the mystery of what clouds could be made of. She conveyed an exhilarated sense of delight in the sound of autumn leaves and the 'greenness' (wondering 'What is green?') of grass. She had even identified friends with whom she could share this framework, and explained that whilst for her the sky was 'holy', she found out that her classmates Kelly and Maggie (p. 102) thought that water and grass suggested a sense of the sacred. In this example, as in many others, one type of context leads to another: child-nature consciousness merges with Louise's desire to be conscious of her friends' perspectives in this area.

Poets have often drawn our attention to the powerful and profound sense of the natural world that one can experience in childhood. Children themselves perhaps need more opportunities to articulate this. A vehicle for spiritual development may exist in experiences of sharing their sense of value and meaning arising in this kind of context with others.

Child-self consciousness. This was expressed in the context of children's sense of relationship with their own identity and their own mental life. As with the other contexts, this was often an important bridge to and from traditionally 'religious' spiritual experiences and expression, but in some cases it stood as a form of spirituality in its own right.

Many of the children talked about the mystery of death: a conundrum that has often given rise to spiritual answers and thus provided a basis for religious traditions. The way in which a context of self-consciousness was suggested in relation to death was by way of comments about it offering a very different and yet unknowable kind of personal consciousness (e.g. Will 'I' know that I'm dead, and in what sense?). A number of children, in both age groups, likened this to their own impossible experiments of trying to consciously observe themselves falling and being asleep.

Ten-year-old Altman had experienced wonder and meaning in a moment of sensing an unusual relationship to his own body and thought. He described this as 'popping out of it' ('it' meaning his own consciousness), and could only account for such an experience as being 'from God'. Similarly much of Jenny's (aged 10) discussion was inspired by existential questions about her sense of identity – 'Why am I here?' 'How did I get here?' – and where her guiding sense of morality came from. She too experienced this in a context of unusually vivid self-consciousness in which she felt herself 'pop out my body and blow somewhere else'. Together with the emotional descriptions of this experience as 'shocking', 'a tingle starting from your head to your feet', and her later explanation that such moments prompted her to 'switch on to God', there appears to be a good case for including certain kinds of consciousness of self as contexts in which children's spirituality could be manifest.

It is necessary to add that of themselves, neither this nor any of the other contexts is suggested as necessarily indicating a spiritual dimension in a child's experience. Rather, the contexts serve as one component amongst other parts in the framework. In combination they help to specify the properties of children's spirituality when revealed as 'relational consciousness'.

Conditions This dimension governed the circumstances in which the core category, in whichever context, was expressed. The varieties of this dimension were characterized by different 'languages' or linguistic environments in which children found ways to articulate their spirituality. By using the term 'language' I mean that children expressed spirituality using a particular 'vocabulary' and often the 'grammar' associated with that. Previous excerpts have already illustrated how some of these languages conditioned the children's talk. The role of religious language was particularly discussed in Chapter 6 and some further illustrations of this and other languages are given below.

Predictably, religious language was mainly Christian, although very often unorthodox or inaccurate in its details when used by 'non-religious' children. The most common alternatives to Christian terms and ideas were Hindu ideas of polytheism and reincarnation. It was not immediately obvious why this particular religious language was a resource for these children, since there were no Hindu children in their classes, very few in their schools and this was not the only faith other than Christianity which they studied in religious education. Nevertheless, it seemed that these ideas were salient in a way in which the details of other faith traditions were not. It is possible that there is a more primal appeal in a polytheistic framework, which appealed to these children's minds struggling in this area. Beth (aged 10), for example, found solace in the opportunity to pray to a specially concerned 'God of Knowledge' as she prepared to sit the Eleven Plus examination.

There is a more obvious source of the children's concern with reincarnation. The topic was debated by characters in the popular television soap opera *Neighbours* in the six months preceding the interviews, and some of the children attributed their ideas to this. As a potent source of social reference and information for young people, this programme had legitimated such language for expressing a sense of the spiritual. It seemed to suggest to these children a logical way of grappling with the mystery of death and their expectation of some kind of identity transformation therein. A straightforward adherence to a Christian framework here might have seemed a more obvious option for young children (e.g. that in death a person simply goes to live in a different place – heaven – with Jesus and the angels). Their comments about this suggested that in many cases they experienced traditional Western beliefs as too prosaic to capture their sense of the mysteries of transformation and continuity of personal identity in life and death.

In general terms (not necessarily religious), the theme of death and the associated language was a popular one in which many children framed their sense of mystery and a perception of an ultimate value in life beyond material achievements and comforts. They experienced a sense of their own finite nature in a more infinite context of life before and after their own existence. The language of death almost never instilled fear, but rather offered a positive resource in which to frame their experiences and explorations.

Some qualities of medieval spirituality were suggested by children's sense of kinship between the living and the dead, highlighting the relational quality in this discourse.[7] This was not merely expressed in terms of 'Grandma looks down on me and helps me when I'm in danger', but also in terms of a raised awareness of relationship for its own sake. For example, a child might regret never having known a grandparent who died before their birth, whilst having a sense of natural connection with such a person nonetheless.

A poignant instance of this use of death language as a condition for spirituality was illustrated in 10-year-old Daniel's case. In his opening remarks he had established that a key 'signature' language for him was that of death and the severing of relationships which such an event inevitably involved. When invited to discuss what he thought 'really mattered' he had replied: 'Like when you are gonna go on to a different land ... like when you die or something like that ...' He frequently referred to his struggle in understanding his parent's marital breakdown, his father's remarriage and the difference all this had made to his relationships with his mum, his dad and his new stepbrother. In his case, these conditions were sources of reflection that prompted 'bigger' questions and a greater awareness of his own philosophy of life's values and meanings. These reflections were collectively symbolized in his profound sense of regret in regard to the grandfather he never met, but with whom a relationship ought naturally to have been formed (just as a 'natural' relationship ought to exist between parents, children and siblings, but didn't in his case). In this instance 'death' helped to articulate Daniel's understanding of interpersonal disconnection, his sadness and bewilderment that natural relationships could seem so undermined by physical separation. The language of death also helped identify a measure beyond this, of enduring relationship or kinship, and a consciousness of relating as an invaluable feeling and personal principle – not just a matter of physical proximity between people.

Autobiographical Language could take the form of a child thinking or fantasizing about his or her own life story and particular events within it. Many children expressed wonder and felt an implicit sense of meaningfulness in their own developmental process from infancy to the present, and in anticipation of their future development.

Louise (aged 10) gave an account of personal transformation and consequent consciousness-raising in autobiographical terms.[8] She described a treasured moment in her development which pivoted upon a moral transgression and her sense of remorse. This in turn prompted a feeling that cannot be merely defined as moral and suggests a shift into the feeling world of spiritual experience. She described this as a 'magic' kind of change in her, a mysterious transformation that could not be accounted for in ordinary terms, nor in terms of her own actions, but suggested something more transcendent:

> When I was being rude to my mum and stuff I ... I felt like I was a new person ... coming out of something like ... like ... I don't know what's wrong with me, though, but I'm a new person from a flower or something. And like I've just grown like a flower or a tree or something. Because I'm going, 'I'm a new person and I'm not going to be rude to my mum.' Makes you feel really, really good actually.

Languages of fiction, as well as *languages of play and games*, were significant ways in which children framed their spirituality for a number of reasons. First, such conditions were necessarily personalized and creative expressions of the child's ideas and feelings. When a child told a story (such as Freddie's account of *Snow White*) or recalled playing a game that captured their attempt to explore a spiritual issue, the fictitious or playful expression was one of their choosing, not imposed by any particular tradition. In this sense one could be more confident that the sentiment being expressed was a genuine response, rather than a product of a learnt religious code of spirituality. Secondly, these languages were important because they afforded considerable flexibility – that is, playfulness – with the material itself. Children who made use of such languages had access to a powerful resource. In contemplating matters of mystery, unintelligibility or exceptional magnitude they had adopted a system of expression that allowed them to be silly and experimental, to be wrong and to be creative.

These types of language were significant for understanding the nature of children's spirituality because fiction and games are such a normal, everyday characteristic of children's lives. Using such language established that spirituality was perceived as something not to be excluded from the child's natural modes of expression, nor reliant on specialized religious knowledge or practices. Other writers have made strong cases against the common neglect of play in children's religious education and nurture,[9] arguing for far greater attention to this as a key to children's most serious 'work'. The three features identified here – play as an internalized and personal response; play's flexible properties; and the instinctive quality of play – ratify these languages as vital to children's spirituality.

The data contain many examples of playfulness, including Beth's (aged 10) imaginary world of a garden which seemed to function like an inner sanctuary for all her spiritual values – namely, peace, beauty, solitude and hope. Another illustration was the religiously precocious John's (aged six; p. 102) modification of the interview into a game in which he interviewed me in the manner of a chat-show host, standing on a chair, holding the microphone as interviewer and clapping wildly as the audience. In this way he was able to articulate a number of questions that were important to him – namely, 'Is it [Christianity] good for everybody?' and what to feel about the spiritual state of 'people who don't believe in good [i.e. non-Christians]'. Much of his spirituality was characterized by his strong sense of Christian identity, personal encounters with God in prayer and vision, and a recognition of a missionary imperative in response to this. Hence these questions about the religious identity and response of others, played out in a game, were indeed close to his heart. Interestingly, these questions were largely left in the air. My role in the game as responding interviewee was not an onerous one, possibly indicating his awareness that these were issues for him to work out, rather than matters to which someone else's answers would be useful.

Some children expressed spirituality through a *language of science and technology*, flouting the conventional expectations of conditions that give rise to spirituality. Science and technology are more often equated with the material world and its values of efficiency, productivity and mechanization stripped of humanity. However, in this language children were able to find an especially legitimate way of expressing ideas and feelings, since they experience it as a powerful and almost unquestioned explanatory framework. In many cases scientific ideas and discoveries were a source of wonder and reverence in themselves. It was often necessary to become detached from one's adult understanding of technology to appreciate the degree to which such feelings were synonymous with spiritual feelings of wonder. Children who were moved to a point of ineffable wonder by the operation of a tap (Louise, aged 10) or a huge satellite dish (Altman, aged 10) were operating from a different perspective to that taken by a plumber or engineer.

The use of the language of science seemed especially fuelled by the popular legitimation conferred by the large amount of science fiction and supernatural fantasy on television. Children's (and adults') appetite for this may in part reflect its function as a powerful contemporary discourse within which, and against which, spirituality can be framed, given the relative demise of conventional spiritual language.

Some of the children made use of scientific language as a source of analogies for spiritual concepts which they could not otherwise grasp. For example, holograms (of people) and parallel universes featured as attempts to explore how a person's soul might be represented. Nevertheless, these analogies, and the whole enterprise of science, were frequently used to suggest the boundary at which the spiritual, as children perceived it, began and ended. Thus holograms were not regarded as sufficient accounts of a human spiritual property. Though the children often gave examples of things which science could account for, the ultimate mystery was that which science was not equipped to explain.

To conclude, our conversations revealed that several different languages can be used by children to give voice to their spirituality. In subtly different ways these conditioned the forms which relational consciousness took. A basic feature of children's spirituality can be seen to emerge. Many of these languages offer 'legitimate' ways of expressing the otherwise 'illegitimate' stuff of spirituality in a predominately materialist, secular, rationalist culture. This implies that children not only need to express themselves in this area in one way or another, but also that they are sensitive to the cultural conditions that may limit it. Even before it expresses itself, children may be subliminally aware that their emerging spirituality is unwelcome or thought to be of little value. Continuing to listen attentively for the ways in which children do find legitimate expression is one way of remedying this. Additionally, identifying the common thread (relational consciousness) that links the use of all of these languages may help to give implicit legitimation to children's spirituality.

Strategies

This dimension of the framework represents an attempt to summarize the activities pursued by children in their attempts to maintain their sense of the spiritual. Many of these strategies were not particularly related to behaviour associated with adult spiritual maintenance, such as meditation, church-going, humanitarian acts and fasting. However, many of the tactics employed by children to protect their spirituality are also familiar to adults. As a psychologist, I was impressed by the children's diversity, range and level of mastery of rather complex mental processes, especially in an area in which formal coaching or instruction about 'how to do it' is rare.

Strategies explicitly used by the children included efforts to mentally and physically withdraw from mundane distractions, attempts to consciously focus or concentrate on a particular subject, seeking relation or communication through prayer, seeking and exploiting aesthetic and sensory experiences, and deliberately 'philosophizing'. As would be expected, older children tended to mention the use of explicit strategies more often than younger children. Sometimes children were specially aware of the role their strategy had played in their spiritual experience. For example, Altman (aged 10) described how he was intrigued by pursuing a mental state of absorbed single focus that created an altered state of awareness, then commented:

> Yeah, and when you click out of it you just notice that you are there, or when you're like concentrating on it, like you just don't

know where you are. [Do you like that feeling?] Yeah, but like recently it just sort of comes when it needs to come. Like if you are upset, it just comes then. [Where do you think it comes from?] God.

The strategies covered a wide range of mental processes, including implicit versions of the explicit activities. For example, rather than comment on how they arrived at a spiritual insight or experience by consciously asking themselves increasingly philosophical questions, the children simply listed their chain of questions. A common pattern for this concerned the origin of the world and human life, often beginning as a simple question about their own identity or name. This led to questions about creation in general and their reactions to different accounts of it in myth and science, and ended in questions about the ontological nature of God himself and, crucially, their emotional and intellectual reaction to such ideas as these and their sense of created order.

In response to the ineffable nature of spiritual experience, evoking imagery and drawing analogies have been time-honoured strategies in most spiritual traditions. These strategies were also employed by the children, and have specially interesting implications for our understanding of their spirituality.

It is likely that most of the children in our sample had not yet reached the Piagetian stage of thinking called 'formal operations' in which abstract ideas and principles can be operated on in the mind. Rather, these children would have 'thought' best in terms of concrete examples or literal images. For this reason it is perhaps not surprising that using imagery was a potent strategy for their spirituality. However, they did not seem 'locked in' by their tendency to create literal imagery; rather it served as a resource that fed other strategies. Nor was all this imagery 'concrete'. In some cases it was creatively combined with more abstract ideas. Six-year-old Andrew's concrete images of heaven and hell as a never-ending circle and a finite 'edged' square respectively, are illustrative of how image-making can give rise to a 'concrete and abstract' combining strategy. His literal imagery was combined with a more abstract level of reasoning concerning the nature of love, and his subsequent insights about human relations and his sense of God.

Another point of interest arising from such strategies concerns whether or not children can understand analogy and metaphor at this stage in cognitive development, let alone use it as a tactic to maintain a sense of the spiritual. Some previous research has suggested that children have fundamental difficulties with the mental processing required to comprehend the nature of analogy. This was a central element in Goldman's argument about children's lack of 'readiness' for religion.[10] More recent work has established that even pre-school children can appreciate analogical relations and can certainly draw on the emotional significance of an analogy, even when unable to express explicitly the nature of the analogical relation between the two components being compared.[11] This helps to make sense of the frequent use of an analogy-making strategy by children expressing spirituality, as a number of examples have already suggested: life's meaning as a 'jigsaw puzzle'; the soul as a 'hologram' and as 'smoke on a misty day'; God as 'eternal love', 'kindness between people' and as amazing places in nature; but also seeing the sacred in an architecturally impressive shopping centre viewed in the dark from a hill![12]

Processes

The 'processes' dimension attempts to chart the local, as well as longer-term, changes in children's spirituality over time; what it was that characterized the way it was turned on or off. Children's ambivalence in using religious language was discussed in Chapter 6, and processes of *avoidance*, *side-tracking*, and changing to a *third-person* perspective all had effects on whether the spiritual chat continued or dried up during our research conversations.

In contrast to the local processes associated with resistance, there were also *processes of magnification*. Children sometimes accepted only a hypothetical notion of the spiritual at first, or could discuss it in terms of what 'other children' might experience, and then gradually or momentarily recognized such properties in their own experience (*identification in the self*). Many children described a process of *interiorizing* their spirituality rather than publicizing it. For some this was thought to be an inherent requirement of 'private' material, whilst others saw it as a protective reaction to avoid ridicule and embarrassment.

Local change in children's spirituality was also shown by the ease with which they could *forget* earlier important material. It was intriguing that when I asked some of the children what they remembered of an earlier interview, though other details of the conversation could be recalled, all the directly spiritual references seemed to have been forgotten. This suggested that at best they were repressed, or perhaps had only a fleeting salience for the children.

Longer-term changes in children's spirituality were equally various. Many mentioned being aware of some change over their lifetime, and none referred to this as a static dimension. For some, an alteration in their spirituality was associated with their increasing knowledge. However, the effects of this were not uniform. A number described their growing knowledge base and increased mental abilities as instrumental in reducing their engagement with the spiritual. For example, they referred to being more gullible when younger and likely to entertain all kinds of extraordinary ideas and readings of experience. Some mentioned the dilution of their spiritual position through exposure to other knowledge frameworks, including effects of learning about other religious traditions. Ruth (aged six; p. 95), for example, described her struggle in response to learning about a creation story from an American Indian spiritual tradition: 'They said, "Ooohh, a raven made the world, darling, not God." Then you try not to believe in that, but you just can't help it.'

In contrast, other children found increasing knowledge and experience had a concentrating effect on their spirituality. Beth (aged 10) felt more equipped to pray and 'properly love' God now that she was older, and others also suggested a process of growing confidence in their spiritual position. Some children made comments about their self-awareness expanding with age and their developing understanding of the complexities of interpersonal relations, all of which would appear to contribute to manifestations of our core category, relational consciousness.

Changes associated with *memory over time* for the spiritual were often noted. Children referred to having had spiritual experiences a long time ago which they had since 'forgotten'. Equally, the features of spiritual experience were less likely to be spontaneously recalled than recognized when presented. These types of process may reflect the difficulties and lack of opportunity children experience in articulating and storing this kind of event in an accessible way.

In general the dynamics of this dimension have a special relevance to those concerned with children's spiritual development. This was not deliberately explored amongst these children, yet we noted a number of salient features about the changing presentation of spirituality in childhood, both within the short-term context of a conversation or over a much longer period. These features may help in appreciating the sensitivity of the area and the pressures on it. They suggest that there is much about spiritual development that will resist the kinds of assessment that depend on measuring linear progression. Standardized forms of appraisal cannot work easily with something as flexible as the dynamics of the spiritual life.

Consequences
The framework would not be a complete account of the dimensions of relational consciousness without a consideration of its effects or consequences. These effects were sometimes explicitly reported but in other cases were inferred from the content of the children's conversation.

At a theoretical level, information concerning 'consequences' suggests one of the few ways in which individuals can be compared and, in a loose sense, the data validated. For example, children's descriptions of the effects of their spirituality included references to deep 'calm', a strange 'fear' combined with 'respect', or a feeling that 'it's all oneness'. Descriptions like this lend the material I have been discussing a degree of validity because of their resemblance to well-established criteria of discernment in adult spirituality.[13]

At the practical level the role of adults in helping children develop their spirituality might usefully include more explicit recognition of some of the different possible consequences, and the provisions these require, so that children can grow from their experience whatever their sense of it.

Positive consequences were the most commonly mentioned, though more negative social effects sometimes qualified these. The list of positive consequences was very varied, including feelings of *calmness*, *peacefulness*, *holiness* and of moral *goodness* (in the child, sometimes outside the child in others, in the world, or more abstractly). Other effects suggested particularly mystical characteristics: a *sense of oneness*, *forgetting self*, and *feeling free*. A number of accounts indicated that the consequences were a reaction to something other or outside, not simply to private experience without external reference. Children spoke of being *impressed*, of an *interested wonder*, a new *desire to search* for understanding or meaning, a *noetic sense* that new understanding had been acquired, a *greater sense of clarity*, and a reaction of *perceiving value* and *feeling grateful*.

Negative consequences most often referred to fear or at least an uncomfortable *strangeness*. Although 'wonder' was frequently a positive consequence, for others this took the form of *frustration*. Another common consequence cited was a *feeling of inner conflict*, often as the experience or ideas were felt to be incompatible with other knowledge the child held.

Children often mentioned experiencing *both* positive and negative consequences, with one type triggering off another in some cases (e.g. wonder turning sour with frustration, or an overwhelming feeling of 'goodness' stimulating 'fear'). Social consequences were uppermost in the minds of many children and these were perceived in almost exclusively negative terms. Children spoke of the danger of feeling either *embarrassed*, *ridiculed* or *undermined* as a result of exposing their experience in the public domain.

Few children had actually shared their spirituality with others, and the negative consequences mentioned above were their imagined predictions of how they would feel if they spoke of it. More worryingly, whilst aware of their own experience, they often admitted that they themselves would be unlikely to speak kindly to others who had the temerity to talk publicly about these matters. Some explained their reluctance as due to an anxiety about not being believed or taken seriously; a few had direct experience of this. Given such sentiments, it is perhaps remarkable and gratifying that they were prepared to be forthcoming in the research conversations.

A number of children in both age groups expressed thanks as well as being intrigued by my interest in the areas probed by the interviews, presumably because it contrasted with their expectations and experiences of the social consequences of sharing their spirituality. A small minority indicated more positive perceptions of the social consequences. Louise (aged 10) had found a *supportive comparison* group amongst her peers to discuss the aspects of nature that gave them a sense of the holy. However, it seemed a sorry reflection on the religious institutions that none of the children who belonged to faith communities felt that these could provide a supportive comparison group for their spiritual ideas, feelings and experiences.

An important difference between the consequences reported in this data and the similar adult characteristics studied by David Hay is that, with the possible exceptions of Freddie (aged six), who talked about Snow White (p. 117), and John (aged six), who told me about his conversion-like sense of God in prayer (p. 102), none of the children suggested that any of these effects had been of life-changing significance.

Possibly children's relatively shorter life span makes it hard for them to frame experiences in such a way: They tend to live more from moment to moment rather than in terms of reflection on sequentially and meaningfully ordered events. Alternatively, this difference is indicative of a distinctive quality in children's spirituality, namely that though perceived as special, it is regarded as altogether more 'ordinary' than most adults assume. In this way, children's spirituality would find support in contemporary theological thinking that has argued against the restriction of the religious (and by extension the 'spiritual') to more extraordinary experiences and interpretations.[14] Children may be the model for adult spiritual development, rather than the reverse, as suggested by the epigraph to this chapter. A task for adult spiritual development may be to recapture the child's more inclusive and all-pervading sense of relation to the spiritual which means that for them it is normally 'everyday' rather than dramatic.

Conclusion

At times the need to selectively extract and to offer an analysis of the children's conversations made me feel as if I was challenging the very nature of what I sought to study. On this point Wordsworth has some cautionary lines:

> Our meddling intellect
> Misshapes the beauteous forms of things: –
> We murder to dissect.[15]

I hope that this analytical framework does not 'murder' spirituality, but offers a helpful and systematic list of how the many features and their roles in children's spirituality can be more easily recognized. My emphasis on the significance of the different parts in the framework being understood as 'spiritual' *only as they relate to each other* is important. It is vital to keep in mind the core category of 'relational consciousness' as a means of seeing the different features and dimensions as members of the whole, held in a dynamic tension with one another. When these other features were shot through with this quality, then what the children said became alive with spirituality.

III

Reflection

8

The Naturalness of Relational

Consciousness

But a Samaritan traveller who came upon him was moved with
compassion when he saw him. He went up and bandaged his
wounds, pouring oil and wine on them. He then lifted him on to
his own mount, carried him to the inn and looked after him.

LUKE 10:33–34

I have put duality away, I have seen that the two worlds are One.
One I seek, one I know, One I see, One I call.

JALAL AL-DIN RUMI[1]

Modern children expressing their relational consciousness
Reading through the transcripts of what the children said, so
rich with spiritual life at both explicit and implicit levels, it is
easy to overlook how hidden and half-forgotten spirituality has
become. In the final chapter I will be suggesting some ways to
assist children to stay in touch with all of that. But the most
important way for teachers to help must surely be to become
aware of the dimensions of children's relational consciousness,

to be sensitive to them when they are expressed, and to respond creatively.

Let me recap some of the findings. What has been disclosed from a disciplined and prolonged immersion in children's conversation is the notion of 'relational consciousness' as the most fundamental feature of their spirituality. From my personal perspective this finding revealed an uncomfortable but ultimately helpful inconsistency in the way we had approached our task. On the one hand, in the opening chapter of this book I gave an account in which it was repeatedly stated quite explicitly that awareness of an holistic relationship with the rest of reality is central to the nature of spirituality. On the other hand, 'relationship' did not even appear as one of the sub-categories of spiritual awareness in our first attempts to give a specification that would be useable in talking to children.

In spite of our omission, as our investigation proceeded the relational dimension began to figure more and more strongly until it came to dominate the data. I felt some relief that our findings had not simply reflected back to us the conscious preconceptions we had brought to the practical side of the research. At the same time I was surprised and somewhat alarmed that such an important element of spirituality could be central to our theoretical dialogue, yet in thinking about the 'hands-on' side of our work it had escaped our notice over several months of planning. Our blindness seems to have been a function of the presuppositions we share in the individualistic society in which we are all immersed. Spirituality points in another more communal direction which only began to emerge when we paid close attention to the children's language.

Language, that most social of human phenomena, is the way spirituality is most obviously brought to public attention. Here orthodox religious vocabulary has traditionally had the central role. It is also here that we found paradoxes when we investigated how, in practice, contemporary children employ language to verbalize their spirituality.

The most straightforward use of language ought to be where children educated within a traditional religious community use its terminology simply and naturally to reflect upon or to express their personal experience. This *can* be the case, more especially amongst six-year-old children, but it is much less common amongst ten-year-olds. At least in contemporary British society the circumstances are often much more equivocal. Some children who are familiar with religious language (I almost said 'jargon') can use it as a means of detaching themselves from the reality of their own experience. They will discourse in a dispassionate way about religious abstractions or 'facts about religion' that they have learned in class. The traditional mode of a pupil in a classroom is one of demonstrating to an adult that you have learned information correctly. It is almost as if shifting into that mode offers a necessary refuge from exposing the vulnerable world of personal relatedness to an outsider. We have seen that the children are already aware that there is a social taboo on speaking about spirituality.

I do not say that privacy is always inappropriate, especially for a child speaking with a comparative stranger in a research conversation. Nevertheless, the distancing suggests a disengagement of language from experience which can in the end be destructive. One may perhaps wonder if in this case religious language is obliquely serving its traditional Marxist function as an instrument of alienation. Later in the chapter I will develop the suggestion that the use of abstract language is associated with a culturally constructed taboo against the expression of spirituality.

We have also seen that in practice relational consciousness can be expressed by children in many other ways than through traditional religious language. The vernacular of science fiction, science itself, ecology or any of the other forms of secular rhetoric listed by Rebecca, can convey a genuine quality of intimate expression which is not necessarily present in more religiously orthodox discourse. Such conversation can be the reverse of trivial, reflecting on the profoundest issues of personal origins, identity and meaningfulness of life. It may also be linked with a strongly stated disavowal of any connection with or approval of religion.

What is happening then, when an enthusiastic young atheist finds himself (it is usually a he) using religious terminology in a self-contradictory manner when discussing 'big questions'? One does not expect a young child to be consistent in the use of language, so the matter at issue is not inconsistency but the source of this particular instance of it. Most obviously it is in part a function of cultural pluralism and the fact that in spite of secularization, religious language is still extremely widespread, not least in the primary school classroom. But there is another more important source; the fragmentariness and insubstantiality of most currently available language, other than religious, which can adequately express relational consciousness at any depth.[2]

Post-religious language and culture are on the whole extremely impoverished in this respect. It is a striking testimony to the vigour of the spiritual life of the children that they are able to to fill the vacuum using the variety of linguistic modes that Rebecca has mentioned. One may even grant that secular means of expression can serve the purpose better than ill-considered religious language, reduced to platitude because it lies outside a coherent cultural context. Even so, amongst thoroughly secularized children it is sometimes as if there were an awareness of a gap or an incompetence in secular language. Religious terminology seems to slip in by default because it expresses the felt sense of what the child is experiencing.

Relational consciousness and altruism
There is something seriously wrong with a schooling which colludes with the impoverishment of language. At times the educational system seems designed to suppress or ignore spirituality as at best an insubstantial extra on the curriculum. In previous pages I have contended that spirituality (and hence spiritual education) is fundamental for the personal and political well-being of the community. Therefore I want to make an emphatic defence of relational consciousness as an entirely natural and universal human predisposition. I am thus returning to the

theme of the first chapter, now reflected upon in the light of the findings reported in Chapters 6 and 7.

Terminology is important, reaching down to only partly apprehended levels of our awareness. It is because of this that something valuable happens to one's understanding of the word 'spirituality' when it is substituted by the term 'relational consciousness'. The concept takes on an elemental quality, an ever-present aspect of being human. At this profound level, relational consciousness is separate from and prior to the discursive intellect, though it is certainly a matter with which the intellect becomes preoccupied. To use the philosopher Martin Heidegger's language, it amounts to the disclosure that we are already immersed in Being, before ever there is an analysis into 'this and that', 'subject and object'.[3] Because it is so primal, it is something that we can see particularly clearly in children.

Recent work on children's implicit understanding of social situations has demonstrated what parents have always known, that they have relational intuitions at an extraordinarily early age. For example, pre-verbal toddlers are well able to engage in teasing games which require insight into what it is for another person to expect to be given something (a toy, a scrap of food) and then to have it snatched away.[4] Similarly, very young children are richly aware of, and have an implicit understanding of their relationship to their environment long before they can name it. When she was learning to walk, my granddaughter Madeleine knew perfectly well that a chair is a thing you pull yourself up on when you are trying to stand. She knew this before she could articulate the word 'chair' or even point to it when the word was repeated by an adult.

This all-pervasive preverbal knowingness, because it predates the potent analytical emphasis of grammar, encompasses an awareness of our indissoluble link with the seamless robe of reality. In principle one would therefore expect relational consciousness to underlie not merely teasing but also care and concern, as I suggested in an earlier chapter. In a total milieu which is so intimately bound up with one's awareness, damage to any part of reality is implicitly perceived as damage to the fabric of which one is a part. Hence I believe that relational consciousness underlies the altruistic impulse. I suggest that every form of self-sacrificing behaviour, whether it is concern for people with whom one has no connection either genetically or socially – or defence of the planetary environment – can be seen as a function of spiritual awareness.

The biology of relational consciousness

This is to say something more than appeared explicitly in the original formulation of Alister Hardy's hypothesis about religious experience, though I think it underlay his conviction that spirituality is of fundamental importance to human survival. He suggested that religious experience (relational consciousness in our terminology) was selected for in the biological evolution of the human species because it has survival value to the *individual*. This is in line with straightforward Darwinian orthodoxy and, as we have seen, modern research repeatedly shows how such experience does indeed appear to confer biological advantage at the individual level.[5]

But the altruism implicit in relational consciousness goes further than this. At the 'religious' end of the range of spirituality, there is a strong and culturally diverse tradition suggesting that high levels of altruistic behaviour are a characteristic outcome of attending in a disciplined manner to relational consciousness.[6] Exercises drawn from many Eastern and Western religions and designed to intensify this dimension of awareness are claimed to lead typically to 'a radical divestiture of possessiveness, self-centredness, and even of ordinary attachments to the results of actions'.[7]

Modern evolutionary theory usually interprets the appearance of self-sacrificing behaviour in highly individualistic terms. In its strictest form the proposal is that the unit of selection or 'replicator' is the gene (Richard Dawkins' famous 'selfish gene').[8] From this perspective the individual animal can be considered as no more than the environment or vehicle of the gene. In the variant of altruism theory known as 'kin selection',[9] action in defence of closely related animals (for example, brothers and sisters, or offspring) is explicable because it protects the shared pool of genes. Studies have shown that the frequency of altruistic behaviour towards another animal does indeed increase in proportion to the closeness of relationship. Hence, although such behaviour may endanger the altruist, it assists in the primary task of ensuring that the shared genes are passed on to the next generation. On the other hand, 'reciprocal altruism'[10] or the hypothesis of 'mutual back-scratching' suggests that animals will act altruistically in relation to others that are not directly related to them if there is the expectation of some kind of return. The potential for mutual benefit rewards the altruists by increasing the likelihood of the survival of their genes.

An apparent difficulty with these explanations is the numerous field observations that have been made of altruistic behaviour in animals which appears to transcend the narrow imperatives of the genes (for example, protecting or helping to save the lives of members of a different species). One way in which this kind of behaviour is explained is by making ever more complex extrapolations from the hypothesis of reciprocal altruism.[11]

But consider the case of a soldier in the army of an authoritarian government who, when ordered to shoot an innocent hostage, refuses to do so because he finds it ethically impossible to kill him. His choice makes no rational sense in terms of reciprocal altruism. Not only will the hostage be killed anyway by someone else, he himself will be shot for refusing to obey an order. The ethical demand made upon him by this stranger is more important than the defence of his own life. Whilst it is probably true that very few people have the courage to make such extreme sacrifices, few of us would fail to recognize the holistic sense of community from which it arises. At this level we appear to be encountering a human predisposition which transcends any form of calculated self-preservation.[12]

Relational consciousness and social evolution

I do not believe that traditional Darwinian orthodoxy adequately explains this phenomenon, and in recent years some uncertainties have been expressed about the explanatory power of altruism theory as it stands. There may be a need to take greater account of a social or cultural component in the evolution of relational consciousness.

Once one creates an image of genes as sentient beings by applying terms like 'selfish' to them, they take on in the mind a spurious 'consciousness' which is the reverse of the intention of the originator of the term. They appear to have, so to speak, the whip hand and it becomes difficult to grasp that survival of the genes may depend on selective processes occurring at many different levels. One alternative proposal is that in human populations the evolution of consciousness, and hence relational consciousness, permits self-sacrificing choices to be made in the context of a greatly enlarged awareness of one's environment. At least potentially an altruism based on relational consciousness might transcend a narrow understanding of what constitutes the 'interests' of the genes.[13]

Associated with this notion is the re-emergence of the idea of 'group selection'. Group selection was originally proposed in 1962 by the Aberdeen zoologist V. C. Wynne-Edwards as a means of explaining the way that animal species appear to control the size and distribution of their populations.[14] At the time it was discarded as unsustainable by more orthodox students of evolution, but recently David Sloan Wilson and Elliott Sober have suggested that the reproductive success of some religious groups can be accounted for in these terms.[15] Their explanation has a bearing on the idea that there is an important cultural component in the evolution of relational consciousness.

The example they use is that of the Hutterites, a fundamentalist Protestant Christian sect whose members fled to North America from persecution in their original home in Germany in the nineteenth century. At the present time the Hutterites have a number of successful colonies in Canada and the United States.[16] By Western standards their community life is markedly ascetic, intentionally isolated from modern technology and guided by strict adherence to biblical norms of self-sacrificing altruism on behalf of the collectivity. Wilson and Sober comment:

> In present day Canada, Hutterites thrive in marginal farming habitats without the benefit of modern technology and almost certainly would displace the non-Hutterite population in the absence of laws that restrict their expansion. The Hutterites' success can also be measured in reproductive terms, since they have the highest birth rate of any known human society.[17]

Wilson and Sober suggest that

> it is possible that humans have evolved to willingly engage in selfless behaviour whenever it is protected by a social organization that constitutes a group-level vehicle of selection. The relatively small group-level vehicles of kinship groups and cooperating dyads are already well recognized. The hypothesis we wish to explore asserts that the Hutterites constitute a less familiar case in which the vehicle is a relatively large group of individuals and families that are genetically unrelated to each other.[18]

In this illustration, successful group selection is based on the interaction of a socially evolved set of cultural beliefs with the process of natural selection, a kind of 'co-evolution'. The Hutterites' beliefs constitute a unit of behaviour or replicator available for cultural selection.[19] Wilson and Sober argue that a form of human life that encourages an exalted level of selfless altruism is well fitted for long-term biological success. The repeated emergence in the human species of the social institution of religion (from my perspective the normal cultural response to relational consciousness), with its highly developed codes for the altruistic maintenance of community, suggest that this is at least plausible.[20]

The co-evolution of relational consciousness

Though natural selection is a dynamic process, in relation to the span of recorded history the evolution of the human species is imperceptibly slow. The predisposition for relational consciousness can therefore be assumed to have remained stable for most of the history of *Homo sapiens*. The phenomena that do vary are the linguistic and cultural tools that lie to hand as media for the expression or, in certain circumstances, suppression of human biological potential.

Recent work on the links between biological and social evolution suggests that there can be various forms of association between the two. In his important book *CoEvolution*,[21] the anthropologist William Durham offers a systematic account of this relationship. Following the suggestion of Richard Dawkins, he proposes that social evolution takes place via a process rather like that of biological evolution through natural selection. Dawkins labelled the units of cultural meaning that are selected in social evolution 'memes', in a conscious reference to certain parallels he felt they have with the role of genes in biological evolution.[22] In Durham's version of the story, memes can vary from the simplest units of connotation (i.e. morphemes – the smallest parts of words that have meaning) through 'complex ideas, beliefs, and values, and on to entire languages, ideologies, symbol systems and cultural pools'.[23] The available variations of particular memes within a human group ('allomemes') provide the possibilities from which selections are made in the process of social evolution.

As in the case of genetic variation, not all variants of memes have equal fitness for survival, and it is this that underpins the mechanism of social selection. Durham suggests that whilst natural selection is 'selection by consequences' – that is, organisms that are unfit simply fail to survive – cultural selection operates 'according to consequences'. On the basis of personal experience, history, or rational reflection the consequences of following a certain pattern of social behaviour are seen to be either helpful or deleterious to survival. The decisions made in the light of these perceptions are loosely analogous[24] to the processes of natural selection in biological evolution. According to Durham the usual result of social evolution is 'a culturally guided mechanism of change ... that tends to promote human survival and reproduction, and does so with considerably greater efficiency than natural selection.'[25]

But this is not always the case. In some circumstances cultural evolution can have the effect of damaging the survival chances of a community, thus contradicting the thrust of biological evolution. Most commonly, says Durham, negative social processes of this kind are imposed from without by powerful groups or individuals who are able to coerce others to behave in a particular way. In so doing, those in power increase their own likelihood of survival and thus of reproductive success, whilst damaging the prospects of the people they have coerced.

Occasionally, says Durham, and sometimes in relation to external imposition, there can be a voluntary acceptance of memes that are unhelpful to survival. There are a number of ways in which this might arise in modern society. There might be 'value blockage' where social values that would normally promote survival are impeded by (for example) continuous propaganda or advertising campaigns by those with economic command of the media, or perhaps through drug addiction or brainwashing. 'Value displacement' contradicts natural selection if values appropriate to survival in one sphere of life are transferred to another inappropriate social context. People may suffer from 'imperception' that there are likely to be damaging consequences of a particular choice of social behaviour. Finally, even when there are destructive consequences following from certain actions, people may simply be 'oblivious of the link' with a particular allomeme.[26]

My suggestion is that the natural relational consciousness, clearly richly present in young children as our research has shown, is currently being obscured, overlaid or even repressed by socially constructed processes which contradict it in just the ways described. I noted earlier the important point made by Durham that in autonomous human groups the normal result of social evolution is a culturally guided mechanism of change. Modern individualist philosophy is an example of the contrary process. It is a meme which has emerged in opposition to the requirements of biological evolution – that is, ultimate reproductive success, in this case the survival of the human species – because of the relentlessly destructive nature of the societies it has produced.

I suggested that the traditional meme which has repeatedly been selected for in human history, because it has concordance with the underlying biological predisposition to relational consciousness, is universalist religion. But in Europe, for historical and political reasons which I have already discussed in an earlier chapter, this meme has been first of all distorted and then displaced.

The processes described by Durham as characteristic of such oppositional displacement are the commonplaces of European history. First, in the case of Christian culture, there has been value blockage at many points throughout its history, bringing about a narrowing of the original universalistic vision. The factors identified as creating the value blockage most famously include:

* The shift of Christianity from being a persecuted sect to the position of Imperial Religion under the influence of Constantine, thus beginning the history of its use as an instrument of political control.
* The assimilation, early in the life of Christianity, of dualistic Greek ideas which came to a head in the philosophy of Descartes.[27]
* The abdication of responsibility by theologians in the seventeenth century for defending religious or spiritual awareness as a valid source of knowledge, as documented by Michael Buckley.[28]

Secondly, there have been value displacements into a domain where they are inappropriate. The most obvious illustration of this is the promotion of the methods of physical science as the pre-eminent means of attaining understanding in realms other than the study of physical phenomena.[29]

Finally, there has been both consequence imperception and cause imperception, where people have failed to see the deleterious consequences of adopting the individualist meme or, having recognized that there has been damage, they have failed to identify the cause. Most obviously the imperception of the spiritual consequences has followed from a focus on the material successes coming from the individualism inherent in 'economic reason'.[30]

The educational problem

There is an important purpose to my rather lengthy theoretical excursus on the link between the biological and social evolution of relational consciousness. The intention of my conjectures on the data we have gathered from the children is to underline my scientific conviction that spirituality, in its full range, including religious awareness, is entirely natural.[31] It grows out of a biological predisposition which can either be obscured or enhanced by culture. More than this, spirituality is the bedrock on which rests the welfare not only of the individual but also of society, and indeed the health of our entire planetary environment. I am speaking of love of humanity, sensuous affinity for the landscapes and life-forms of our world, awe before the immensity of the universe in which we find ourselves, awareness of an interfusing presence through all of these. They are just as constrained by our biology as the emotions of protective love we feel towards our kin or those who reciprocate our altruism.

Arbitrarily to cut off any of this range of human experience as mere social construction, either illusory or infinitely malleable, because it does not fit easily with a particular philosophical theory is to deny humanity its wholeness. William James, whose most famous book *The Varieties of Religious Experience* was in some editions significantly subtitled 'A Study in Human Nature', put the same point nearly a hundred years ago: 'A rule of thinking which would absolutely prevent me from acknowledging certain kinds of truth, if those kinds of truth were really there, would be an irrational rule.'[32]

James was trying to defend religious belief. But there is a deeper issue than the defence of religion. It is a concern which was expressed by people like Margaret Knight and other humanists who were aware that our spiritual heritage, both religious and secular, is rapidly being eroded. This is more than merely destructive of religion, as I think Margaret Knight intuitively felt but was unable to articulate. It creates an artificial gulf between two paradigms of knowing – that is, relational consciousness and the supposedly detached methods of empirical science. It is a gulf that remains extremely powerful in the popular imagination, in spite of recent efforts to bridge it.[33]

When I explained to a friend what I was attempting to do in this book he responded pessimistically that I would fail because I am attempting to contradict the general impetus of an entire culture. In my view there is more awareness of the issue than my friend assumes. The evidence of rich relational consciousness in children that has been presented in Chapters 6 and 7 shows this to be so. But the difficulty is that social pressures hostile to relational consciousness can quickly sabotage children's sense of community. Furthermore, the most powerful influences on our presuppositions must be those of which we are least aware. They are so axiomatic that they often fail to enter into conscious reflection. Transcending these constraints is extremely difficult, and even with goodwill it is not always achieved.[34]

Recent attempts by British educators at the national level to attend to children's spirituality have not always escaped these limitations. In spite of being painfully aware of their responsibility, the documents produced in recent years by the British School Curriculum and Assessment Authority (now the QCA) have not yet brought Spiritual Education into an appropriate relationship with Moral Education. This is mainly because they have not taken full account of the universality, fragility and yet potential motivating power of relational consciousness. If this is not taken seriously it is rather easy to fall into the trap of sidestepping the issue and replacing it with a set of moral injunctions.

The final report of the SCAA Forum in 1996 presented a list of admirable values and principles for action to develop understanding of Society, Relationships, the Self and the Environment, all of them self-evidently aspects of relational consciousness. I suspect that without further advice and training, teachers will be tempted to approach these didactically, or at best through the medium of class discussion. The problem is that any child can learn off a list of such moral imperatives; can debate moral problems in specially arranged workshops; perhaps even obtain an 'A' grade in an examination for demonstrating proficient understanding of them. At the end of the process they may still have a boredom or detachment, even a cynicism about what they have learned. Without insight, words remain words, however well they are manipulated. The primary task must be to gain insight into how these values grow out of spiritual awareness.

It is important to note that I am not suggesting the replacement of moral education or that spirituality should be taught in its place. The purpose is to develop the spiritual insight which underlies and gives plausibility to moral education. It is in fact somewhat inaccurate to refer to the teaching spirituality. Strictly speaking, it cannot be taught, since relational consciousness is a biologically in-built constituent of what it is to be human.[35]

What the teacher *can* do is to help children to become 'aware of their awareness' and to reflect on this experience in the light of the language and culture within which it emerges.[36] The intractable problem which faces and frequently stifles contemporary education is the lack of a social context which gives permission for an open acceptance of spirituality. To summarize much of the argument of this book, three important dimensions of this intractability are:

1. The language of spirituality in the Western world is overwhelmingly Christian. This produces paradoxical consequences in children's use of language. We have seen that even those children who are culturally very remote from Christianity will quite often resort to the use of fragments of traditional religious language in relation to their own spirituality.

2. Because of the dominance of Christian language, spirituality is usually linked in children's heads with religion. At the same time, for complex historical reasons which are the subject matter of secularization theory in sociology, Christianity has come to seem implausible or out of touch with a majority of children at least in Britain (and, I suspect, in most of Western Europe), especially as they reach the end of primary school.[37] Hence spirituality tends to be damaged by association. On the other hand, we encountered 10-year-old children who, as part of the process of cutting their links with religion, create a 'macho' defensiveness against their own spiritual awareness.

3. Popular culture espouses extreme forms of competitive individualism and consumerism which pervert the communal and environmental values that grow out of spiritual awareness. John Macmurray interpreted this as the unconscious expression of a philosophical conception of the world which ultimately derives from Cartesian dualism.[38] Combined with the dominance of Christian language in reference to spirituality and the large-scale rejection of Christianity, what often results is a culturally constructed suppression or even repression of spirituality. Whilst most people know they have a spiritual life, they are usually embarrassed about it, fearing they will be thought stupid, foolish or even mentally unbalanced if they speak about it in public. Our research has shown that a similar shyness is already evident in most children by the age of 10, including those who are religiously practising.

We have thus arrived at a point where the workings of European social history have constructed an impasse. For many children in primary school their natural spiritual awareness undergoes a process of becoming orphaned, steadily isolated to a greater or lesser degree from two of the major modes of cultural expression. It is isolated from religious tradition through the operation of secularization and also because the religious institutions sometimes seem to have forgotten their spiritual roots. Spirituality is also often cut off from science, the dominant contemporary mode of reflective discourse, because conservative forms of empirical science claim to distance themselves from human subjectivity, and in some cases to deny its importance or even its reality.[39]

This isolation is a learned isolation into which children are educated. I am not now thinking only of schools where, from an official perspective, the education is judged to be mediocre or poor. The problem may be equally great in so-called 'good' schools which lay emphasis on a thorough grounding in forms of knowledge which can be given a grade in performance league tables. Judging the spiritual adequacy of the education provided by a school is notoriously difficult,[40] with the result that there is a 'backwash' effect. Contestants in a competitive league do not bother with what is not easily measurable. They go after high scores on the concrete criteria that enable them to win. That is how they maintain their morale and their financial support. In this kind of competition empirically verifiable data are paramount, objective knowledge matters more than subjective knowledge, rationality more than emotional insight.

But what if I am right? What if Hardy and Macmurray are on to something (and perhaps I could add the Marx of the 1844 Manuscripts, with his emphasis on 'species being')? What if spirituality supports people in time of trial and illuminates them in times of joy? What if it is spiritual awareness that truly sustains human community? What if it has a profound political function, underlying our moral sense and our desire for social justice? In that case spirituality is too important to be dealt with piecemeal by the educational system – a bit of poetry here, a touch of music there, a passing reference in the RE class. It needs some more global, holistic treatment in the school.

The formidable measure against which an adequate spiritual education must be judged is this. In all traditional communities – that is, those that are the bearers of Selznick's 'sustaining ideas' – the normal way in which spirituality is nourished is by:

❖ Directing formal attention daily (sometimes several times a day) to those aspects of human experience through which spiritual awareness most easily comes to light (e.g. worship, prayer, silence, contemplation, meditation, mantras, koans etc.).

* The provision of a context of ritual, communal narrative, doctrine and social teaching which both focuses attention on and gives concrete expression to spiritual insight. In this way spirituality diffuses through and influences the whole of life in a coherent manner.

Without the coherence and plausibility provided by such a set of sustaining ideas, either the spiritual life becomes privatized or secret, or spirituality itself becomes discredited. One pathological result of this process is that children grow up alienated or embarrassed by their own relational consciousness. It therefore ceases to feed into political legislation and the creation of true human community. In Yeats' words, the best lack all conviction, feel weak and become unsure of themselves, while the worst are full of passionate intensity.

This destructive process is not inevitable; it has been socially constructed. In the final chapter I will begin to suggest some ways in which teachers can go about the task of deconstruction.

The Spirit of the Child

9

Nurturing the Spirit of the Child

Love for our neighbour, being made of creative attention, is
analogous to genius.

SIMONE WEIL[1]

Spiritual education ignored
What happens to a child whose spiritual education is damaged or
utterly ignored? Let me take an extreme example. At the beginning of 1996 two American children aged ten and eleven were
sentenced in court for killing an even younger child, five-year-old
Eric, by dropping him from a fourteenth-floor window. Their
explanation for their action was Eric's refusal to steal some sweets
for them. Barbara Kimes Myers, who brings this story to our
attention,[2] comments on the difficulty of fathoming the nature of
the life experience of two boys who judged the life of another
child to be of less value than candy. It seems doubtful that the two
children had themselves been part of a caring home community
during their short lives, quite apart from any schooling they
might have had.

This story will raise uncomfortable recognitions in a British audience. Fortunately, damage to relational consciousness only very rarely leads to such tragic consequences.[3] But the threadbare texture of community in many parts of our society impoverishes a much more substantial number of children, to the point where they begin to lose touch with their spirituality. Relational consciousness seems to lie at a deep, almost primeval level, easily overlooked or mislaid. In effect the children forget who they are.

A moving example of such forgetfulness and how it was overcome, is provided by the drama teacher Jonathan Tafler.[4] He was attempting to help a young man with a poor verbal delivery to develop more expression – that is, to find his 'true voice':

> He was very constrained in everything he did, he wasn't following through to the end of thoughts but delivering everything in little gobbets of words, very fractured, no flow through. He had a Cockney accent which was not right for the character that he was attempting to inhabit and which anyway was rather grating, as was the rest of his 'cheeky chappie' personality ... I suggested he might try the piece in a different accent, something broader and more expansive than his own ... He thought perhaps he might be able to do the accent from where he lived when he was a little boy, deep in (I think) deepest Hampshire ... He took a few moments, then started again, in his new voice. The transformation was extraordinary. Not only the accent had changed, but he was producing it differently – it was coming from deep down, it had flow and power, suddenly he was conveying emotion. So much so that after a few seconds, tears were falling down his face as he was speaking.

Tafler goes on to explain that the man's family had split up when he was a small boy, and he went to live with his mother in a rough part of the East End of London. There he was persecuted mercilessly because of his country accent. He knew he needed to protect himself and he developed his new hard persona, the cheekie Cockney, as a shield. It was not his true voice or personality, which is probably why it grated so much.

The Spirit of the Child

It seems that the boy had been forced into membership of a 'tribe' which did not represent his true self. The despair that follows the loss of spiritual awareness often leads to the creation of false communities, the tribalisms – ethnic, religious, national, political, sporting – that are symptomatic, sometimes murderously so, of the destruction of relational consciousness. There is a difference between the individuality which is free to exist in genuine human relationship and the conformity that underlies false community. Tribalism is based on a fear-filled crushing out of individuality for the sake of tribal membership. The frailty and instability of the tribe means there is a permanent need to reinforce solidarity by generating anger in the face of real or imagined danger from outsiders.

This kind of difficulty suggests that it is important for educators to look carefully at how tribalisms which inhibit genuine sociality are created during the early years of schooling. I am thinking here especially of the social construction of a type of masculinity which our research has shown is already evident in some boys by the time they are 10 years old. The ideal of tough self-sufficiency has an admirable aspect to it, but it can be falsely and fearfully assumed by children who, in the process, lose contact with their more genuine feelings of vulnerability, dependency and need for relationship.[5]

Of course, one must not be naive about this. As in the case of Jonathan Tafler's pupil, there is a political and environmental context lying behind every child's adoption of a personal style. The 'macho' individualism of many boys (and some girls) may be a characteristic that is taken on by them as an unfortunate necessity. They may feel, perhaps only half awarely, that they need it to survive. In such circumstances even the best efforts of an individual teacher to create a spiritually aware community may have only limited success. The problem is one of 'structural evil' which ultimately can only be resolved by a cultural change in the school. This requires leadership of a high order from the senior staff and eventually, political change in the community as a whole.[6]

A four-point plan

What can the teacher do? There is as yet no widely available cross-curricular programme of spiritual education for schools. This is a weakness which needs to be remedied, but since I cannot offer a syllabus, I wish to convey a mood, a perspective from which a future programme can be constructed. Devising teaching methods is important, but nurturing the spiritual life of children is much more about the realities of human relationship than it is about detailed lesson plans.[7]

It ought to be self-evident that when adults are working with children they are primarily communicating a way of being human – how they themselves approach life. Nevertheless, the importance of relationship can be almost entirely concealed from teachers who think of their task primarily as one of processing information, or training in thinking skills. I know this to be the case from observing many young people on teaching practice and experiencing the sterile – sometimes hostile – atmosphere generated by someone who is either fearful of genuine human contact or forgets its centrality in their relationship with their class. Spirituality cannot be nurtured where education is purveyed as just another commodity distributed at arm's length, so that the subjectivity of the teacher is safely concealed from the children. Contemporary overconcern with scores on academic league tables makes it tempting to forget this. What is conveyed is a lack of spiritual awareness, sometimes paraded as a virtue.

A second point concerns the connection I have been exploring at length between spirituality and religion. Although I maintain that religious belief is a characteristic outcome of relational consciousness, I am concerned with nurturing a human predisposition rather than with any specific religious (or secular) system of belief. The fact has to be faced that by the time they are 10 years old a substantial number of children living in a secularized community harbour a shyness or embarrassment about anything closely linked with religion. Our research has demonstrated that this is so. But relational consciousness is a human universal that cannot be claimed by any one belief system. Once this is clear, spiritual education can free itself both from children's misgivings and the suspicion of secular humanists that it is a thinly disguised attempt to indoctrinate children into religious beliefs with which they are at odds.

The purpose of spiritual education is in fact the reverse of indoctrination.[8] The task of nourishing spirituality is one of releasing, not constricting children's understanding and imagination. It is to help children to emancipate themselves from the grip of historically created social pressures which damage the wholeness of their personalities. What is implied is practical activity, analogous to the practical work that goes on in a science laboratory. In this case the investigation is not of physical matter, but of what it is to be an aware and reflective human being. The teacher has four major responsibilities: (a) helping children to keep an open mind, (b) exploring ways of seeing, (c) encouraging personal awareness, and (d) becoming personally aware of the social and political dimensions of spirituality.

(a) Helping children to keep an open mind What I have said so far means that there is a major preparatory task before spiritual education, proper, can be embarked upon. Looked at logically, such education begins by gently encouraging or re-awakening children's natural disposition to spiritual awareness. But allowing oneself to become aware of one's relational consciousness at any depth requires a personal freedom and self-confidence that we have seen is not always available to children. This is particularly true if they have been psychologically damaged by poor parenting, or targeted from an early age by social pressures which have the effect of directing attention towards other more self-alienating concerns. The matters that can be closed off in the classroom or the school yard include discovering a purpose in life, understanding their dependency on the community in which they find themselves, what it means to be just, facing the reality of their own death, the need for meaning, what it is to be a free human being and how to stand alone.[9]

Creation of an environment where children feel themselves to be respected can begin very simply by making the physical

surroundings attractive. But even the best of physical circumstances will not be helpful if the children do not esteem themselves as worthwhile people.[10] They will be unable to get in
touch with or to express their individuality.[11] Awareness is always
personal, the vision of a uniquely embodied individual. A simple
way of demonstrating individuality to a group of children is to
get them sitting in a circle and ask them to 'observe' silently and
write down what they observe.[12] When they read out what they
have written after the five minutes are up they discover that
nobody's list is the same. Sometimes this is simply because children sitting in different parts of the circle see different things in
front of them. It is also, more importantly, because every child
has different preoccupations. Some lists are just that, an enumer-
ation of objects in the room. Some children write down things
about the other children they can see, others about the weather
outside the room, still others write about their 'inner weather',
how they are feeling inside themselves.

The extraordinary variety of personal and emotional narratives that exists in every group of children can very soon be concealed by the pressure to conform to some externally imposed
set of rules. Sometimes this is because a teacher has a rather
limited conception of the range of human possibility which they
try to impose on the children for whom they have responsibility.
A more probable influence pushing children towards conformity is the multitude of images drawn from the commercial media
which dictate with extraordinary rigidity their own standards of
dress code, conduct and belief.

Teachers can counter this pressure. Tom Limb of Wood-
borough Woods School in Nottinghamshire tells how he used a
Russian *matrioshka* doll to help junior pupils to explore 'the real
me' in the safety of the classroom:

> I started the lesson by taking the doll apart as I talked about
> the different sides of our individual natures. I said that we're all
> rather like this doll since we each have an outside, exterior, self
> which everyone can see. Deep down inside, however, we've got a
> very private self which is what we are when we are on our own.

Then there are shades of our personality which are in between the private and the public self. Next we used movement and dance to reflect on the public image of ourselves. The class was in the hall and ready to let off some steam so I played disco music and asked them to show how they behaved at the last school disco. After a few questions to help them consider that side of their character they tried body sculpture to portray their private self. They moulded partners into a position which showed what they, the moulder, did in private. Each sculptor admired the work of the other sculptors, spotting readers, games players and computer-buffs ... Everyone had the chance to be both model and sculptor as well as looking at the work of other people. I asked them what it felt like to model an activity they didn't normally do and then suggested that this could give a glimpse of what it's like to be your partner.[13]

(b) Exploring ways of seeing   Another way of countering the narrowing of perspectives is to help children to develop insight into alternative ways of seeing. There are many ideas for introducing this in the classroom, using ambiguous figures, metaphors and exercises in empathy.[14] One approach which I have found to be especially revealing has been used with children as young as six as well as with adults. The idea was developed by the American phenomenologist Don Ihde[15] using a well-known ambiguous figure, the Necker Cube (Figure 1).

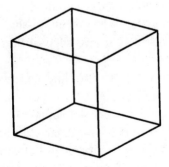

Figure 1

I have asked many groups to describe this diagram. No-one has ever named it as anything other than a cube. The cube differs in appearance according to the story you tell yourself about it (for example, that you are standing below the cube looking up at it, or above the cube looking down on it). But as Ihde points out, it could equally well be interpreted in several other ways. Perhaps it is a pyramid shape with sloping sides and the tip cut off, in which case the base must be flat. But it might also be seen as an oddly cut diamond, in which case there is an assumption that on the side of the diamond not visible to the viewer there are other sloping facets. Or it might be a rather badly made lampshade with sloping sides and a gap in the middle. Is the top of the lampshade nearest to the viewer or farthest away? It could even be seen as a flat figure, though usually children say it is difficult to see it in that way.

Why is it so hard to see this figure as flat? After all, it consists of a set of lines on a plane surface. One plausible interpretation might be that everyone in the Western world has lived inside or been surrounded by cuboidal structures since birth and this 'cultural construction' leads us to see a cube as the most obviously represented figure. Suppose then, says Ihde, that we imagine being brought up in a tribe of people living in the Amazonian rainforest who have never seen a cube. They all belong to a clan whose totem is an insect. Everyone in the clan, from the day they are born, is required to wear a badge representing this insect. It is thus the most prominent human artefact in the community. The badge is a highly stylized representation of an insect with a somewhat diamond-shaped body and six legs sticking out sideways to the edge of the hexagonal badge (Figure 2).

When they are told this story, children usually say that they can see the figure as flat, at least for a moment or two, but then it 'flips' back to being a cube. But suppose we were to show a cube to the members of the Amazonian tribe and point out that the insect badge could be interpreted that way? Ihde's guess is that something rather striking would happen that tells us something about the power of social construction. The Amazonians

The Spirit of the Child

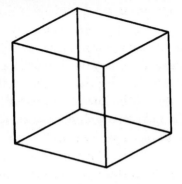

Figure 2

would probably say that they could see the diagram briefly as a cube, but that it quickly returns to looking like a flat insect badge.

Broad social agreement about the way things are is a necessity for the smooth operation of society. The point of this exercise is not to criticize the inevitability of social construction. It is to illustrate how powerfully it conditions our experience of reality, both consciously and unconsciously. Nobody brainwashes children into seeing the diagram as a cube, or the hypothetical Amazonians into seeing it as an insect badge. There is, however, a danger in this 'cultural sedimentation' of a single perspective. It can become a dogmatism which closes off other equally legitimate ways of seeing. After having had it pointed out that the diagram can be seen in other ways than as a cube, some children become quite angry or irritated that these ways are taken seriously. For them, it really is just a cube and other interpretations are foolish or frivolous.

By analogy, there is a strong temptation to dogmatic individualism in contemporary Western culture. As they grow older, children are enticed into treating holistic spiritual awareness as an illegitimate or, at best, a trivial alternative way of experiencing reality which gives way rather quickly to the dominant mode of seeing. Relational consciousness has to struggle for legitimacy against forces that give licence to the individualism necessary for the operation of a society driven by the norms of economic reason. There is a narrowing down of the selfless impulse in the human species. Altruism in its higher reaches ceases to seem natural or is even seen, as T. H. Huxley interpreted it, as a struggle fought by reason against our biologically based instincts.[16] Exercises which help to free children from this dogmatism open the way for them to consider their relational consciousness as a mature and important dimension of their biological make-up.

(c) Encouraging personal awareness As our research has shown, when they are very young most children are perfectly well aware that they have a spiritual dimension to their experience of life. The task of the teacher is therefore not at all abstract, though spiritual education has something of a subversive quality to it, since it is encouraging children to question the isolation and individualism which is bequeathed upon them by European social history. It is to give permission for spiritual awareness to continue to flourish by pointing to it in the children themselves and relating it to its cultural expressions in the great ethical and religious traditions of humanity.

A self-confident spirituality is unlikely to develop in a child unless parents or teachers provide what Barbara Kymes Myers refers to as 'hospitable space', and I would call compassionate concern. Yet relational consciousness is so deeply a part of being human that in one sense it merely requires someone to direct our attention for it to become obvious. It is said of Rainer Maria Rilke that when he was a young man in Paris, frustrated by his early attempts at writing poetry, he was advised by the sculptor Rodin, 'Why don't you just go and look at something – for example, at an animal in the Jardin des Plantes, and keep on looking at it till you're able to make a poem of it?'[17] The result was his poem 'The Panther':

> His gaze, going past those bars, has got so misted
> with tiredness, it can take in nothing more.
> He feels as though a thousand bars existed,
> and no more world beyond them than before.

Those supply powerful paddings, turning there
in tiniest of circles, well might be
the dance of forces round a centre where
some mighty will stands paralyticly.

Just now and then the pupils' noiseless shutter
is lifted. – Then an image will indart,
down through the limbs' intensive stillness flutter,
and end its being in the heart.[18]

What seems to be happening in this poem is an empathy, even
an identification with the panther and the awakening of a compassion which also reveals something of Rilke to himself. In a
nutshell this awakening is the primary task of the teacher concerned with spiritual education.[19]

A few years ago, with a group of colleagues, I attempted to
create a structured experiential approach to this domain, in the
context of a new approach to Religious Education. In practice
the methods we devised apply to the process of understanding
any cultural expression of relational consciousness, religious
or secular. They were tested out by teachers in a total of 24
different English primary and secondary schools before being
published.[20]

At the heart of the exercises lies the immediacy I discussed in
an earlier chapter; Margaret Donaldson's 'point mode'. There
is no need to labour this with younger children since, as
Donaldson has shown, they spend much of their time in the
here-and-now of their experience. Indeed it may be prudent not
to pay too much attention to this theme, since what is important
for children at this stage is to develop a clearly structured
understanding of the environment with which they are becoming acquainted for the first time.

With older children there is a gradual and necessary withdrawal from this mode for the sake of attaining an understanding of their environment that is more structured, analytical and
reflective. The practical necessities of life require that time is
spent reflecting on the meaning of past experience and planning

for the future in the light of events. In addition, time and energy are saved by going about the routine of daily tasks on 'automatic pilot' rather than attending with intense awareness to each moment of experience.

The danger associated with this necessary constriction of awareness is that it can cut us off from the recognition of our immediate consciousness of our relation to the outside world (what we can immediately see, hear, touch, taste and smell). It also isolates us from awareness of our relationship with the inside world (what is going on inside our bodies).[21] For this reason there comes a time when it is necessary to remind children of the immediacy which was once their permanent possession.

The practical exercises that are most appropriate in helping them to pay attention to their awareness are very simple and rather more relaxed in mode than what follows the traditional teacher's request to 'pay attention'. Sitting still with the eyes closed and attending to the here-and-now, even for a minute or two can be an extraordinarily revealing experience for children, putting them in touch with aspects of their environment of which they were completely unaware.

A good example of this type of exercise was devised by Dr Patrick Pietroni, primarily for use with adults investigating holistic living, though it is perfectly usable with children.[22] I have chosen it as an illustration firstly because of its simplicity and immediacy. It is also interesting because the form which Pietroni gives to the activity invites us to move beyond immediacy to connect it with an holistic context.

The exercise begins by inviting people to experience as fully as possible the physical act of eating a piece of fruit. Children are not always able to be explicit about their experience, though they are often clearly moved.[23] The following adult's account of participating in a similar class exercise may hint at some aspects of a child's experience:

Feeling a bit silly, giggly; this is a daft thing to do. The mood continues amongst the clumsy slipping noises and bangs as people cut their apples up. Then eyes closed – breathing out tiredness into the darkness; slacking off a bit. Still a bit naff though, being told to experience the apple as if I've never met one before. Fumbling around on the plate for one of the pieces ... it feels bigger than I expected. A seed slides away on my finger as it passes over the core ... careful to let it fall onto the plate, not the floor. I prefer the skin, it's smooth and not so cold on my fingers as the cut flesh. Lifting to my nose ... perfumed skin, more so than the inside; that's a surprise ... the room is filled with perfume, like the bouquet of a wine. The skin feels greasy on my lips; the rough cut surface wipes across my mouth, across my cheek ... Then I'm looking at the vague reflections of the window, the lights, my head as a dark shadow in the depths of the green skin ... colour leaking into the adjacent flesh ... extraordinarily beautiful curving lines and folds in the surfaces of the core, catching the light ... A sense of change, fleetingness, as the edges begin to turn brown. Now biting; the sound of the skin breaking with a small pop as it gives way to the pressure of my teeth ... an odd feeling of ethical uneasiness, of not being sure if I have permission to do this to the apple. Crushing against my back teeth – I hadn't noticed I'm a right-handed chewer ... the sound spreads up through the skull into my head. Substance against substance, resisting each other, then the apple gives way, liquid running down the gums. The consciousness is watching this, amazed. Swallowing, all kinds of movements in my throat, the apple marking its presence in sensation all the way to my stomach.

This account is very different in content from most everyday experiences of eating, especially when children are hurriedly rushing through a school dinner before moving on to the next activity. Sometimes we, children and adults, are so unaware that we can't even remember what we ate at our last meal. Another interesting discovery is that eating awarely means we need less food to be satisfied. Participants in a class exercise often say that a whole apple is too much to eat.

So far, Pietroni's exercise has similarities to the simple instructions given to a beginner in *vipassana* meditation.

It could also be related to the doctrine of the 'sacrament of the present moment'. There are many other simple exercises available which can be used with children to give them insight into the here-and-now of their experience. What they engender when they succeed is a re-examination of everyday life, now returned to and, in T. S. Eliot's phrase, 'known for the first time'.

(d) Becoming personally aware of the social and political dimensions of spirituality The novel feature that Pietroni has introduced in his exercise is to place the act of eating into its social (and perhaps political) context. He suggests that the participants continue with eyes closed and imagine as concretely as possible a sequence, beginning with the fruit in the shop. They then go on to imagine the apple having been supplied by the wholesaler to the shop; the wholesaler having bought the apple from a farmer; the harvest when the apple was collected from a particular tree, branch and twig. They imagine the tree being planted and the seed from which the tree grew coming from the core of another apple. Then the imagination turns round and moves forward in time: seed – sapling – tree – apple – farmer – harvest – market – wholesaler – shop – to reflect upon the piece of fruit they now continue to eat, as it nourishes and becomes part of the body.

Spirituality by definition is always concerned with self-transcendence. It requires us to go beyond egocentricity to take account of our relatedness to other people, the environment and, for religious believers, God. Without an examination of the cultural context in which they are presented, awareness exercises would remain unintegrated with the texture of the children's personal and social life.

Every human culture abounds with symbolism which through rituals, stories, music, poetry, art and architecture offers a means of attempting to articulate the inexpressible. In this holistic dimension of education the role of the teacher has been well described by the Soviet psychologist Lev Vygotsky.[24] It is to offer a necessary scaffolding of language and cultural understanding that will enable children to come to grips with their spirituality – that is, their understanding of themselves in relation to the rest of reality.

A primary consequence of taking up this perspective is the realization that spirituality quite evidently is not the preserve of Religious Education. It affects the politics of the curriculum and concerns the entire culture of the school. As will be evident from reflection on Pietroni's exercise, all experience taken at depth has a spiritual aspect. Probably most teachers when they are talking with children about subjects like English or History are aware of its link with relational consciousness. They may perhaps make a point of the necessity for entering into imaginative dialogue with the stories and events that are being investigated. But it may be, as it certainly was in my own case, that school subjects like science and mathematics have a greater potential to arouse awe and amazement at the reality with which we are all intimately related.

The problem facing the framers of the curriculum when they consider spiritual education is not puzzling out where it might or might not fit in. The deeper issue which has been pointed out by Barbara Kymes Myers is to do with the essentially holistic nature of spirituality – its universality. The fragmentation of the school curriculum for the sake of efficiency, specialization or the need to improve examination results is potentially very damaging. This is another example of how the ethos of a school not only creates but also destroys. Myers remarks that:

> Splitting children into numerous unconnected components needs to be seen for what it is – a metaphorical and cultural perspective. We exist within culturally approved constructions of reality. We take part in compartmentalization both in relation to human development, and in the ways we approach and understand our westernized institutions ... Yet we take all of our being and all of the ways we make sense out of our reality into these various institutions, and what happens in any one of them is complex and related to what happens in the others. We are not compartmentalized people nor are our youngest children.

If we understand spirituality as the way we ascribe meaning to the deeper level of existence that surrounds us and is in us and our relationships, then we cannot lock spirituality out of any institution that wants to do what is culturally expected – teach, heal, help, serve.[25]

The concept of a National Curriculum has to be treated with caution. There is a balance to be made between the legitimate requirements of an education system on the one hand and attention to the spiritual growth of the children within it. The untidy and unpredictable realities of children's lives mean that an over-rigid curriculum may be anti-human. It ignores the real coherences of the children's experience to which the sensitive teacher naturally responds, and replaces it with an appearance of consistency which in practice may turn out to be damagingly spurious. The temptation to think of one's curricular area as compartmented off from other areas or from the personal life of the child can lead to an emptying out of meaning from that academic area. Spiritual education as the underpinning of the curriculum acts as a permanent reminder of the absolute necessity to aim for coherence.

What I have just said about the cross-curricular nature of spiritual education does not negate the importance of understanding relational consciousness as it expresses itself through its traditional manifestations. We have seen how even highly secularized children resort to religious language to express their spiritual insights. Nevertheless, an insistence on learning factual information about a culture as the first task of spiritual education often means a kind of 'learning at second hand'. In practice this can seem to imply a divorce of culture from down-to-earth experience.

This is particularly obvious in poorly executed approaches to religious education which undertake an externalized study of various dimensions of religious activity (ritual, mythology, doctrine, ethics, social practice) whilst keeping them at a distance from the personal life of the child. Such learning approximates to an imperialist foray into other people's supposedly mistaken ways of making sense of reality. It detaches children from the understanding that they are exploring aspects of a universal quest, in which they also are engaged by virtue of being human.

Conclusion

In most state education systems spiritual education as a cross-curricular element is still a distant dream. For it to become a practical reality there will have to be a radical change in educational culture. It requires the creation and testing of appropriate teaching materials, right across the syllabus, as well as guidance to schools and teacher training institutions. At the very least, this will need the backing of a policy directive at a national level.

Measures also need to be taken to ensure that spiritual education is taken seriously. The spiritual health of a school community cannot be assessed in any straightforward manner.[26] As I mentioned previously, easily measured attainment targets notoriously have a backwash effect on classroom practice. Teachers naturally enough tend to choose to work with material that can be assessed with a minimum of difficulty by those outside agencies that have power over their professional future. Government bodies charged with inspecting standards in schools have a considerable responsibility here. The inspectorate is unlikely to take this obligation seriously unless it is demonstrated in concrete ways that spiritual education has thoroughly practical educational and social consequences.

This is not an empty hope. National research bodies in most Western countries are showing increasing, even urgent, interest in the sources of social integration.[27] But there is a need to be wary here. 'Social integration' can be a euphemism for social control; in extreme cases, a call for dictatorship. Genuine social integration arises from another source: a widespread awareness that relational consciousness is the bedrock of a free and humane society. In such a society the primary task of education is the nurture of the spirit of the child.

Notes

Chapter 1: What Is Spirituality and Why Is It Important?

1. Margaret Chaterjee, *The Concept of Spirituality* (Ahmedabad: Allied Publishers, 1989).
2. Adolphe Tanquerey ss, DD, *The Spiritual Life: A Treatise on Ascetical and Mystical Theology*, tr. Herman Branderis (Tournai, Paris, Rome, New York: Desclee & Co., 1923). Forty years ago copies of Tanquerey would have been found in most Roman Catholic convents and seminaries around the world.
3. Ibid., pp. 5–6.
4. Quoted by Jack Priestley in 'The Spiritual in the Curriculum' in P. Souper, *The Spiritual Dimension in Education* (Occasional Papers Series No. 2, University of Southampton, Department of Education, 1985).
5. See David Hay, 'Memories of a Calvinist childhood' in W. Gordon Lawrence (ed.), *Roots in a Northern Landscape* (Edinburgh: Scottish Cultural Press, 1996).
6. The crassness of much reporting on religion, even in the broadsheet newspapers, has been commented on forcefully by the Religious Affairs Editor of *The Guardian*. See Madeleine Bunting, 'God's media image', *The Tablet*, 16 Nov. 1996, pp. 1505–6.
7. Karl Marx, 'Contribution to the Critique of Hegel's Philosophy of Right', reprinted in K. Marx and F. Engels, *On Religion* (Moscow: Progress Publishers, 1957), p. 38.
8. Nancy Bancroft offers the following definition: 'Species being ... is Marx's term for the deepest center or spirit of humankind as a

collective. The term asserts that there is no division between individual and society: "Human" means precisely social. In Marx's view, we complete our individual and species character only by social interaction and over time.' In Benjamin B. Page (ed.), *Marxism and Spirituality: An International Anthology* (Westport and London: Bergin & Garvey, 1993). Marx's fullest account of 'species being' is in the *Economic and Philosophical Manuscripts of 1844*, published in *Marx and Engels: Collected Works*, Vol. 3 (London: Lawrence & Wishart, 1975).

9. The term 'holism' was popularized in the 1920s by Jan Christiaan Smuts in his book *Holism and evolution* (Westport, Conn.: Greenwood Press, 1973; reprint of the 1926 edn published by Macmillan, London). Although some of his ideas are very dated, his general stance is recognizable in modern ecological and 'Green' politics.

10. This was in the second of two series of Gifford Lectures on 'Science, Natural History and Religion' delivered in the Natural History Department of Aberdeen University by Sir Alister Hardy FRS and published as *The Divine Flame: An Essay Towards a Natural History of Religion* (London: Collins, 1966). The ideas put forward in the Gifford Lectures are developed further in *The Spiritual Nature of Man* (Oxford: Clarendon Press, 1979).

11. Freud repeats this assertion in many places, perhaps most accessibly in *The Future of an Illusion* (London: Hogarth Press, 1928).

12. See Émile Durkheim, *The Elementary Forms of the Religious Life*, tr. J. W. Swain (London: George Allen & Unwin, 1915).

13. Representative texts by these authors are, Friedrich Schleiermacher, *On Religion: Speeches to its Cultured Despisers*, tr. John Oman, with an introduction by Rudolf Otto (New York: Harper & Row, 1958); also Schleiermacher, *Glaubenslehre* (2nd edn), tr. H. R. Mackintosh as *The Christian Faith* (Edinburgh: T. & T. Clark, 1928); William James, *The Varieties of Religious Experience: A Study in Human Nature* (New York: Longmans, 1902); Ernst Troeltsch, 'Das Wesen der Religion und der Religionsgeschichte', tr. Robert Morgan and Michael Pye, in *Ernst Troeltsch: Writings on Theology and Religion* (Atlanta: John Knox Press, 1977); Rudolf Otto, *The Idea of the Holy*, tr. J. W. Harvey (Oxford University Press, 1950); Joachim Wach, *The Comparative Study of Religions* (New York: Columbia University Press, 1958).

14. *The Elementary Forms of the Religious Life*, op. cit., p. 416.

15. Ibid., p. 417.

16. R. R. Marrett, *Psychology and Folklore* (London: Methuen & Co., 1920), p. 166.

17. Up to the time of his death in 1985, Hardy was working on an autobiography containing a number of lyrical descriptions of his own mystical experience. The unfinished text is held in London by the National Cataloguing Unit for the Archives of Contemporary Scientists.

18. See George Lindbeck, *The Nature of Doctrine: Religion and Theology in a Post-Liberal Age* (Philadelphia: The Westminster Press, 1984), ch. 2, p. 31.

19. This is something in which sociologists have taken an increasing interest in recent years. Cf. Chris Shilling, *The Body and Social Theory* (London: Sage Publications, 1993).

20. This argument has been pressed for some considerable time. See, e.g., Steven T. Katz (ed.), *Mysticism and Philosophical Analysis* (New York: Oxford University Press, 1978).

21. See, e.g., Eugene Gendlin, *Experiencing and the Creation of Meaning* (Chicago: Free Press of Glencoe, 1962).

22. See David Hay, 'Religious experience and its induction' in L. B. Brown (ed.), *Advances in the Psychology of Religion* (Oxford: Pergamon Press, 1985).

23. See, e.g., D. T. Suzuki, *Mysticism Christian and Buddhist* (London: George Allen & Unwin, 1957); Thomas Merton, *Zen and the Birds of Appetite* (New York: New Directions, 1968); Aelred Graham, *Conversations: Christian and Buddhist* (New York: Harcourt Brace Jovanovich, 1968); William Johnson, *Silent Music: The Science of Meditation* (London: Collins, 1974); J. K. Kadowaki SJ, *Zen and the Bible: A Priest's Experience* (London: Routledge & Kegan Paul, 1980).

24. See Karl Popper, *Conjectures and Refutations: The Growth of Scientific Knowledge* (London: Routledge & Kegan Paul, 1963).

25. See David Hay, *Religious Experience Today: Studying the Facts* (London: Cassell/Mowbrays, 1990); David Hay, '"The biology of God": What is the current status of Hardy's hypothesis?', *International Journal for the Psychology of Religion* 4 (1), 1994, pp. 1–23.

26. As assessed by the Bradburn Balanced Affect Scale. See Norman M. Bradburn, *The Structure of Psychological Wellbeing* (Chicago: Aldine, 1969). The validity of this scale has been reviewed recently by Bowling. Whilst self-report of psychological well-being does not necessarily equate to an individual's level of mental health, the Bradburn scale appears to be a valid measure when used with a large population. See A. Bowling, *Measuring Health: A Review of Quality of Life Measurement Scales* (Buckingham: Open University Press, 1991).

27. Freud's ambiguity about spiritual experience makes it difficult to pin him down. He believed that religious belief and practice were symptomatic of neurosis but added the tantalizing comment that to suffer from this 'universal neurosis', so to speak, absolved the person from the pains of an 'individual neurosis'. But the criticism of religious belief as symptomatic of neurosis depends in turn on the philosophical assumption that religious interpretations of reality are erroneous. In making that assumption Freud moves out of the realm of scientific investigation into a metaphysical speculation which is the subject of continuing strong controversy. Regarded from within the field of empirical science, his argument is circular.

28. See David Hay and Ann Morisy, 'Secular society/religious meanings: A contemporary paradox', *Review of Religious Research*, 26 (3), 1985, pp. 213–27.

The Spirit of the Child

29. David Hay and Gordon Heald, 'Religion is good for you', *New Society*, 17 Apr. 1987, pp. 20–22.

30. David Hay, 'Religious experience amongst a group of postgraduate students: a qualitative study', *Journal for the Scientific Study of Religion*, 18 (2), 1979, pp. 164–82; Hay and Morisy, 1985, op. cit.; David Lewis, 'All in good faith', *Nursing Times*, 18–24 Mar. 1985, pp. 40–43.

31. Certainly this is true of Marx, whose use of the term 'spirit' has close analogies to the understanding I have been proposing. See Nancy Bancroft, op. cit.

32. See David Lewis, op. cit.

33. See especially Andrew M. Greeley, *The Sociology of the Paranormal: A Reconnaissance* (Sage Research Papers in the Social Sciences, Studies in Religion and Ethnicity Series No. 90-023; Beverly Hills and London: Sage Publications, 1975); Robert Wuthnow, *The Consciousness Reformation* (Berkeley: University of California Press, 1976).

34. Address delivered to the Royal Institute of Philosophy in Oct. 1948.

35. Karl Rahner, 'The experience of God today' in *Theological Investigations XI*, tr. David Bourke (London: Darton, Longman & Todd, 1974), ch. 6, pp. 149–65.

Chapter 2: The Social Destruction of Spirituality

1. Ernest Rénan, *The Life of Jesus* (London: The Temple Publishing Company, n.d.), p. 96.

2. Owen Chadwick, *The Secularisation of the European Mind in the Nineteenth Century* (Cambridge University Press, 1975).

3. H. W. Wardman, *Ernest Rénan: A Critical Biography* (London: The Athlone Press, 1964).

4. See Auguste Comte, *A Discourse on the Positive Spirit*, tr. Edward Spencer Beesley (London: William Reeves, 1903).

5. Marx, *Economic and Philosophical Manuscripts of 1844*, op. cit., ch. 1.

6. From 'Intimations of Immortality from Recollections of Early Childhood', in *William Wordsworth: The Poems*, ed. John O. Hayden (London: Penguin Books, 1990).

7. The classic exposition of this use of the word in relation to Britain is Bryan Wilson's *Religion in Secular Society* (London: Watts, 1966).

8. See *The Secularisation of the European Mind*, op. cit.

9. David Hay and Ann Morisy, 'Secular society/religious meanings: a contemporary paradox', *Review of Religious Research*, 26 (3), 1985, pp. 213–27.

10. During my research career I have quite often had the disconcerting experience of listening to someone, shame-faced and stammering, reluctantly using orthodox Christian language to speak to me of what has quite obviously been a moment of great importance to them in their spiritual life.

11. The phrase 'archaeologists of knowledge' is borrowed from Michel Foucault. See *The Order of Things: An Archaeology of the Human Sciences*

(New York: Vintage Books, 1973).

12. Samuel Preus, *Explaining Religion: Criticism and Theory from Bodin to Freud* (Yale University Press, 1987).

13. For an account of 'methodological atheism' as the appropriate stance for a sociologist of religion, and an assessment of the human cost of doing so, see Peter Berger, *The Social Reality of Religion* (London: Faber and Faber, 1969), especially ch. 4, 'Religion and alienation', pp. 81–101 and Appendix II, 'Sociological and Theological Perspectives', pp. 179–88.

14. See *The Life of Edward, First Lord Herbert of Cherbury*, written by himself, edited with an introduction by J. M. Shuttleworth (London: Oxford University Press, 1976).

15. Pointed out by J. M. Shuttleworth in his preface to the *Life*, op. cit.

16. Herbert, *Life*, op. cit., pp. 120–21.

17. Vico, Giambattista, *The new science of Giambattista Vico* (*La scienza nuova*), tr. from the 3rd edn (1744) by Thomas Goddard Bergin and Max Harold Fisch (Ithaca, NY: Cornell UP, 1948).

18. Preus, *Explaining Religion*, op. cit., p. 77.

19. See David Hume, *Principal writings on religion including Dialogues Concerning Natural Religion and The Natural History of Religion*, edited with an introduction by J. C. A. Gaskin (Oxford University Press, 1993).

20. Preus, op. cit., p. 210.

21. Michael J. Buckley SJ, *At the Origins of Modern Atheism* (New Haven and London: Yale University Press, 1987).

22. It has been pointed out that it is the lack of embeddedness of the Thomistic proofs in a religious form of life, much more than their philosophical deficiencies that makes them look thin to modern eyes. Within faith communities, not only Christianity but also in Hindu and Islamic religion, philosophical proofs have their primary purpose as aids to conceptual analysis. See John Clayton, 'Piety and the proofs', *Religious Studies*, 26, (1), 1990, pp. 19–42.

23. The curious mixture of the denial of the possibility of sincere atheism, combined with a fear of its existence is well brought out in David Berman, *A History of Atheism in Britain: from Hobbes to Russell* (London: Croom Helm, 1988).

24. For a history of Enthusiasm, see Ronald Knox, *Enthusiasm: A Chapter in the History of Religion with special reference to the XVII and XVIII Centuries* (Oxford University Press, 1950).

25. From John Locke's *Essay Concerning Human Understanding*, ed. Peter A. Nidditch (Oxford: Clarendon Press, 1975), bk IV, ch. 19.

26. A discussion of Newton's attitudes towards 'Enthusiasm' is contained in Frank E. Manuel, *The Religion of Isaac Newton* (Oxford: Clarendon Press, 1974), especially pp. 66, 87.

27. Buckley, op. cit., p. 343.

28. Ibid., p. 360.

The Spirit of the Child

29. Owen Chadwick, *The Secularisation of the European Mind*, op. cit.
30. Ibid., p. 11.
31. The last proposition in the last section condemned the doctrine that the Pope 'can and ought to reconcile himself with progress, with liberalism and with modern civilisation'.
32. William Paley, *Natural Theology; or, Evidences of the Existence and Attributes of the Deity, Collected from the Appearances of Nature* (New Edition) (London: C. & J. Rivington; J. Nunn; Longman, Hurst, Rees, Orme, and Co.; et al., 1825).
33. Charles Darwin, *On the Origin of Species by Means of Natural Selection: Or, the Preservation of Favoured Races in the Struggle for Life* (London: John Murray. Reprinted with an introduction by Ernst Mayr, Cambridge, Mass.: Harvard University Press, 1964).
34. See Adrian Desmond and James Moore, *Darwin* (London: Penguin Books, 1992), ch. 41. Nevertheless, the repudiation of Paley as a means of discrediting religious belief is still a popular academic pastime. Cf. Richard Dawkins, *The Blind Watchmaker* (London: Longman Scientific & Technical, 1986); Daniel C. Dennett, *Darwin's Dangerous Idea: Evolution and the Meanings of Life* (London: Allen Lane, 1995).
35. *At the Origins of Modern Atheism*, op. cit., p. 360.
36. Though scientific discovery is, of course, commonly associated with profound moments of wonder, similar or identical to what I would call spiritual awareness. Cf. Michael Polanyi, *Personal Knowledge* (London: Routledge & Kegan Paul, 1962).
37. Vítezlav Gardavsky, *God Is Not Yet Dead*, tr. from the German by Vivienne Menkes (London: Penguin Books, 1973), pp. 83–4.
38. Pascal's biographer, Ernest Mortimer, is somewhat sceptical: 'There is the story of the accident on the Neuilly Bridge, of which Voltaire made capital at the expense of Pascal's sanity. He had it from some unnamed person who claimed to have had it from d'Arnauld de Saint Victor as having been reported by the Prior de Barillon as from Mme Périer.' In *Blaise Pascal: The Life and Work of a Realist* (London: Methuen & Co., 1959).
39. English translation reproduced from J. M. Cohen's Introduction to Pascal's *Pensées* (London: Penguin Books, 1961), p. 15.
40. The most eminent student of the influence of Calvin's theology on European history is the sociologist Max Weber. His thesis that it underlay the rise of modern capitalism is contained in *The Protestant Ethic and the Spirit of Capitalism*, tr. Talcott Parsons (London: George Allen & Unwin, 1930).
41. See Michael Watts, *The Dissenters* (Oxford: Clarendon Press, 1978).
42. Perkins, quoted in the introduction to *The Work of William Perkins*, edited with an introduction by Ian Breward (Appleford: Sutton Courtney Press, 1970).
43. The psychology of Puritan religious experience is discussed in depth in Charles Lloyd Cohen's book *God's Caress* (Oxford University Press,

1986). It is significant that almost up to the present day, those students of religion who have taken up an interpretation of it which roots it in spiritual or religious experience come overwhelmingly from a Protestant Pietist or Calvinist background (cf. Schleiermacher, Otto, Troeltsch, James, Hall, Starbuck, Wach).

44. Jonathan Edwards, *The Religious Affections*, first published in 1746 (Edinburgh: The Banner of Truth Trust, 1986), p. 15.
45. R. D. Stock, *The Holy and the Daemonic from Sir Thomas Browne to William Blake* (Princeton University Press, 1982).
46. In *William Wordsworth: The Poems*, op. cit.
47. Stephen Gill, *William Wordsworth: A Life* (Oxford University Press, 1990), p. 154.
48. I have been struck by the frequency with which works of art which seem to me to carry a very powerful spiritual message are attacked for their alleged immorality by the popular media (for example, films like *Trainspotting* or *Pulp Fiction*).
49. 'The first anniversarie: An anatomy of the world', from John Donne, *The Epithalamions, Anniversaries and Episedes*, ed. W. Milgate (Oxford: Clarendon Press, 1978).
50. William Butler Yeats, 'The Second Coming', reprinted in *The Penguin Book of English Verse*, ed. John Hayward (London: Penguin Books, 1956).
51. See Philip Selznick, *The Moral Commonwealth: Social Theory and the Promise of Community* (Berkeley: University of California Press, 1992).
52. Amitai Etzioni, *The Spirit of Community: Rights, Responsibilities and the Communication Agenda* (London: Fontana Press, 1995).
53. Ibid., pp. x–xi.
54. Now Lord Dearing.
55. Margaret Knight, *Morals Without Religion*, and other essays (London: Dobson, 1955).
56. *The Sunday Graphic*, 7 Jan. 1955.
57. See the OFSTED publication, *Religious Education and Collective Worship 1992–1993: A Report from the Office of H.M. Chief Inspector of Schools, 1994* (London: HMSO).

Chapter 3: Children's Spirituality – What We Know Already

1. Thomas à Kempis, *The Imitation of Christ*, tr. Ronald Knox and Michael Oakley (London: Burns Oates, 1960), p. 19.
2. See Benjamin Beit-Hallahmi, 'Psychology of religion 1880–1930: the rise and fall of a psychological movement', *Journal of the History of the Behavioral Sciences*, 10, 1974, p. 84; also David Hay, 'Interpreting conversion: the role of psychology in the rise of the hermeneutics of suspicion in the United States', unpublished paper.
3. See Ronald Goldman, *Religious Thinking from Childhood to Adolescence* (London: Routledge & Kegan Paul, 1964).

4. Ibid., p. 14.

5. See the following articles: Kenneth Hyde, 'The critique of Goldman's research', *Religious Education*, 63, 1968, pp. 429–35; A. A. Langdon, 'A critical examination of Dr Goldman's research study on religious thinking from childhood to adolescence', *Journal of Christian Education*, 12, 1969, pp. 37–63; Leslie Francis, *An enquiry into the concept of 'Readiness for religion'*, unpublished Ph.D. thesis, University of Cambridge, 1976; Roger Murphy, *An Investigation into some aspects of the development of Religious Thinking in Children aged between six and eleven years*, unpublished Ph.D. thesis, University of St Andrews, 1980; Andrew McGrady, 'Metaphorical and operational aspects of religious thinking: research with Irish Catholic pupils', Part 1, *British Journal of Religious Education*, 16 (3), 1994, pp. 148–63, Part 2, *British Journal of Religious Education*, 17 (1), 1995, pp. 56–62.

6. See, James Fowler, *Stages of Faith* (New York: Harper & Row, 1980); James Fowler, K. E. Nipkow and F. Schweitzer (eds), *Stages of Faith and Religious Development: Implications for Church, Education and Society* (London: SCM Press, 1991).

7. Fritz Oser and K. Helmut Reich, 'Moral judgment, religious judgment, world views and logical thought: a review of their relationship', *British Journal of Religious Education*, 12, 1990, pp. 94–101, 172–81.

8. Gote Klingberg, 'A study of religious experience in children from 9 to 13 year of age', *Religious Education*, 54, 1959, pp. 211–16.

9. D. and S. Elkind, 'Varieties of religious experience in young adolescents', *Journal for the Scientific Study of Religion*, 2, 1962, pp. 102–12.

10. D. Long, D. Elkind and B. Spilka, 'The child's conception of prayer', *Journal for the Scientific Study of Religion*, 6, 1967, pp. 101–9.

11. See G. Stanley Hall, *Adolescence: its psychology and its relations to physiology, anthropology, sociology, sex, crime, religion, and education* (New York: D. Appleton, 1904); also Edwin D. Starbuck, *The Psychology of Religion* (London: Walter Scott, 1901).

12. Edward Robinson, *The Original Vision* (New York: Seabury Press, 1983).

13. Edwin Muir, *An Autobiography* (London: Methuen, 1964), p. 33.

14. David Heller, *The Children's God* (University of Chicago Press, 1986).

15. Joanne Taylor, *Innocent Wisdom: Children as Spiritual Guides* (New York: Pilgrim Press, 1989).

16. Robert Coles, *The Spiritual Life of Children* (London: HarperCollins, 1992).

17. Ana-Maria Rizzuto, *The Birth of the Living God: A Psychoanalytic Study* (University of Chicago Press, 1979).

18. D. W. Winnicott, 'Transitional objects and transitional phenomena', *International Journal of Psycho-Analysis*, 34, 1953, pp. 89–97; reprinted in D. W. Winnicott, *Playing and Reality* (London: Tavistock, 1971).

19. The plausibility of considering Winnicott's 'transitional space' as the region in which spiritual or religious experience occurs is discussed

helpfully in James W. Jones, *Contemporary Psychoanalysis and Religion: Transference and Transcendence* (New Haven and London: Yale University Press, 1991).

20. See Kalevi Tamminen, 'Religious experiences in childhood and adolescence: a viewpoint of religious development between the ages of 7 and 20', *International Journal for the Psychology of Religion*, 4, 1994, pp. 61–85.

21. A. Vergote and A. Tamayo, *Parental Figures and the Representation of God: A Psychological and Cross-Cultural Study* (The Hague: Mouton Press, 1981).

22. A. Godin and M. Hallez, 'Parental images and divine paternity' in A. Godin (ed.), *From Religious Experience to Religious Attitude* (Chicago: Loyola University Press, 1965); J. P. Deconchy, 'God and parental images' in A. Godin (ed.), *From Cry to Word* (Brussels: Lumen Vitae Press, 1968); B. Spilka, J. Addison and M. Rosensohn, 'Parents, self and God: a test of competing theories of individual-religion relationships', *Review of Religious Research*, 6, 1975, pp. 28–36.

23. Theophil Thun, *Die Religione des Kindes* (2nd edn, Stuttgart: Ernst Klett, 1964; 1st edn, 1959).

24. Rudolf Otto, *The Idea of the Holy*, tr. J. W. Harvey (Oxford University Press, 1950).

25. Theophil Thun, *Die religiöse Entscheidung der Jugend* (Stuttgart: Ernst Klett, 1963).

26. Maria Bindl, *Das religiöse Erleben im Spiegel der Bildgestaltung: Eine Entwicklungs-psychologie Untersuchung* (Freiburg: Herder, 1965).

27. Ludwig Klages, 'Die "religiöse Kurve" in der Handschrifte', *Zeitschrifte für Menschenkunde*, 2, 1927, pp. 1–8.

28. See David M. Wulff, *Psychology of Religion: Classic and Contemporary Views*, 2nd edn (New York: John Wiley, 1996), p. 569.

29. See Susan Bach, *Life Paints its own Span: On the significance of spontaneous pictures by severely ill children* (Zurich: Daimon Verlag, 1990); also Greg Furth, *The Secret World of Children's Drawings: Healing through Art* (Boston: Sigo Press, 1988).

30. Kalevi Tamminen, *Religious Development in Childhood and Youth: An Empirical Study* (Helsinki: Suomalainen Tiedeakatemia, 1991).

31. Leslie Francis, 'The decline in attitudes towards religion among 8–15 year olds', *Educational Studies*, 13 (2), 1987, pp. 125–34.

32. F. Schweitzer, 'Developmental views of the religion of the child: Historical antecedents' in J. Fowler, K. E. Nipkow and F. Schweitzer (eds), *Stages of Faith and Religious Development: Implications for Church, Education and Society*, op. cit., pp. 67–81.

33. For an exposition of this point, see C. Dykstra and S. Parks (eds), *Faith Development and Fowler* (Birmingham, Alabama: Religious Education Press, 1986).

34. Henri Bissonnier, 'Religious expression and mental deficiency' in A. Godin (ed.), *From Religious Expression to Religious Attitude* (Brussels:

The Spirit of the Child

Lumen Vitae Press, 1965), pp. 143–54.

35. Jean-Marie Jaspard, 'Comprehension of religious rituals among male and female mentally handicapped adults', paper presented at the Sixth European Symposium for the Psychology of Religion, University of Lund, June. 1994.

36. Elsewhere I have noted that 'From an evolutionary perspective the holistic awareness underlying spirituality can be understood as a consequence of the need to survive within the multi-faceted intricacy of the natural environment. This has been an important theme amongst sociobiologists in recent years. In his pioneering study of the evolution of consciousness, John Crook demonstrated through comparative studies of the life of other modern primates, how living and hunting in communities as our forebears did leads to the need for a brain that can process, prioritise and make speedy decisions on the basis of the well-nigh infinite mass of data constantly entering the sensory apparatus. Such a process cannot follow the dictates of linear logic, which depends on a watertight set of arguments following sequentially and unidimensionally from a static point in time. It cannot even depend on multi-dimensional logical sequences such as could be generated by a computer, because the flow of data is far too large and dynamic to be processed in this way.' See David Hay, 'Dreams and spirituality' in David Armstrong and Burkhardt Sievers (eds), *Discovering Social Meanings* (unpublished).

37. Hans-Günther Heimbrock, 'The development of symbols as a key to the developmental psychology of religion', *British Journal of Religious Education*, 8, 1986, pp. 150–54.

38. Hans-Günther Heimbrock, 'Religious development and the ritual dimension' in J. W. Fowler, K. E. Nipkow and F. Schweitzer, (eds), *Stages of Faith and Religious Development: Implications for Church, Education and Society*, op. cit., pp. 192–205.

39. Lorelei Farmer, 'Religious experience in childhood: a study of adult perspectives in early spiritual awareness', *Religious Education*, 87, 1992, pp. 259–68.

40. Edward Robinson, *The Original Vision*, op. cit.

41. See Noam Chomsky, *Syntactic Structures* (The Hague: Mouton Press, 1957).

42. Karl Rahner, 'The experience of God today' in *Theological Investigations XI*, tr. David Bourke (London: Darton, Longman & Todd, 1974), pp. 149–65.

43. Peter Berger, *A Rumour of Angels* (London: Allen Lane at the Penguin Press, 1967).

44. Elaine McCreery, 'Talking to children about things spiritual' in Ron Best (ed.), *Education, Spirituality and the Whole Child* (London: Cassell, 1996).

45. See Edward Robinson, *The Original Vision*, op. cit.

46. Clive and Jane Erricker, 'Where angels fear to tread: discovering

children's spirituality' in Ron Best (ed.), *Education, Spirituality and the Whole Child*, op. cit. For a full account of the Children and Worldviews Project, see Clive Erricker, Jane Erricker, Danny Sullivan, Cathy Ota and Mandy Fletcher, *The Education of the Whole Child* (London: Cassell, 1997).

47. Clive Erricker, Danny Sullivan, Jane Erricker, John Logan and Cathy Ota, 'The development of children's worldviews', *Journal of Beliefs and Values*, 15 (2), 1994, pp. 3–6.

Chapter 4: A Geography of the Spirit

1. Karl Rahner sj, 'The experience of God today' in *Theological Investigations XI*, tr. David Bourke (London: Darton, Longman & Todd, 1974), pp. 149–65.

2. I want to underline the fact that I have no intention to contradict the orthodox Christian doctrine of Grace. One can maintain a positive stance towards divine transcendence and the action of Grace (as in fact I do), whilst asserting that the human context within which the spiritual life most fruitfully develops can nevertheless be the subject of scientific investigation.

3. See Margaret Donaldson, *Human Minds* (London: Allen Lane, Penguin Press, 1992).

4. Vygotsky believed that this occurs at the point where pre-verbal thought and pre-conceptual speech are brought together, causing a change of consciousness in the child. This consolidation is described, somewhat misleadingly, as the emergence of 'inner speech', of which Vygotsky says that 'it is so saturated with sense that many words would be required to explain it in external speech.' Hence, 'inner speech' should not be confused with the running dialogue one has in one's head when thinking about something. See Lev Vygotsky, *Thought and Language* (Cambridge, Mass.: MIT Press, 1962), especially ch. 7, p. 119.

5. Taken from *101 Zen Stories*, transcribed by Nyogen Senzaki and Paul Reps (London: Rider, 1939).

6. Jean Pierre de Caussade sj, *Self Abandonment to Divine Providence* (London: Collins/Fontana, 1971), p. 66.

7. See Alfred Schutz, 'Making music together: a study in social relationship' in Arvid Brodersen (ed.), *Collected Papers II: Studies in Social Theory* (The Hague: Martinus Nijhoff, 1964), pp. 135–58.

8. Mary Jo Neitz and James V. Spickard, 'Steps toward a sociology of religious experience: the theories of Mihaly Csikszentmihalyi and Alfred Schutz', *Sociological Analysis*, 51 (1), 1990, pp. 15–33.

9. See Edward Robinson, *The Original Vision*, op. cit., ch. 3.

10. Edward Robinson and Michael Jackson, *Religion and Values at 16+* (Oxford: Alister Hardy Research Centre/Christian Education Movement, 1985).

11. See Mihaly Csikszentmihalyi, *Beyond Boredom and Anxiety* (San Francisco: Jossey-Bass, 1975).

12. Reproduced from Mihaly Csikszentmihalyi, Kevin Rathunde and Samuel Whalen, *Talented Teenagers: The Roots of Success and Failure* (Cambridge University Press, 1993).

13. See Isabella Csikszentmihalyi, 'Flow in a historical context: the case of the Jesuits' in Mihaly Csikszentmihalyi and Isabella Csikszentmihalyi (eds), *Psychological Studies of Flow in Consciousness* (New York: Cambridge University Press, 1988), pp. 232–48.

14. See, Eugene Gendlin, *Experiencing and the Creation of Meaning* (Illinois: Free Press of Glencoe, 1963); *Focusing* (Toronto: Bantam Books, 1981).

15. See Peter Campbell and Edwin McMahon, *Biospirituality: Focusing as a Way to Grow* (Chicago: Loyola University Press, 1985).

16. The deficiencies of Cartesian dualism have often enough been exposed during this century. One of the most readable and convincing critiques, which also has a strong bearing on the nature of spirituality, is that of the Edinburgh philosopher John Macmurray in *The Self as Agent* (London: Faber & Faber, 1957; reissued with an introduction by Stanley M. Harrison in 1995).

17. Kalevi Tamminen, *Religious Development in Childhood and Youth: An Empirical Study*, op. cit., ch. 3.

18. This is a theme discussed by Karl Rahner in 'Experience of self and experience of God' in *Theological Investigations XIII*, tr. David Bourke (London: Darton, Longman & Todd, 1975), ch. 8, pp. 122–31.

19. Rudolf Otto, *The Idea of the Holy*, tr. John W. Harvey (Oxford University Press, 1950).

20. Immanuel Kant, *Critique of Practical Reason and Other Writings in Moral Philosophy*, translated and edited with an introduction by Lewis White Beck (University of Chicago Press, 1949), p. 258.

21. In adult life I reappropriated this experience as spiritual when I first read Gerard Manley Hopkins' poem on 'The Blessed Virgin Compared to the Air we Breathe': 'Wild air, world-mothering air, / Nestling me everywhere, / That each eyelash or hair / Girdles; goes home betwixt / The fleeciest, frailest-flixed / Snowflake.' From *Poems and Prose of Gerard Manley Hopkins*, selected with an introduction and notes by W. H. Gardner (London: Penguin Books, 1953), p. 54.

22. See Karl R. Popper, *The Logic of Scientific Discovery* (London: Hutchison, 1959).

23. James Watson, *The Double Helix* (London: Penguin Books, n.d.).

24. See Janet Soskice, *Metaphor and Religious Language* (Oxford: Clarendon Press, 1985).

25. George E. Ganss sj, *The Spiritual Exercises of St Ignatius: A Translation and Commentary* (St Louis: The Institute of Jesuit Sources, 1992).

26. See Carmen Blacker, 'Deliberate religious transformation in Japanese Buddhism: methods of symbolic imitation in Shingon and Zen' in

Victor C. Hayes (ed.), *Religious Experience in World Religions* (Bedford Park: Australian Association for the Study of Religions, 1980), pp. 112–21.

27. See Mircea Eliade, *Shamanism: Archaic techniques of ecstasy* (New York, 1964).

28. Recommendations for the use of fantasy in Religious Education are contained in Hammond, Hay et al., *New Methods in RE Teaching: An Experiential Approach* (London: Longmans/Oliver & Boyd, 1990). For wise advice on the sensitive use of fantasy with children see particularly chs 12, 14 in Eric Hall, Carol Hall and Alison Leech, *Scripted Fantasy in the Classroom* (London: Routledge, 1990). See also Eric Hall, 'Fantasy in religious education: a psychological perspective', *British Journal of Religious Education*, 10 (1), 1988, pp. 41–8.

29. In *Human Minds*, op. cit.

30. In *The Self as Agent*, op. cit.

31. Laurence Kohlberg, *The Philosophy of Moral Development; Moral Stages and the Idea of Justice* (San Francisco: Harper & Row, 1981).

32. 'The Ascent of Mount Carmel' in St John of the Cross, *Collected Works*, tr. Kieran Kavanaugh OCD and Otilio Rodriguez OCD (Washington DC: Institute of Carmelite Studies, 1973).

33. See Jean Piaget, *The Language and Thought of the Child* (New York: Harcourt Brace, 1926).

34. Peter Berger, *A Rumour of Angels* (London: Allen Lane/Penguin Press, 1970).

35. Ibid., p. 72.

36. Ibid., p. 73.

37. The relation between childhood experience and images of God is impressively analysed in Ana-Maria Rizzuto's book, *The Birth of the Living God*, op. cit., ch. 3.

38. See James Fowler, *Stages of Faith* (San Francisco: Harper & Row, 1981).

39. See C. Daniel Batson, P. Schoenrade and L. W. Ventis, *Religion and the Individual: A Social Psychological Perspective* (New York: Oxford University Press, 1993).

Chapter 5: How Do You Talk with Children about Spirituality?

1. Hans-Georg Gadamer, 'Truth in the Human Sciences' in Brice R. Wachterhauser (ed.), *Hermeneutics and Truth* (Evanston: Northwestern University Press, 1994; first published in German in 1954).

2. The Exercises were originally given continuously over a period which was theoretically 30 days. In the 19th of a set of introductory annotations to the Exercises, Ignatius suggests that they can be undertaken by people involved in 'public affairs or pressing occupations' over a much longer period, though still with the assistance of an experienced guide. See *The Spiritual Exercises of St Ignatius*, translation and

commentary by George E. Ganss SJ (St Louis: Institute of Jesuit Sources, 1992), p. 27.

3. And indeed in empirical science. The lengthy modern debate about the nature of scientific rationality was initiated by Thomas Kuhn's book *The Structure of Scientific Revolutions* (Chicago: University of Chicago Press, 1962).

4. See *The Future of an Illusion* (London: Hogarth Press, 1928), p. 56.

5. Entertainingly discussed in Martyn Hammersley and Paul Atkinson, *Ethnography* (London: Routledge, 1995).

6. See Wilhelm Schmidt, *The Origin and Growth of Religion*, tr. H. J. Rose (London: Methuen, 1931).

7. The possibility of a position which lies beyond the false dichotomy of objectivism and relativism has been explored with clarity in Richard Bernstein's *Beyond Objectivism and Relativism: Science, Hermeneutics and Praxis* (Philadelphia: University of Pennsylvania Press, 1985).

8. Yoshikawa provides a very interesting account of the nature of the difficulties which deals with both Far-Eastern and European insights into the problems of cross-cultural communication. See Muneo Jay Yoshikawa, 'The double-swing model of intercultural communication between the East and the West' in D. Lawrence Kincaid (ed.), *Communication Theory: Eastern and Western Perspectives* (San Diego: Academic Press, 1987).

9. Hans-Georg Gadamer, *Truth and Method*, 2nd edn, translation revised by Joel Weinsheimer and Donald G. Marshall (London: Sheed and Ward, 1989).

10. See Herbert Blumer, 'Sensitising concepts', *American Sociological Review*, 19, 1964, pp. 3–10.

11. The fieldwork was undertaken by Rebecca, who had considerable previous experience of conversing with young children whilst working as a researcher into children's theory of mind at Birmingham University.

12. Clive Erricker, Jane Erricker, Danny Sullivan, Cathy Ota and Mandy Fletcher, *The Education of the Whole Child* (London: Cassell, 1997).

13. See David Hay, *Exploring Inner Space*, 1st edn (London: Penguin Books, 1982), pp. 157–60.

14. If the sociologist Peter Berger is right, very often the social pressure felt by those belonging to a 'cognitive minority' will lead them to defect from their community, unless protective measures such as the setting up of a ghetto are undertaken. See Berger, *A Rumour of Angels*, op. cit., ch 1.

15. The discussion by John Macmurray of the 'rationality of feeling' predates some of the insights of Gadamer on the limitations of the methods of traditional empirical science as a means of achieving truth. See especially John Macmurray, *Reason and Emotion* (London: Faber & Faber, 1935; new edition 1995).

16. The conversations were all transcribed and analysed using a piece of computer software, QSR.NUD.IST, developed at La Trobe University in Australia. NUD.IST facilitates the storage and retrieval of transcribed material and field notes, whilst allowing very fast coding and organization of the textual data in the process of theory construction. See the *User's Guide for QSR.NUD.IST (Revision 3 for Apple Macintosh)* (London: Sage Publications Software SCOLARI, 1996).

Chapter 6: Listening to Children Talking

1. 'Heart speaks to heart', the motto chosen by J. H. Newman when he was made a Cardinal.
2. See P. Maykut and R. Morehouse, *Beginning Qualitative Research: A Philosophical and Practical Guide* (London: Falmer Press, 1994).
3. The children's names have been changed to preserve their anonymity.
4. Robert Coles refers obliquely to the 'spiritual psychology' of each child in *The Spiritual Life of Children* (London: HarperCollins, 1991). James Fowler draws on Kegan's account of personality development as being amongst the key factors in the characterization of a person's faith. See James Fowler, *Faith Development and Pastoral Care* (Philadelphia: Fortress Press, 1987). See also J. Fowler, K. Nipkow and F. Schweitzer (eds), *Stages of Faith and Religious Development: Implications for Church, Education and Society* (London: SCM Press, 1991). For a description of Kegan's approach to personality development, see R. Kegan, *The Evolving Self: Problems and Process in Human Development* (Cambridge: Harvard University Press, 1982).
5. Anticipating the subject of Chapter 9, I think it is really helpful for people working with children's spirituality to have some kind of record (written, audio or audio-visual) on which to reflect. Of course, it is impractical to suggest that every teacher, parent or children's minister records and transcribes every conversation they have. But there is much to be learnt from the experience of attempting this on at least one occasion. It wakes one up to the layers of spirituality in children's conversations, and to their own sensitivities (and insensitivities) to that.
6. Many of the contributors to Edward Robinson's study of adult recollections of childhood religious experience reported similar parental rejections of their interpretation of events. See Edward Robinson, *The Original Vision* (New York: Seabury Press, 1983).
7. For a discussion of the taboo, see David Hay's book *Religious Experience Today: Studying the Facts* (London: Mowbray/Cassell, 1990).
8. See Rudolf Otto, *The Idea of the Holy* (Oxford University Press, 1950).
9. The Jungian account of a religious core of the unconscious (the God image as an archetype of the Self), and the role of dreams as communications to our consciousness, would be a way of establishing a theoretical parallel in this case with the more explicitly religious expressions of

other children. E.g. see C. G. Jung, *Man and His Symbols* (Garden City, NY: Doubleday, 1989).

Chapter 7: Identifying the Core of Children's Spirituality

1. Jean-Paul Sartre, *Being and Nothingness* (New York: Philosophical Library, 1956).
2. For a straightforward account of the methodology, see Anselm Strauss and Juliet Corbin, *Basics of Qualitative Research: Grounded Theory Procedures and Techniques* (Newbury Park: Sage Publications, 1990).
3. Some readers may wish to have more details about the nature and particular processes of analysis that gave rise to this result. It must be emphasized that this kind of qualitative approach does not make the same kinds of claims to validity and certainty (qua statistical probability) as is typical of quantitative methodologies. One may not 'prove' that relational consciousness is the most apt way to refer to the spirituality revealed in these conversations; it is offered as a conclusion that at least made sense of the data to the researchers involved. The emergence of 'relational consciousness' as the core category from this data reflected extensive qualitative analysis of the conversations and a growing corpus of commentary (the 'data trail') about them. This ranged from indexing and cataloguing themes and styles suggested from line by line analysis of whole transcripts, similarly detailed re-indexing of selected key passages of different kinds of data (as referred to in the previous chapter), as well as analysis of the emerging analytical products themselves, such as lengthy case-study memos outlining the main features and 'story' which each child in the sample represented. As this was conducted using the on-line skills of a computer programme (NUD.IST), the otherwise overwhelming number of details and cross-references was kept at a manageable level and the information was always accessible at the push of a button. Obviously, given the character of the material, the computer was not employed to analyse the meaning suggested by the data; this remained a subjectively informed process, progressively more informed and tutored by such close acquaintance with the data. However, in moving towards the identification of the core category it was helpful to exploit the computer's assistance for comparing and contrasting the extent to which different indexed themes appeared, as well as where they appeared and in what forms. The proposed core category is thus a result of exhaustive, but essentially creative, analysis; no more and no less. Its debt to 'grounded theory' is reflected in (amongst other things) its emergence from the data (and reflection on that data) rather than as part of an a priori set of predictions about the nature of children's spirituality. It is worth noting that there had been nothing bearing obvious resemblance to this category in the set of guideline categories in Chapter 4 that were drawn up in advance to help the data collection process.

Once this core category seemed to suggest itself, reiterative study was made of large portions of the data afresh, to 'test the fit' of this organizing idea against a variety of cases. This served both to confirm the usefulness of 'relational consciousness' as a heuristic for describing the general characteristics of the data, and to suggest the particular dynamics and intricacies of that core category.

4. The term 'mental' is not used to suggest that this phenomenon is only an intellectual or cognitive quirk, but rather gathers together the psychological functions of cognition, emotion, action and sensation.

5. At another level a link between the Disney story and the Christian beliefs he has just mentioned may be suggested. The dawning, transforming self-consciousness of Grumpy as a consequence of Snow White's unjust death at the hands of the evil witch and her subsequent 'resurrection', echo the Christian story, at least in the way Freddie unconventionally retells the story. Such a link may have unconsciously resonated in him allowing the Disney account to stand alongside his account of his religious conceptions and sentiments. This also finds parallel in Fowler's account of the mythic-literal stage of faith.

6. This was not wonder in the sense of wanting to know their physical constitution, but rather wonder inspired by her sense that such knowledge was impossible knowledge.

7. See R. Brooke and C. Brooke, *Popular Religion in the Middle Ages* (London: Thames and Hudson, 1984). The religious practices of the Middle Ages suggest that people had a greater sense of kinship that extended across the boundaries of generations, living and dead. The poor depended in part on the financial support of the departed in the form of money which was paid to them to offer prayers and attend masses for the dead person. Equally, the dead were seen as dependent on the living in order that their souls could be sufficiently prayed for. This sense of interdependency fostered a kinship-based sense of spirituality.

8. Compare this with six-year-old Freddie's semi-autobiographical language describing his experience of self-transformation which was more obviously a case of employing a language of fiction.

9. See J. Berryman, *Godly Play* (Minneapolis: Augsburg Fortress, 1995); also S. Cavalletti, *The Religious Potential of the Child* (New York: Paulist Press, 1983).

10. See R. Goldman, *Readiness for Religion* (London: Routledge & Kegan Paul, 1965).

11. See U. Goswami, *Analogical Reasoning in Children* (Hove: Lawrence Erlbaum Associates, 1992).

12. Two children referred to experiences of profound awe in response to seeing the large Merry Hill shopping complex in Dudley, West Midlands, illuminated and attracting them inside on a dark winter's evening.

13. E.g. see D. Hay, *Exploring Inner Space*, 2nd edn (Oxford: Mowbrays Press, 1987).

14. E.g. see Nicholas Lash, *Easter in Ordinary* (London: SCM Press, 1988).
15. Quoted by Jack Priestley, in 'The Spiritual in the Curriculum' in P. C. Souper (ed.), *The Spiritual Dimension of Education* (Southampton: Department of Education, Occasional Paper Series No. 2).

Chapter 8: The Naturalness of Relational Consciousness

1. Quoted in Mircea Eliade, *From Primitives to Zen* (London: Collins, 1967).
2. The major exception to this generalization is the language of poetry.
3. Martin Heidegger, *Being and Time*, tr. John Macquarrie and Edward Robinson (New York: Harper & Row, 1962).
4. I am indebted here to Rebecca Nye's expertise in the contemporary field of research into children's theory of mind; in particular for pointing me to Harris' work on psychological understanding in children. See P. Harris, *Children and Emotion: the Development of Psychological Understanding* (Oxford: Blackwells Press, 1989).
5. About 50 per cent of the accounts on file in the Alister Hardy Centre in Oxford relate to moments of personal stress, often of an extreme kind – i.e. fear of death, loss of a loved one, personal destitution or despair. Typically the effect of the experience is to reduce stress, thus enabling the person to cope better with the difficulty. See David Hay, *Exploring Inner Space: Scientists and Religious Experience* (London: Penguin Books, 1982). The hypothesis that spiritual experience has a problem-solving function in stressful situations has recently been put forward by Jackson and Fulford. See Mike Jackson and K. W. M. Fulford, 'Spiritual experience and psychopathology', *Philosophy, Psychiatry & Psychology*, 4 (1), 1997, pp. 41–66.
6. Much research on the relationship between religious belief and ethical behaviour suggests an unflattering link with punitiveness, racism and other socially undesirable traits. For a summary of this work, see C. D. Batson, P. Schoenrade and L. W. Ventis, *Religion and the Individual: A Social Psychological Perspective* (New York: Oxford University Press, 1993). Whilst this implies an equivocal connection between religious belief and altruism, spirituality, as I have been at pains to point out, is not the same as religion.
7. See Richard Woods, 'Mysticism and social action: the mystic's calling, development and social activity', *Journal of Consciousness Studies*, 3 (2), 1996, pp. 158–71.
8. Richard Dawkins, *The Selfish Gene* (Oxford University Press, 1976).
9. The modern development of the idea of kin selection is usually traced to W. D. Hamilton. See, e.g., W. D. Hamilton, 'The genetical evolution of social behaviour (I & II)', *Journal of Theoretical Biology*, 7, 1964, pp. 1–16, 17–52.
10. See R. L. Trivers, 'The evolution of reciprocal altruism', *Quarterly Review of Biology*, 46, 1971, pp. 35–57.

11. See, e.g., Frans de Waal, *Good Natured: The Origins of Right and Wrong in Humans and Other Animals* (Cambridge: Harvard University Press, 1996); Matt Ridley, *The Origins of Virtue* (London: Viking, 1996).

12. The significance of this demand has been central to the ethical writing of the philosopher Emmanuel Levinas. The example I have chosen is discussed in detail in the context of a reflection on the philosophy of Levinas by the Dominican theologian Edward Schillebeeckx. See *On Christian Faith: The Spiritual, Ethical and Political Dimensions* (New York: Crossroad, 1987), especially pp. 55–65.

13. See, e.g., Dawkins, *The Selfish Gene*, op. cit. Here we are entering the contentious territory of sociobiology, where my personal stance resembles that of John Crook: 'Sociobiology explains why human behaviour is not arbitrary, why it is structured in a broadly characteristic way wherever people are, but it does not proceed to reduce all descriptions of individual human action to biological causation ... Cultural evoltion thus comprises a historical process that provides human beings with the sociological environment within which the basic biological strategies of the species are worked out.' See John H. Crook, *The Evolution of Human Consciousness* (Oxford: Clarendon Press, 1980), pp. 186–7.

14. See V. C. Wynne-Edwards, *Animal Dispersion in Relation to Social Behaviour* (Edinburgh: Oliver & Boyd, 1962).

15. See David Sloan Wilson and Elliott Sober (and commentators), 'Re-introducing group selection to the human behavioural sciences', *Behavioural and Brain Sciences*, 17, 1994, pp. 585–654; and further comment in *Behavioural and Brain Sciences*, 19, 1996, pp. 777–87.

16. What was, no doubt, a somewhat Utopian idea of the mode of life in such a community was portrayed in the film *The Witness*.

17. Wilson and Sober, op. cit., p. 605. The question of whether high birth rates ultimately contribute to human survival or the protection of the planetary environment is, of course, highly debatable. I myself have written a book which highlights the issue of overpopulation. But the very existence of the debate suggests that relational consciousness enters into the process of social evolution. At this stage of human evolution it may seem highly appropriate to consider the global community in the light of the ethos arising from relational consciousness.

18. Ibid., p. 602.

19. Dawkins, *The Selfish Gene*, op. cit.

20. I am indebted to Arthur Peacocke for indicating that this point had already been made more than 20 years ago. In an address given to the American Psychological Association in 1975 the anthropologist Donald Campbell, speaking as a 'hard line neo-Darwinian', suggested that the social evolution of religion had been the primary means of optimizing the functioning of society against the narrow interests of the selfish gene. See Donald T. Campbell, 'On the conflicts between biological and

social evolution and between psychology and moral tradition', *Zygon* 11, 1976, pp. 167–208. My only addition to Campbell's remarks would be to insist that the relational consciousness that provides the constraints for social evolution is itself the product of biological evolution.

21. William H. Durham, *CoEvolution: Genes, Culture and Human Diversity* (Stanford University Press, 1991).

22. Dawkins, *The Selfish Gene*, op. cit.

23. Durham, op. cit., p. 421.

24. The analogy must not be taken too far. The danger of taking the notion of memes as the equivalent of genes was pointed out several years ago by Arthur Peacocke in his Bampton Lectures. See *Creation and the World of Science* (Oxford: Clarendon Press, 1979), pp. 177–8.

25. Durham, op. cit., p. 363.

26. One of the examples chosen by Durham as an illustration of this kind of opposition is particularly relevant to the current crisis in Britain over meat eating because of the epidemic of BSE in cattle. Over the past 100 years the practice of 'endo-cannibalism' (the eating of dead relatives) evolved amongst the Fore people of the Eastern Highlands of New Guinea. One of its unforeseen consequences was the spread of *Kuru*, a lethal nerve-degeneration disease with similarities to BSE, through the eating of infected human nervous tissue. *Kuru* was particularly devastating to the female population, presumably because social custom dictated that at mortuary feasts where pork was also available, men were given prior rights to the pork. The central government of Papua-New Guinea banned cannibalism in the 1950s, and since that time there has been a steady decline in deaths attributable to *Kuru*. See Durham, pp. 393–414.

27. The sense of individual isolation which this produced in the European consciousness has been powerfully analysed by John Macmurray. See the two volumes of Macmurray's Gifford Lectures at Glasgow University, *The Self as Agent and Persons in Relation* (republished by Faber & Faber in 1995).

28. Michael Buckley, *At the Origins of Modern Atheism*, op. cit., ch. 2.

29. This has been devastatingly criticized by Gadamer. See Hans-Georg Gadamer, *Truth and Method*, op. cit., ch. 5.

30. The irrationalities of this are discussed most revealingly by the economist André Gorz. See his *Critique of Economic Reason*, tr. Gillian Handyside and Chris Turner (London: Verso, 1989).

31. One of my colleagues who read a version of this chapter felt that even the highest levels of altruism can be explained in terms of straightforward Darwinian orthodoxy. I am not so sure, but if he is correct this simply adds to my conviction that I am writing about a natural human predisposition.

32. William James, *The Will to Believe* (London: Longmans, Green, 1904), p. 28.

33. For a particularly clear account of the problems produced by this

antithesis, see Richard Bernstein, *Beyond Objectivism and Relativism: Science, Hermeneutics and Praxis*, op. cit., ch. 5.

34. In the introduction to his Gifford Lectures, *The Form of the Personal*, John Macmurray remarks that the philosophical dualism bequeathed to us by Descartes is so deeply within our cultural consciousness that though his lectures are dedicated to combat dualism, he fears that he will not always escape from its assumptions even in the process of combating them. Even so, from Gadamer's perspective, Macmurray's prejudice forms the platform from which a fruitful engagement with our cultural history does become possible. See Macmurray, *The Self as Agent*, op. cit., p. 14.

35. Modern biological theory on the origins of altruism is sometimes seen as a threat to spiritual conceptions of reality. This misconception is based on a confusion between spirituality and religion.

36. For an example of this approach, see John Hammond, David Hay et al., *New Methods in RE Teaching: An Experiential Approach* (London: Longmans/Oliver & Boyd, 1990).

37. There is at least anecdotal evidence that the secularizing forces that have affected Judaism and Christianity for several hundred years are also damaging adherence to more recent arrivals in Europe like the Indian religions.

38. Macmurray, op. cit.

39. E.g., the views of behaviourist psychologists. It is not so long ago that the opinions of B. F. Skinner had a dominant role in the image of psychology held by the general public.

40. For a courageous discussion of the problems, see Jasper Ungoed-Thomas, 'Inspecting spiritual, moral, social and cultural development', *Pastoral Care*, Dec. 1994, pp. 21–5.

Chapter 9: Nurturing the Spirit of the Child

1. Simone Weil, quoted by John Berger in 'The Man in the Street', *The Guardian*, Thu. 19 Dec. 1991, p. 21.

2. The story is recounted in Barbara Kimes Myers' book *Young Children and Spirituality* (New York and London: Routledge 1997).

3. See the British Home Office report *1996 British Crime Survey* (HMSO).

4. I am grateful to Jonathan Tafler for giving me permission to use this story which I first heard on *The Afternoon Shift*, BBC Radio 4, Fri. 21 Nov. 1997.

5. There are now many books dealing with this issue. One which touches in an autobiographical way on the social construction of masculinity is David Jackson's *Unmasking Masculinity* (London: Unwin Hyman, 1990). Roy McCloughry's *Men and Masculinity: From Power to Love* looks at the construction of masculinity from a specifically Christian perspective.

6. Though there are some striking examples of success in highly unpromising environments. See, e.g., the account of Frank Walters' work as Headmaster of Bergen Street Middle School in Newark, NJ reported in a BBC documentary, *The Transformers*, 1990. An illustration from the adult world will make the difficulty clear. Reflecting in 1995 about the attempts by the Sandinista government in Nicaragua to effect democratic land reform with the peasantry, Fernando Cardenal writes of how the government gave the rural workers land, tools, technical assistance and capital, but still the experiment failed. The material conditions were insufficient; there also needed to be a cultural renewal. Cardenal pointed out that in Latin America the history of physical domination by wealthy landowners has made the poor passive, lacking in confidence and fearful of change. Most peasants in Nicaragua saw their material wellbeing as dependent on becoming the client of a rich or powerful protector. Liberty was sacrificed for the sake of the supposed security offered by a patron. When the Contras overturned the Sandinista regime it turned out that the fearfulness of the peasants was well founded. But, tragically, their fearfulness colluded with the overthrow of those who sought their freedom. See Fernando Cardenal, 'La renovación necesaria: desarrollo humano', *Christus* (Mexico), 60, 1995, pp. 74–9. I am grateful to my friend Fr Cyril Lovett ssc for bringing this article to my attention.

7. In fact many of the exercises used in Personal and Social Education have a direct reference to spirituality as I have defined it. Any future syllabus will certainly draw upon this source. At the same time a word of caution is appropriate. The methodology used in PSE should not be undertaken without proper training, since insensitive use of the exercises can do more harm than good. The Centre for the Study of Human Relations, Nottingham University, Nottingham NG7 2RD, has been providing training in these methods for many years.

8. Religious education is not indoctrination either, when it takes place in a secular milieu. Rather, it opens up alternative ways of understanding reality. A more likely candidate as indoctrinatory is secularism, since its cultural norms are so all-pervasive as to generate 'single vision'.

9. These matters are explored with great sensitivity in Irving D. Yalom's book *Existential Psychotherapy* (New York: Basic Books, 1980). Children's reflections on such existential issues are beautifully portrayed in Lennart Pasborg's film *You and I* (1994), which listens in on the profound philosophizing of four young Danish children. Available (with English subtitles) from Magic Hour Films, The Danish Film Studio, Blomstervaenget 52, DK-2800, Lyngby, Denmark.

10. Nowadays there are many handbooks of advice for enhancing children's self-esteem in the classroom. One that I have found very helpful over a number of years is Canfield and Wells' book *100 Ways to Enhance Self-Concept in the Classroom* (Englewood Cliffs, N.J.: Prentice-Hall, 1976). Another example is Robert W. Reasoner's hand-

book *Building Self-Esteem: Elementary Edition* (Palo Alto: Consulting Psychologists' Press, 1982).

11. In certain circumstances children will express their despair by becoming disruptive or violent. Some years ago I had a valuable, though at the time extremely painful, opportunity to work with a group of very disruptive pupils in an inner-city school. They had been withdrawn from normal classes because the teachers had refused to have them in the room with the other pupils because they were unteachable. It was true; I did no better than their regular teachers. In desperation I decided to have private conversations with each of them to try to find out something about them as individuals. What I discovered behind the loud, bragging, smart-ass exterior of every one of them was someone without a sense of self-worth who felt lost and thoroughly alienated from their natural community. At least one of them had taken steps to join a 'tribe' by becoming a member of the National Front.

12. This exercise is borrowed from Karl Popper, who used it with students of the philosophy of science to demonstrate that no one ever approaches reality from an unbiased perspective. See *The Logic of Scientific Discovery* (London: Hutchinson Press, 1959).

13. Taken from John Hammond, David Hay et al., *New Methods in RE Teaching*, op. cit., Chapter 8, pp. 99–100.

14. Many exercises of this type are to be found in *New Methods in RE Teaching*, op. cit.

15. See Don Ihde, *Experimental Phenomenology* (New York: Paragon Books, 1979).

16. See T. H. Huxley's 1893 Romanes Lecture, 'Evolution and ethics: prolegomena', republished in T. H. Huxley's *Collected Essays*, 9 volumes, 1894–1908 (London: Macmillan & Co.), vol. 9, pp. 46–116.

17. The story is told by J. B. Leishman in his introduction to *Rilke: Selected Poems*, translated with an introduction by J. B. Leishman (London: Penguin Books, 1964).

18. Ibid., p. 33.

19. The process of reading and re-reading transcripts of the conversations which Rebecca had with children taught us a lot about attention. Following an interview which had seemed to be devoid of interest, we quite often found that giving prolonged attention to the text opened up deeper aspects of the conversation of which we had been unaware. It may be a revealing exercise for teachers to tape-record some of their conversations with children and to listen to them at this meditative level of attentiveness.

20. For a more detailed account of the rationale and practical approach of the project, see John Hammond, David Hay, et al, *New Methods in RE Teaching*, op. cit., Chapter 8.

21. I intend to continue using the terms 'inside' and 'outside', referring to an inner and an outer world, in spite of accusations of dualism by some of my critics. These terms recognize the physical facts of everyday

The Spirit of the Child

human experience and do not imply the espousal of a Cartesian split in reality to which I do not subscribe. See David Hay and John Hammond, '"When you pray, go to your private room": a reply to Adrian Thatcher', *British Journal of Religious Education*, 14 (3), 1992, pp. 145–50.

22. This exercise is adapted from an idea by Dr Patrick Pietroni in his book *Holistic Living* (London: J. M. Dent, 1986).

23. I have been struck by how often teachers tell me that awareness exercises are surprisingly successful with children normally thought of as difficult or disruptive. It is as if the exercises respond to a felt need for – what? Space? Silence? Even discovering a relationship with reality?

24. Vygotsky may seem a surprising choice in relation to spiritual education. Yet it is clear when reading an account of his life that one of the stronger influences was the reading of William James' *Varieties of Religious Experience*.

25. See Barbara Kymes Myers, *Young Children and Spirituality* (New York and London: Routledge, 1997), especially p. 62.

26. See Jasper Ungoed-Thomas, 'Inspecting Spiritual, Moral, Social and Cultural Development', op. cit., ch. 8.

27. E.g., the British Economic and Social Science Research Council produced an updated 'Thematic Priorities' document in 1997 which highlighted as one of its major research priorities an investigation into the causes of 'Social Integration and Exclusion'. The Thematic Priorities Document is available from Polaris House, North Star Avenue, Swindon SN2 1UJ. It is also available on the ESRC Internet site: http://www.esrc.ac.uk/th9

Bibliography

Bach, S. (1990). *Life Paints its own Span: On the Significance of Spontaneous Pictures by Severely ill Children*. Zurich: Daimon Verlag.

Bancroft, N. (1993). 'Spirituality in Marxism: A Communist View' in Benjamin B. Page (ed.), *Marxism and Spirituality: An International Anthology*. Westport and London: Bergin & Garvey.

Barbour, I. (1974). *Myths, Models and Paradigms*. London: SCM Press.

Batson, C. D., Schoenrade, P. and Ventis, L. W. (1993). *Religion and the Individual: A Social Psychological Perspective*. New York: Oxford University Press.

Beit-Hallahmi, B. (1974). 'Psychology of religion 1880–1930: the rise and fall of a psychological movement', *Journal of the History of the Behavioral Sciences*, 10, pp. 84–90.

Berger, J. (1991). 'The Man in the Street', *The Guardian*, Thu. 19 Dec. 1991, p. 21.

Berger, P. (1969). *The Social Reality of Religion*. London: Faber and Faber.

Berger, P. (1967). *A Rumour of Angels: Modern Society and the Rediscovery of the Supernatural*. London: Allen Lane/Penguin Press.

Berman, D. (1988). *A History of Atheism in Britain: from Hobbes to Russell*. London: Croom Helm, 1988.

Bernstein, R. (1985). *Beyond Objectivism and Relativism: Science, Hermeneutics and Praxis*. Philadelphia: University of Pennsylvania Press.

Berryman, J. (1995). *Godly Play*. Minneapolis: Augsburg Fortress.

Best, R. (ed.) (1996). *Education, Spirituality and the Whole Child*. London: Cassell.

Bindl, M. (1965). *Das religiöse Erleben im Spiegel der Bildgestaltung: Eine Entwicklungs-psychologie Untersuchung*. Freiburg: Herder.

Bissonnier, H. (1965). 'Religious expression and mental deficiency' in A. Godin (ed.), From *Religious Expression to Religious Attitude*. Brussels: Lumen Vitae Press.

Blacker, C. (1980). 'Deliberate religious transformation in Japanese Buddhism: methods of symbolic imitation in Shingon and Zen' in Victor C. Hayes (ed.), *Religious Experience in World Religions*. Bedford Park: Australian Association for the Study of Religions.

Blumer, H. (1964). 'Sensitising concepts', *American Sociological Review*, 19, pp. 3–10.

Bowling, A. (1991). *Measuring Health: A Review of Quality of Life Measurement Scales*. Buckingham: Open University Press.

Bradburn, N. (1969). *The Structure of Psychological Wellbeing*. Chicago: Aldine.

Brooke, R. and Brooke, C. (1984). *Popular Religion in the Middle Ages*. London: Thames and Hudson.

Buckley, M., SJ (1987). *At the Origins of Modern Atheism*. New Haven and London: Yale University Press.

Bunting, M. (1996). 'God's media image', *The Tablet*, 16 Nov. 1996, pp. 1505–6.

Campbell, D. T. (1976). 'On the conflicts between biological and social evolution and between psychology and moral tradition', *Zygon* 11, pp. 167–208.

Campbell, P. and McMahon, E. (1985). *Biospirituality: Focusing as a Way to Grow*. Chicago: Loyola University Press.

Cardenal, F. (1995). 'La renovación necesaria: desarrollo humano', *Christus* (Mexico), 60, pp. 74–9.

de Caussade, J. P., SJ (1971). *Self Abandonment to Divine Providence*. London: Collins/Fontana.

Cavalletti, S. (1983). *The Religious Potential of the Child*. New York: Paulist Press.

Chadwick, O. (1975). *The Secularisation of the European Mind in the Nineteenth Century*. Cambridge University Press.

Chaterjee, M. (1989). *The Concept of Spirituality*. Ahmedabad: Allied Publishers.

Chomsky, N. (1957). *Syntactic Structures*. The Hague: Mouton Press.

Clayton, J. (1990). 'Piety and the proofs', *Religious Studies*, 26, pp. 19–42.

Cohen, C. L. (1986). *God's Caress*. New York: Oxford University Press.

Coles, R. (1992). *The Spiritual Life of Children*. London: HarperCollins.

Comte, A. (1903). *A Discourse on the Positive Spirit*, tr. Edward Spencer Beesley. London: William Reeves.

Crook, J. H. (1980). *The Evolution of Human Consciousness*. Oxford: Clarendon Press.

Csikszentmihalyi, I. (1988). 'Flow in a historical context: the case of the Jesuits' in Mihaly Csikszentmihalyi and Isabella Csikszentmihalyi (eds),

Psychological Studies of Flow in Consciousness. New York: Cambridge University Press.

Csikszentmihalyi, M. (1975). *Beyond Boredom and Anxiety.* San Francisco: Jossey-Bass.

Csikszentmihalyi, M., Rathunde, K. and Whalen, S. (1993). *Talented Teenagers: The roots of success and failure.* Cambridge University Press.

Darwin, C. (1964). *On the Origin of Species by Means of Natural Selection: Or, the Preservation of Favoured Races in the Struggle for Life.* London: John Murray. Reprinted with an introduction by Ernst Mayr, Cambridge, Mass.: Harvard University Press.

Dawkins, R. (1976). *The Selfish Gene.* Oxford University Press.

Dawkins, R. (1986). *The Blind Watchmaker.* London: Longman Scientific & Technical.

Deconchy, J. P. (1968). 'God and parental images' in A. Godin (ed.), *From Cry to Word.* Brussels: Lumen Vitae Press.

Desmond, A. and Moore, J. (1992). *Darwin.* London: Penguin Books.

Dennett, D. (1995). *Darwin's Dangerous Idea: Evolution and the Meanings of Life.* London: Allen Lane/Penguin Press.

Donaldson, M. (1992). *Human Minds.* London: Allen Lane/Penguin Press.

Donne, J. (1978). *The Epithalamions, Anniversaries and Episides,* ed. W. Milgate. Oxford: Clarendon Press.

Durham, W. H. (1991). *CoEvolution: Genes, Culture and Human Diversity.* Stanford University Press.

Durkheim, É. (1915). *The Elementary Forms of the Religious Life,* tr. J. W. Swain. London: George Allen & Unwin.

Dykstra, C. and Parks, S. (eds) (1986). *Faith Development and Fowler.* Birmingham, Alabama: Religious Education Press.

Edwards, J. (1986). *The Religious Affections* (first published in 1746). Edinburgh: The Banner of Truth Trust.

Eliade, M. (1964). *Shamanism: Archaic techniques of Ecstasy,* translated from the French by Willard R. Trask. London: Routledge & Kegan Paul.

Eliade, M. (1967). *From Primitives to Zen.* London: Collins.

Elkind, D. and Elkind, S. (1962). 'Varieties of religious experience in young adolescents', *Journal for the Scientific Study of Religion,* 2, pp. 102–12.

Erricker, C., Sullivan, D., Erricker, J., Logan, J. and Ota, C., (1994). 'The development of children's worldviews', *Journal of Beliefs and Values,* 15 (2), pp. 3–6.

Erricker, C. and Erricker, J. (1996). 'Where angels fear to tread: discovering children's spirituality' in Ron Best (ed.), *Education, Spirituality and the Whole Child.* London: Cassell.

Erricker, C., Erricker, J., Sullivan, D., Ota, C. and Fletcher, M. (1997). *The Education of the Whole Child.* London: Cassell.

Etzioni, A. (1995). *The Spirit of Community: Rights, Responsibilities and the Communication Agenda.* London: Fontana Press.

Farmer, L. (1992). 'Religious experience in childhood: a study of adult perspectives in early spiritual awareness', *Religious Education*, 87, pp. 259–68.

Foucault, M. (1973). *The Order of Things: An Archaeology of the Human Sciences*. New York: Vintage Books.

Fowler, J. (1980). *Stages of Faith*. New York: Harper & Row.

Fowler, J. (1987). *Faith development and Pastoral Care*. Philadelphia: Fortress Press.

Fowler, J., Nipkow, K. E. and Schweitzer, F. (eds). *Stages of Faith and Religious Development: Implications for Church, Education and Society*. London: SCM Press.

Francis, L. (1976). *An enquiry into the concept of 'Readiness for religion'*. Unpublished Ph.D. thesis, University of Cambridge.

Francis, L. (1987). 'The decline in attitudes towards religion among 8–15 year olds', *Educational Studies*, 13 (2), pp. 125–34.

Freud, S. (1928). *The Future of an Illusion*. London: Hogarth Press.

Furth, G. (1988). *The Secret World of Children's Drawings: Healing through Art*. Boston: Sigo Press.

Gadamer, H.-G. (1989). *Truth and Method*, 2nd edn, translation revised by Joel Weinsheimer and Donald G. Marshall. London: Sheed & Ward.

Gadamer, H.-G. (1994). 'Truth in the Human Sciences' in Brice R. Wachterhauser (ed.), *Hermeneutics and Truth*. Evanston: Northwestern University Press. ('Truth in the Human Sciences' was first published in German in 1954.)

Ganss, G. E., SJ (1992). *The Spiritual Exercises of St Ignatius: A Translation and Commentary*. St Louis: The Institute of Jesuit Sources.

Gardavsky, V. (1973). *God Is Not Yet Dead*, tr. from the German by Vivienne Menkes. London: Penguin Books.

Gendlin, E. (1962). *Experiencing and the Creation of Meaning*. Chicago: Free Press of Glencoe.

Gendlin, E. (1981). *Focusing*. Toronto: Bantam Books.

Gill, S. (1990). *William Wordsworth: A Life*. Oxford University Press.

Godin, A. and Hallez, M. (1965). 'Parental images and divine paternity' in A. Godin (ed.), *From Religious Experience to Religious Attitude*. Chicago: Loyola University Press.

Goldman, R. (1964). *Religious Thinking from Childhood to Adolescence*. London: Routledge & Kegan Paul.

Goldman, R. (1965). *Readiness for Religion*. London: Routledge & Kegan Paul.

Gorz, A. (1989). *Critique of Economic Reason*, tr. Gillian Handyside and Chris Turner. London: Verso.

Goswami, U. (1992). *Analogical Reasoning in Children*. Hove: Lawrence Erlbaum Associates.

Graham, A. (1968). *Conversations: Christian and Buddhist*. New York: Harcourt Brace Jovanovich.

Greeley, A. (1975). *The Sociology of the Paranormal: A Reconnaissance* (Sage Research Papers in the Social Sciences, Studies in Religion and

Ethnicity Series No. 90-023). Beverly Hills and London: Sage Publications.

Groome, T. H. (1980). *Christian Religious Education: Sharing our Story and Vision*. San Francisco: Harper & Row.

Hall, E. (1988). 'Fantasy in religious education: a psychological perspective', *British Journal of Religious Education*, 10 (1), 1988.

Hall, E., Hall, C. and Leech, A. (1990). *Scripted Fantasy in the Classroom*. London: Routledge.

Hall, G. S. (1904). *Adolescence: its psychology and its relations to physiology, anthropology, sociology, sex, crime, religion, and education*. New York: D. Appleton.

Hammersley, M. and Atkinson, P. (1995). *Ethnography*. London: Routledge.

Hamilton, W. D. (1964). 'The genetical evolution of social behaviour (I & II)', *Journal of Theoretical Biology*, 7, pp. 1–16, 17–52.

Hammond, J., Hay, D., Moxon, J., Netto, B., Raban, K., Straugheir, G. and Williams, C. (1990). *New Methods in RE Teaching: An Experiential Approach*. London: Longmans/Oliver & Boyd.

Hardy, A. (1966). *The Divine Flame: An Essay Towards a Natural History of Religion*. London: Collins.

Harris, P. (1989). *Children and Emotion: the Development of Psychological Understanding*. Oxford: Blackwells Press.

Hay, D. (1979). 'Religious experience amongst a group of postgraduate students: a qualitative study', *Journal for the Scientific Study of Religion*, 18 (2), pp. 164–82.

Hay, D. (1982). *Exploring Inner Space: Scientists and Religious Experience*. London: Penguin Books.

Hay, D. (1985). 'Religious experience and its induction' in L. B. Brown (ed.), *Advances in the Psychology of Religion*. Oxford: Pergamon Press.

Hay, D. (1990). *Religious Experience Today: Studying the Facts*. London: Cassell/Mowbrays.

Hay, D. (1994). '"The biology of God": What is the current status of Hardy's hypothesis?', *International Journal for the Psychology of Religion*, 4 (1), pp. 1–23.

Hay, D. (1996). 'Memories of a Calvinist childhood' in W. Gordon Lawrence (ed.), *Roots in a Northern Landscape*. Edinburgh: Scottish Cultural Press.

Hay, D. (1997). 'Interpreting conversion: the role of psychology in the rise of the hermeneutics of suspicion in the United States'. Unpublished paper.

Hay, D. (1997). 'Dreams and spirituality'. Unpublished paper.

Hay, D. and Hammond, J. (1992). '"When you pray, go to your private room": a reply to Adrian Thatcher', *British Journal of Religious Education*, 14 (3), pp. 145–50.

Hay, D. and Heald, G. (1987). 'Religion is good for you', *New Society*, 17 Apr.

Hay, D. and Morisy, A. (1985). 'Secular society/religious meanings: A contemporary paradox', *Review of Religious Research*, 26 (3), pp. 213–27.

Heidegger, M. (1962). *Being and Time*, tr. John Macquarrie and Edward Robinson. New York: Harper & Row.

Heimbrock, H.-G. (1986). 'The development of symbols as a key to the developmental psychology of religion', *British Journal of Religious Education*, 8, pp. 150–54.

Heller, D. (1986). *The Children's God*. University of Chicago Press.

Home Office (1998). *1996 British Crime Survey*. HMSO.

Hopkins, G. M. (1953). *Poems and Prose of Gerard Manley Hopkins*, selected with an introduction and notes by W. H. Gardner. London: Penguin Books.

Hume, D. (1993). *Principal writings on religion including Dialogues Concerning Natural Religion and The Natural History of Religion*, ed. with an introduction by J. C. A. Gaskin. Oxford: Oxford University Press.

Hyde, K. (1968). 'The critique of Goldman's research', *Religious Education*, 63, pp. 429–35.

Ihde, D. (1979). *Experimental Phenomenology*. New York: Paragon Books.

Jackson, D. (1990). *Unmasking Masculinity*. London: Unwin Hyman.

Jackson, M. and Fulford, K. W. M. (1997). 'Spiritual experience and psychopathology', *Philosophy, Psychiatry & Psychology*, 4 (1), pp. 41–66.

James, W. (1902). *The Varieties of Religious Experience: A Study in Human Nature*. New York: Longmans.

James, W. (1904). *The Will to Believe*. London: Longmans, Green.

Jaspard, J. M. (1994). 'Comprehension of religious rituals among male and female mentally handicapped adults'. Paper presented at the Sixth European Symposium for the Psychology of Religion, University of Lund.

John of the Cross, St. (1973). 'The Ascent of Mount Carmel', in St John of the Cross, *Collected Works*, tr. by Kieran Kavanaugh OCD and Otilio Rodriguez OCD. Washington DC: Institute of Carmelite Studies.

Johnson, W. (1974). *Silent Music: The Science of Meditation*. London: Collins.

Jones, J. W. (1991). *Contemporary Psychoanalysis and Religion: Transference and Transcendence*. New Haven and London: Yale University Press.

Jung, C. G. (1989). *Man and His Symbols*. Garden City, NY: Doubleday.

Kadowaki, J. K., SJ (1980). *Zen and the Bible: A Priest's Experience*. London: Routledge & Kegan Paul.

Kant, I. (1976). *Critique of Practical Reason, and Other Writings in Moral Philosophy*, tr. and ed. with an introduction by Lewis White Beck. New York: Garland Publications.

Katz, S. (ed.) (1978). *Mysticism and Philosophical Analysis*. New York: Oxford University Press.

Kegan, R. (1982). *The Evolving Self: Problems and Process in Human Development*. Cambridge: Harvard University Press.

à Kempis, T. (1960). *The Imitation of Christ*, tr. Ronald Knox and Michael Oakley. London: Burns & Oates.

Klages, L. (1927). 'Die "religiöse Kurve" in der Handschrifte', *Zeitschrifte für Menschenkunde*, 2, pp. 1–8.

Klingberg, G. (1959). 'A study of religious experience in children from 9 to 13 years of age', *Religious Education*, 54, pp. 211–16.

Knight, M. (1955). *Morals Without Religion, and other essays*. London: Dobson.

Knox, R. (1950). *Enthusiasm: A Chapter in the History of Religion with special reference to the XVII and XVIII Centuries*. Oxford University Press.

Kohlberg, L. (1981). *The Philosophy of Moral Development; Moral Stages and the Idea of Justice*. San Francisco: Harper & Row.

Kuhn, T. (1962). *The Structure of Scientific Revolutions*. Chicago: University of Chicago Press.

Langdon, A. A. (1969). 'A critical examination of Dr Goldman's research study on religious thinking from childhood to adolescence', *Journal of Christian Education*, 12, pp. 37–63.

Lash, N. (1988). *Easter in Ordinary*. London: SCM Press.

Lewis, D. (1985). 'All in good faith', *Nursing Times*, 18/24 Mar., pp. 40–43.

Lindbeck, G. (1984). *The Nature of Doctrine: Religion and Theology in a Post-Liberal Age*. Philadelphia: The Westminster Press.

Locke, J. (1975). *An Essay Concerning Human Understanding*, ed. Peter A. Nidditch. Oxford: Clarendon Press.

Long, D., Elkind, D. and Spilka, B. (1967). 'The child's conception of prayer', *Journal for the Scientific Study of Religion*, 6, pp. 101–9.

Macmurray, J. (1935). *Reason and Emotion*. London: Faber & Faber. New edition 1995.

Macmurray, J. (1957). *The Self as Agent*. London: Faber & Faber. Reissued with an introduction by Stanley M. Harrison in 1995.

Macmurray, J. (1961). *Persons in Relation*. London: Faber & Faber. Reissued with an introduction by Frank G. Kirkpatrick in 1995.

Manuel, F. E. (1974). *The Religion of Isaac Newton*. Oxford: Clarendon Press.

Marrett, R. R. (1920). *Psychology and Folklore*. London: Methuen & Co.

Marx, K. (1957). 'Contribution to the Critique of Hegel's Philosophy of Right', reprinted in K. Marx and F. Engels, *On Religion*. Moscow: Progress Publishers.

Marx, K. (1975). *Economic and Philosophical Manuscripts of 1844*, published in *Marx and Engels: Collected Works*, Vol. 3. London: Lawrence & Wishart.

McCloughry, R. (1992). *Men and Masculinity: From Power to Love*. London: Hodder & Stoughton.

McCreery, E. (1996). 'Talking to children about things spiritual' in Ron Best (ed.), *Education, Spirituality and the Whole Child*. London: Cassell.

McGrady, A. (1994–5). 'Metaphorical and operational aspects of religious thinking: research with Irish Catholic pupils', Part 1, *British Journal of Religious Education*, 16 (3), 1994, pp. 148–63; Part 2, *British Journal of Religious Education*, 17 (1), 1995, pp. 56–62.

Maykut, P. and Morehouse, R. (1994). *Beginning Qualitative Research: A Philosophical and Practical Guide*. London: Falmer Press.

Merton, T. (1968). *Zen and the Birds of Appetite*. New York: New Directions.

Milgram, S. (1965). 'Some conditions of obedience and disobedience to authority', *Human Relations*, 18 (1), pp. 57–75.

Milgram, S. (1992). *The Individual in a Social World: Essays and Experiments*, 2nd edn. New York: McGraw-Hill.

Mortimer, E. (1959). *Blaise Pascal: The Life and Work of a Realist*. London: Methuen & Co.

Muir, E. (1964). *An Autobiography*. London: Methuen.

Murphy, R. (1980). *An Investigation into some aspects of the development of Religious Thinking in Children aged between six and eleven years*. Unpublished Ph.D. thesis, University of St Andrews.

Myers, B. K. (1997). *Young Children and Spirituality*. New York and London: Routledge.

Neitz, M. J. and Spickard, J. V. (1990). 'Steps toward a sociology of religious experience: the theories of Mihaly Csikszentmihalyi and Alfred Schutz', *Sociological Analysis*, 51 (1), pp. 15–33.

Nye, R. (1998). *Psychological Perspectives on Children's Spirituality*. Unpublished Ph.D. thesis submitted to the University of Nottingham.

OFSTED (1994). *Religious Education and Collective Worship 1992–1993: A Report from the Office of Her Majesty's Chief Inspector of Schools*. London: HMSO.

Oser, F. and Reich, K. H. (1990). 'Moral judgment, religious judgment, world views and logical thought: a review of their relationship', *British Journal of Religious Education*, 12, pp. 94–101, 172–81.

Otto, R. (1950). *The Idea of the Holy*, tr. J. W. Harvey. Oxford University Press.

Paley, W. (1825). *Natural Theology; or, Evidences of the Existence and Attributes of the Deity, Collected from the Appearances of Nature*, new edition. London: C. & J. Rivington; J. Nunn; Longman, Hurst, Rees, Orme, and Co; et al.

Pascal, B. (1961). *Pensées*, tr. with an introduction by J. M. Cohen. London: Penguin Books.

Peacocke, A. (1979). *Creation and the World of Science*. Oxford: Clarendon Press.

Perkins, W. (1970). *The Work of William Perkins*, ed. with an introduction by Ian Breward. Appleford: Sutton Courtney Press.

Piaget, J. (1926). *The Language and Thought of the Child*. New York: Harcourt Brace.

Pietroni, P. (1986). *Holistic Living*. London: J. M. Dent.

Polanyi, M. (1962). *Personal Knowledge*. London: Routledge & Kegan Paul.

Popper, K. (1959). *The Logic of Scientific Discovery*. London: Hutchison.

Popper, K. (1963). *Conjectures and Refutations: The Growth of Scientific Knowledge*. London: Routledge & Kegan Paul.

Preus, S. (1987). *Explaining Religion: Criticism and Theory from Bodin to Freud*. Yale University Press.

Priestley, J. (1985). 'The Spiritual in the Curriculum' in Souper, P., *The Spiritual Dimension in Education*. Occasional Papers Series No. 2, University of Southampton, Department of Education.

QSR NUD.IST (1996). *User's Guide*. London: Sage/SCOLARI.

Rahner, K. (1974). 'The experience of God today', *Theological Investigations XI*, tr. David Bourke. London: Darton, Longman & Todd.

Rahner, K. (1975). 'Experience of self and experience of God', *Theological Investigations XIII*, tr. David Bourke. London: Darton, Longman & Todd.

Rénan, E. (n.d.). *The Life of Jesus*. London: The Temple Publishing Company.

Ridley, M. (1996). *The Origins of Virtue*. London: Viking.

Rilke, R. M. (1964). *Rilke: Selected Poems*, tr. with an introduction by J. B. Leishman. London: Penguin Books.

Rizzuto, A.-M. (1979). *The Birth of the Living God: A Psychoanalytic Study*. University of Chicago Press.

Robinson, E. (1983). *The Original Vision*. New York: Seabury Press.

Robinson, E. and Jackson, M. (1985). *Religion and Values at 16+*. Oxford: Alister Hardy Research Centre/Christian Education Movement.

Sartre, J.-P. (1956). *Being and Nothingness*. New York: Philosophical Library.

Schillebeeckx, E. (1987). *On Christian Faith: The Spiritual, Ethical and Political Dimensions*. New York: Crossroad.

Schleiermacher, F. (1928). *Glaubenslehre*, 2nd edn, tr. H. R. Mackintosh as *The Christian Faith*. Edinburgh: T. & T. Clark.

Schleiermacher, F. (1958). *On Religion: Speeches to its Cultured Despisers*, tr. John Oman, with an introduction by Rudolf Otto. New York: Harper & Row.

Schmidt, W. (1931). *The Origin and Growth of Religion*, tr. H. J. Rose. London: Methuen.

Schutz, A. (1964). 'Making music together: a study in social relationship' in Arvid Brodersen (ed.), *Collected Papers II: Studies in Social Theory*. The Hague: Martinus Nijhoff.

Schweitzer, F. (1991). 'Developmental views of the religion of the child: Historical antecedents' in J. Fowler, K. E. Nipkow and F. Schweitzer (eds), *Stages of Faith and Religious Development: Implications for Church, Education and Society*. London: SCM Press.

Selznick, P. (1992). *The Moral Commonwealth: Social Theory and the Promise of Community*. Berkeley: University of California Press.

Senzaki, N. and Reps, P. (eds) (1939). *101 Zen Stories*. London: Rider.

Shilling, C. (1993). *The Body and Social Theory*. London: Sage Publications.

Shuttleworth, J. (ed.) (1976). *The life of Edward, First Lord Herbert of Cherbury, written by himself*. London: Oxford University Press.

Smuts, J. C. (1926). *Holism and evolution*. London: Macmillan.

Soskice, J. (1985). *Metaphor and Religious Language*. Oxford: Clarendon Press.

Spilka, B., Addison, J. and Rosensohn, M. (1975). 'Parents, self and God: a test of competing theories of individual-religion relationships', *Review of Religious Research*, 6, pp. 28–36.

Starbuck, E. D. (1901). *The Psychology of Religion*. London: Walter Scott.

Stock, R. D. (1982). *The Holy and the Daemonic from Sir Thomas Browne to William Blake*. Princeton University Press.

Strauss, A. and Corbin, J. (1990). *Basics of Qualitative Research: Grounded Theory Procedures and Techniques*. Newbury Park: Sage Publications.

Suzuki, D. T. (1957). *Mysticism Christian and Buddhist*. London: George Allen & Unwin.

Tamminen, K. (1991). *Religious Development in Childhood and Youth: An Empirical Study*. Helsinki: Suomalainen Tiedeakatemia.

Tamminen, K. (1994). 'Religious experiences in childhood and adolescence: a viewpoint of religious development between the ages of 7 and 20', *International Journal for the Psychology of Religion*, 4, pp. 61–85.

Tanquerey, A. (1923). *The Spiritual Life: A Treatise on Ascetical and Mystical Theology*, tr. Herman Branderis. Tournai, Paris, Rome, New York: Desclee & Co.

Taylor, J. (1989). *Innocent Wisdom: Children as Spiritual Guides*. New York: Pilgrim Press.

Thun, T. (1964). *Die Religione des Kindes*, 2nd edn. Stuttgart: Ernst Klett. (First edition 1959.)

Thun, T. (1963). *Die religiöse Entscheidung der Jugend*. Stuttgart: Ernst Klett.

Trivers, R. L. (1971). 'The evolution of reciprocal altruism', *Quarterly Review of Biology*, 46, pp. 35–57.

Troeltsch, E. (1977). 'Das Wesen der Religion und der Religionsgeschichte', tr. Robert Morgan and Michael Pye, in *Ernst Troeltsch: Writings on Theology and Religion*. Atlanta: John Knox Press.

Ungoed-Thomas, J. (1994). 'Inspecting spiritual, moral, social and cultural development', *Pastoral Care*, Dec., pp. 21–5.

Vergote, A. and Tamayo, A. (1981). *Parental Figures and the Representation of God: A Psychological and Cross-Cultural Study*. The Hague: Mouton Press.

Vico, G. (1948). *The new science of Giambattista Vico (La scienza nuova)*, tr. from the 3rd edn (1744) by Thomas Goddard Bergin and Max Harold Fisch. Ithaca, NY: Cornell UP.

Vygotsky, L. (1962). *Thought and Language*. Cambridge, Mass.: MIT Press.

de Waal, F. (1996). *Good Natured: The Origins of Right and Wrong in Humans and Other Animals*. Cambridge: Harvard University Press.

Wach, J. (1958). *The Comparative Study of Religions*. New York: Columbia University Press.

Wardman, H. (1964). *Ernest Rénan: A Critical Biography*. London: The Athlone Press.

Watson, J. (1968). *The Double Helix: a personal account of the discovery of the structure of DNA*. London: Weidenfeld & Nicolson.

Watts, M. (1978). *The Dissenters*. Oxford: Clarendon Press.

Weber, M. (1930). *The Protestant Ethic and the Spirit of Capitalism*, tr. Talcott Parsons. London: George Allen & Unwin.

Wilson, B. (1966). *Religion in Secular Society*. London: Watts.

Wilson, D. S. and Sober, E. (and commentators) (1994). 'Re-introducing group selection to the human behavioural sciences', *Behavioural and Brain Sciences*, 17, pp. 585–654.

Wilson, D. S. and Sober, E. (and further commentators) (1996). 'Re-introducing group selection to the human behavioural sciences', *Behavioural and Brain Sciences*, 19, pp. 777–87.

Winnicott, D. W. (1953). 'Transitional objects and transitional phenomena', *International Journal of Psycho-Analysis*, 34, pp. 89–97. Reprinted in D. W. Winnicott, *Playing and Reality* (London: Tavistock, 1971).

Wordsworth, W. (1990). *Wordsworth: The Poems*, ed. John O. Hayden. London: Penguin Books.

Woods, R. (1996). 'Mysticism and social action: the mystic's calling, development and social activity', *Journal of Consciousness Studies*, 3 (2), pp. 158–71.

Wulff, D. (1996). *Psychology of Religion: Classic and Contemporary Views*, 2nd edn. New York: John Wiley.

Wuthnow, R. (1976). *The Consciousness Reformation*. Berkeley: University of California Press.

Wynne-Edwards, V. C. (1962). *Animal Dispersion in Relation to Social Behaviour*. Edinburgh: Oliver & Boyd.

Yalom, I. D. (1980). *Existential Psychotherapy*. New York: Basic Books.

Yeats, W. B. (1956). 'The Second Coming', reprinted in *The Penguin Book of English Verse*, ed. John Hayward. London: Penguin Books.

Yoshikawa, M. J. (1987). 'The double-swing model of intercultural communication between the East and the West' in D. Lawrence Kincaid (ed.), *Communication Theory: Eastern and Western Perspectives*. San Diego: Academic Press.

Index

Aberdeen University, 9, 148, 177
Addison, J., 184
alienation, 18, 63, 143, 180
altruism, 144, 146–9, 153, 193
   kin selection, 146, 193
   reciprocal altruism, 147, 193
Aquinas, St Thomas, 28
archaeology of knowledge, 25, 179
atheism, 8, 30, 82, 116, 144
Atkinson, Paul, 189
awareness, 4, 8–10, 12, 14, 16–18,
   22–4, 26, 31, 39, 41–6, 48, 49, 51,
   52, 54–66, 68, 71, 74, 87–91, 100,
   105, 106, 113–15, 125, 126, 128,
   130, 142, 144–6, 148, 152–7, 161–3,
   167, 168, 170, 172, 173, 175, 181,
   185
'awareness sensing', 87
awe, 67, 97, 153, 173, 192

Bach, Susan, 49, 184
backwash effect, 175
Bancroft, Nancy, 176, 179
Batson, Daniel, 73, 188, 193
BBC, 38, 197

behaviourism, 41, 196
Beit-Hallahmi, Benjamin, 182
Berger, Peter, 54, 71, 72, 180, 185,
   188, 189
Berman, David, 180
Bernstein, Richard, 189, 196
Berryman, Jerome, 192
Bible, 14, 41, 69, 104, 178
Bindl, Maria, 48, 49, 184
biology, 9, 14, 146, 153, 178
Birmingham, 79, 84, 184, 189
Bissonnier, Henri, 51, 184
Blacker, Carmen, 187
Blumer, Herbert, 189
Bowling, A., 178
Bradburn, Norman M., 178
brainstorming, 6, 7, 13
Brittany, 22
Buckley, Michael, 28–31, 152, 180, 195
Buddhism, 9, 14, 61, 178
   Shingon, 69, 187
   Sutras, 14
   Theravada, 61
   vipassana, 9, 61, 172
   Zen, 15, 178, 186, 187, 193

Bunting, Madeleine, 176

Calvin, John, 33, 181
Campbell, Donald, 194
Campbell, Peter, 187
Cardenal, Fernando, 197
Caussade, Jean Pierre de, 62, 186
Chadwick, Owen, 21, 30, 179, 181
Chaterjee, M., 3, 176
Cherbury, Lord Herbert of, 25, 180
Child-God, 119
Child-Self, 123
Children's God, The, 45, 183
Chomsky, Noam, 53, 185
Christianity, 3, 4, 6, 9, 13, 15, 30, 31,
    33, 38, 42, 46, 48, 53, 54, 58, 62, 66,
    69, 70, 86, 97, 102, 122, 124, 125,
    128, 148, 152, 155, 156, 177, 178,
    179, 180, 186, 192, 194, 196
  Calvinism, 4, 33, 176, 182
  Church of England, 23, 35, 84, 85,
    95
  Protestant, 11, 47, 148, 181, 182
  Roman Catholicism, 4, 48, 52, 85,
    176

Clayton, John, 180
co-evolution, 149, 150
cognition, 29, 41, 51, 52, 68, 70, 73,
    74, 100, 132, 192
Cohen, Charles L., 181
Cohen, John M., 181
Coles, Robert, 46, 47, 183, 190
Comenius, John Amos, 50
community, 8, 22, 35–7, 39, 44, 57,
    81, 89, 143, 144, 147–9, 151, 154,
    157–9, 160–3, 166, 175, 194, 199
Comte, Auguste, 22, 23, 179
Constantine, 22, 152
conversion, 4, 32, 33, 40, 44, 182
Corbin, Juliet, 191
Critique of Practical Reason, 67, 187
Crook, John H., 185, 194
Csikszentmihalyi, Isabella, 64, 187
Csikszentmihalyi, Mihaly, 63, 64, 187
cultural construction, 4, 143, 156
cultural sedimentation, 167

Darwin, Charles, 30, 31, 181

Dawkins, Richard, 146, 150, 181, 194,
    195
Dearing, Lord, 37, 182
death, 26, 32, 48, 54, 55, 96, 123, 125,
    126, 163, 177, 192, 193
Deconchy, J.P., 184
deconstruction, 25
Dennett, Daniel C., 181
Descartes, René, 29, 66, 152, 196
Desmond, Adrian, 181
disintegration, social, 35
Disneyesque, 56
dogmatism, 167, 168
Donaldson, Margaret, 60–2, 70, 71,
    169, 186
Donne, John, 35, 182
Dorpat (Tartu), 48
Double Helix, The, 68, 187
drawings, 46, 48, 49
dreams, 69, 107, 116, 190
durée, 63
Durham, William, 150–2, 195
Durkheim, Émile, 10, 12, 15, 16, 17,
    177
Dykstra, C., 184

economic reason, 153, 168
Edinburgh University, 30
Education
  moral, 155
  religious, 169, 173, 174, 182–6,
    188, 199
  spiritual, 4–6, 20, 35, 39, 53, 74, 84,
    144, 154, 157, 159, 162, 163,
    168, 169, 173–5, 199
Education Reform Act, 6, 39, 53
Edwards, Jonathan, 33, 34, 182
Elementary Forms of the Religious Life,
    12, 177
Eliade, Mircea, 188, 193
Elkind, David, 43
embodiment, 14, 164
'enthusiasm', 29, 180
Erikson, Erik, 52
Erricker, Clive, 55–6, 86, 185, 186,
    189
Erricker, Jane, 55–6, 185, 186, 189
ESRC, 37, 182, 199
Essay Concerning Human Understanding,
    29, 180

Ethics, 17, 18, 147, 168, 171, 193, 194
    and social cohesion, 18
Etzioni, Amitai, 36, 37, 182
Explaining Religion, 25, 180

Farmer, Lorelei, 52, 53, 185
'felt sense', 65, 66, 144
'flow', 63, 64, 187
focusing, 65, 66, 94, 187
Foucault, Michel, 179
Fowler, James, 41, 73, 183, 184, 185,
    188, 190, 192
Francis, Leslie, 49, 183, 184
Francke, August Hermann, 50
Freud, Sigmund, 10, 15, 16, 17, 47, 80,
    177, 178, 180
Fulford, K.W.M., 193
Furth, Greg, 184

Gadamer, Hans-Georg, 79, 83, 188,
    189, 196
Gallup Polls, 16
Ganss, George E., 187, 189
Gardavsky, Vitezlav, 181
Gendlin, Eugene, 65, 66, 178, 187
'genres', 55, 56
Gifford Lectures, 9, 30, 177, 195, 196
Gill, Stephen, 35, 182
Girgensohn, Karl, 48
God, 8, 18, 19, 26, 28, 31–4, 38, 42,
    43, 45–9, 51, 54, 57, 58, 62, 71,
    95–9, 102–8, 113–19, 121–5, 128,
    131–3, 136, 172, 176, 178, 179, 181,
    183–8, 190
Godin, André, 184
'God-talk', 54, 57, 87
Goldman, Ronald, 41, 43, 44, 54, 132,
    182, 183, 192
Gorz, André, 195
Goswami, U., 192
Graham, Aelred, 178
Greeley, Andrew M., 179

Hall, Canon, 5
Hall, Carol, 188
Hall, Eric, 188
Hall, G. Stanley, 40, 44, 183
Hallez, M., 184
Hamilton, W.D., 193
Hammersley, Martyn, 189

Hammond, John, 188, 196, 198, 199
Hardy, Alister, 9, 10, 12, 13, 15–17, 20,
    42, 44, 53, 73, 146, 157, 177, 178,
    186, 193
Harris, P., 193
Harvard University, 11, 46, 181, 190,
    194
Hay, David, 59, 136, 176, 178, 179,
    182, 185, 186, 188, 189, 190, 192,
    193, 196, 198, 199
Hayes, Victor C., 188
Heald, Gordon, 179
Heidegger, Martin, 145, 193
Heimbrock, Hans-Günther, 52, 185
Heller, David, 45, 183
'here-and-now', 60–2, 169, 170, 172
Hinduism, 124, 180
holism, 9, 51, 53, 57, 66, 68, 71, 72, 90,
    142, 147, 157, 167, 170, 173, 185
holograms, 129
Holy Spirit, 102, 115
Homo sapiens, 9, 10, 150
Hopkins, Gerard Manley, 187
Hume, David, 27, 180
Hutterites, 148, 149
Huxley, Thomas Henry, 168, 198
Hyde, Kenneth, 183

Ignatius Loyola, St, 64, 69, 79–80, 187,
    188, 189
Ihde, Don, 165, 166, 198
imagination, 52, 68, 69, 70, 95, 154,
    163, 172
implicit spirituality, 106
    associative, 107, 108
    isolated, 4, 107, 108, 109, 149, 156
individualism, 18, 36, 153, 156, 161,
    167, 168
indoctrination, 163
innate ideas, 26, 27
Innocent Wisdom, 46, 183
Internet, 81, 199
Islam, 55, 56, 67, 85

Jackson, David, 196
Jackson, Michael, 63, 186, 193
James, William, 11, 40, 41, 63, 68, 73,
    153, 154, 177, 181–4, 186–8, 190,
    195, 199
Jaspard, Jean-Marie, 51, 185

Jerusalem, 22
Jesuits, 19, 28, 62, 64, 187, 189
Jesus, 21, 22, 32, 48, 125, 179
John of the Cross, St, 4, 71, 188
Johnson, William, 178
Jones, James W., 105, 184
Jung, Carl Gustav, 68, 69, 191

Kadowaki, J.K., 178
Kant, Immanuel, 67, 187
Katz, Steven T., 178
Kegan, R., 178, 181, 182, 190, 192
Kempis, Thomas à, 40, 182
Klages, Ludwig, 49, 184
Klingberg, Gote, 42, 43, 47, 183
Knight, Margaret, 38, 39, 154, 182
Knox, Ronald, 177, 180, 182
Kohlberg, Lawrence, 52, 70, 188
Kuhn, Thomas, 189

language of science and technology,
    128
language acquisition device, 54
Lash, Nicholas, 193
Leech, Alison, 188
Leishman, J.B., 198
Lessius, Leonard, 28
Levinas, Emmanuel, 194
Lewis, David, 179
Life of Jesus, 22, 179
Lindbeck, George, 13, 177
line mode, 61
Locke, John, 29, 34, 50, 180
Logan, John, 186
Lovett, Cyril, 197
Luther, Martin, 50

Macmurray, John, 70, 156, 157, 187,
    189, 195, 196
Madonna, 72
Manuel, Frank E., 180
Marrett, R.R., 12, 177
Marx, Karl, 8, 23, 176
Marxism, 30, 32, 143
masculinity, 161, 196
Maykut, P., 190
McCloughry, Roy, 196
McCreery, Elaine, 54, 55, 185
McGrady, Andrew, 183
McMahon, Edwin, 187

memes, 150–2, 153, 195
Memorial, Pascal's, 32
Mersenne, Marin, 28
Merton, Thomas, 178
meta-consciousness, 114
metaphor, 55, 174
methodological atheism, 25, 180
modernity, 23
Moore, James, 181
Morehouse, R., 190
Morisy, Ann, 24, 178, 179
Mortimer, Ernest, 181
Muir, Edwin, 45, 182
Murphy, Roger, 182
Myers, Barbara Kimes, 159, 168, 173,
    196, 199
mysterium fascinans, 48
mysterium tremendum, 48

National Curriculum, 174
Natural History of Religion, 27, 177, 180
natural philosophy, 28
natural selection, 9, 11, 31, 149–51,
    194
natural theology, 30, 181
Necker Cube, 165
Neitz, Mary Jo, 63, 186
New England, 33, 40, 42, 44
Newman, John Henry, 190
Newton, Isaac, 29, 180
Nipkow, K.E., 183, 184, 185, 190
Nottingham University, 56
Nye, Rebecca, 59, 67, 79, 83, 186, 193

OFSTED, 182
Origin of Species, The, 31
Original Vision, The , 44, 183, 185, 186,
    190
Oser, Fritz, 41, 52, 183
Ota, Cathy, 186, 189
Otto, Rudolf, 11, 48, 67, 105, 177,
    182, 184, 187, 190
Oxford University, 9

Paley, William, 30, 31, 73, 181
Panther, The, 168–9
Paris, 3, 28, 168, 176
Parks, S., 184
Parliament, 5, 6
Pasborg, Lennart, 197

Pascal, Blaise, 32, 33, 35, 181
Peacocke, Arthur, 195
Pensées, 33, 181
performance league tables, 157
Perkins, William, 33, 181
photographs, 87, 88
physics, 28, 32
Piaget, Jean, 41, 52, 70, 71, 188
pietist, 11
Pietroni, Patrick, 170, 171, 172, 173, 199
point mode, 60, 61, 62, 169
Polanyi, Michael, 181
Politics and spirituality, 5, 11, 17, 19, 20, 25, 28, 29, 35, 37, 39, 82, 144, 152, 157, 158, 161, 168, 172
polytheism, 97, 124
Pope Pius IX, 30
Popper, Karl, 15, 68, 178, 187, 198
postmodernism, 14, 23, 81, 82
prayer, 3, 4, 6, 9, 15, 26, 42, 43, 48, 62, 69, 88, 98, 121, 128, 130, 136, 157, 183
predestination, 33
Preus, Samuel, 25–8, 35, 180
Priestley, J., 5, 193
primary school, 84, 92, 144, 156
projection, 47, 88
psychoanalysis, 41
psychology, 33, 41, 48, 51, 52, 59, 70, 80, 93, 99, 113, 119
Puritanism, 33, 40, 181

QSR.NUD.IST, 190

Rahner, Karl, 19, 20, 31, 54, 57, 74, 179, 185, 186, 187
Rathunde, Kevin, 187
reductionism, 10, 15
Reformation, 25, 28, 33, 35, 179
Reich, K. Helmut, 183
reincarnation, 97, 124, 125
relational consciousness, 113–15, 118–21, 124, 129, 130, 134, 137, 141–6, 148–55, 158, 160–3, 168, 169, 173, 174, 175, 191, 192, 194, 195
relativism, 38, 81, 189
Religion
    and contemplation, 4, 9, 15, 51, 62, 68

and meditation, 6, 9, 15, 43, 61, 69, 130, 157, 172
and science, 30
and spirituality, 6, 7, 10, 13, 19, 20, 24, 35, 162, 197
and the 'common core', 13
and truth claims, 13
as neurosis, 10, 16, 35, 178
development of, 49, 50, 52
experiential-expressive dimension of, 13
hypotheses about, 10
language of, 35, 55, 57, 58, 87, 103, 105–8, 117, 118, 124, 132, 143, 144, 155, 174
natural, 25
Religious Affections, The, 34, 182
religious experience, 9, 10, 14, 16, 17, 40–2, 44, 48, 73, 88, 99, 101–3, 114, 119, 146
as effervescence, 10, 16
Religious Experience Research Unit, 44
Religious Thinking from Childhood to Adolescence, 41, 182
Renaissance, 10, 24
Rénan, Ernest, 21–4, 35, 81, 179
Ridley, Matt, 194
Rilke, Rainer Maria, 168, 169, 198
ritual, 51, 52, 64, 67, 158, 175, 185
Rizzuto, Ana-Maria, 46, 47, 183, 188
Robinson, Edward, 44–6, 54, 63, 183, 185, 186, 190, 193
Romanticism, 10, 34
Rome, 3, 23, 29, 176
Rosensohn, M., 184
Rousseau, Jean-Jacques, 50
Rumi, Jalal Al-Din, 141
Rumour of Angels, A, 71, 185, 188, 189

Samuel, Lord, 19, 25, 35, 180, 187
Sartre, Jean-Paul, 112, 191
SCAA Forum, 155
Schillebeeckx, Edward, 194
Schleiermacher, Friedrich, 10, 177, 182
Schmidt, Wilhelm, 81, 189
Schoenrade, P., 188
school, 5, 7, 39, 40–2, 47, 48, 53, 54, 56, 66, 84, 86, 88–90, 92, 93, 95,

109, 117, 124, 144, 156, 157, 161–3, 165, 172, 173, 175, 198

School Curriculum and Assessment Authority (SCAA), 37, 38, 154, 155

Schutz, Alfred, 62, 63, 186

Schweitzer, F., 50, 183, 184, 185, 190

science fiction, 129, 143

Scottish Enlightenment, 27

Secular Society, British, 6, 179

secularism, 25, 30

'selfish gene', 146, 194

Selznick, Philip, 36, 39, 157, 182

Shamanism, 69

Shilling, Chris, 178

Sikhism, 55

Smuts, Jan Christiaan, 177

Snow White, 117, 127, 136, 192

Sober, Elliott, 148, 149, 194

social construction, 15, 25, 30, 153, 161, 166, 167, 198

Soskice, Janet, 187

Southampton, 55, 176

'species-being', 8, 23

Spickard, James, 63, 186

Spilka, Bernard, 43, 183, 184

Spiritual Exercises, 65, 69, 79–80, 187, 188

Spiritual Life of Children, The, 46, 183, 190

Starbuck, Edwin Diller, 182, 183

Stock, R.D., 34, 182

Strauss, Anselm, 191

structural evil, 161

Sullivan, Danny, 186, 189

sustaining ideas, 36, 39, 157, 158

Suzuki, Daisetsu T., 178

Sweden, 42, 43

Syllabus of Errors, 30

synaesthesia, 96

taboo, 89, 143, 153, 190

Tafler, Jonathan, 160, 161, 196

Tamayo, A., 184

Tamminen, Kalevi, 47, 49, 50, 66, 184, 187

Tanquerey, A., 3, 4, 8, 176

Tate, Nicholas, 38

Taylor, Jo-Anne, 46, 183

Temple, W., 5, 105, 179

Theresa, St, 4

Thun, Theophil, 47, 48, 184

Tintern Abbey, 34

Tom Limb, 164

transcendence, 27, 31, 49, 54, 66, 186
signals of, 54

'transitional space', 46, 51, 183

Trivers, R.L., 194

Troeltsch, Ernst, 11, 177, 182

tuning, 62, 63

Ungoed-Thomas, Jasper, 196, 199

United States, 36, 37, 40, 43, 148

Value-sensing, 70

Varieties of Religious Experience, The, 153, 177

Ventis, L.W., 188

Vergote, Antoine, 184

Vico, Giambattista, 26, 27, 180

vipassana, 9, 61, 171

Vygotsky, Lev, 61, 172, 186, 199

Waal, Frans de, 194

Wach, Joachim, 11, 177, 182

Wardman, H.W., 179

Watson, James, 68, 187

Watts, Michael, 179, 181

Weber, Max, 181

Weil, Simone, 159, 196

Whalen, Samuel, 187

Whitehead, Alfred North, 18

Wilson, Bryan, 179

Wilson, David Sloan, 148, 194

Winnicott, Donald, 46, 51, 72, 183

wonder, 67

Woods, Richard, 164, 193

Wordsworth, William, 23, 34, 35, 45, 137, 179, 182

Wulff, David M., 184

Wynne-Edwards, Vero C., 148, 194

Yalom, Irving D., 197

Yeats, William Butler, 36, 158, 182

Yoshikawa, Muneo Jay, 189